A Sociological Yearbook of Religion in Britain · 5

A Sociological Yearbook of Religion in Britain · 5

Edited by Michael Hill

SCM PRESS LTD

334 01555 3

First published 1972
by SCM Press Ltd
56 Bloomsbury Street London

© *SCM Press Ltd 1972*

Printed in Great Britain by
Northumberland Press Ltd, Gateshead

CONTENTS

THE CONTRIBUTORS

JAMES A. BECKFORD Lecturer in Sociology, University of Reading

JAMES BENTLEY Rector of All Saints', Stretford

COLIN CAMPBELL Lecturer in Sociology, University of York

ROBERT W. COLES Lecturer in Sociology, University of York

ALAN DEACON Lecturer in Social Administration, University of Leeds

HILARY GRAHAM Graduate Student, Department of Sociology, University of York

MICHAEL HILL Lecturer in Sociology, London School of Economics and Political Science

R. K. JONES Staff Tutor in Sociology, North West of England and Northern Ireland, Open University

DAVID MARTIN Professor in Sociology, London School of Economics and Political Science

CHRISTINE PARKIN Salvation Army Officer

W. S. F. PICKERING Senior Lecturer in Sociology, University of Newcastle

ANDREW RIGBY Lecturer in Sociology, University of Aberdeen

MARGARET SCOTFORD ARCHER Lecturer in Sociology, University of Reading

BRYAN S. TURNER Lecturer in Sociology, University of Aberdeen

MICHALINA VAUGHAN Senior Lecturer in Sociology, London School of Economics and Political Science

R. G. WADDELL Research Student in Sociology, London School of Economics and Political Science

BERYL WRIGHT Sometime Lecturer in Sociology, University of Natal, Durban, South Africa

PREFACE

YEARBOOK number five follows the general pattern of previous editions and thus includes theoretical, historical and empirical material. Since we aim to cover a broad readership the approach is above all eclectic, with a solid sociological core. In answer to the reviewer who did not see how the Yearbook could 'hang together', I would simply state that apart from the sociological emphasis the only thing which keeps the collection hanging together is its binding.

This year's theoretical article is a spirited – and very necessary – defence and restatement of Weber's concept of charisma. Against the stream of 'cultural drift', through which dogmatic distortions of Weber's original formulation have come to be accepted as Weber's own ideas, Waddell argues for a more precise understanding of the concept in terms of (1) originality; and (2) its recognition. The so-called psychological bias of charisma is strongly rejected.

Charisma also features in Beckford's article on the organizational development of the sect of Jehovah's Witnesses. He suggests that a full interpretation of this development cannot be subsumed under any of the available sociological models of religious group-formation but rather that it must include an idiosyncratic combination of features, one of which was a charismatic founder. The origins of the sect as an evangelistic publishing concern and its growth into an exclusivist body are given a detailed interpretation. Another kind of development is analysed in Pickering's article on the secularized Sabbath. Taking a broad historical perspective, he shows how Christian notions of the Sabbath crystallized about the same time that the church became institutionalized and have persisted in various forms ever since. Both secular and sacred definitions of Sunday are identified from the start.

The article on F. D. Maurice sets in a sociological framework the various attitudes to education of the different schools of church-manship in the Church of England. In the thought of F. D. Maurice the relative weight of Christian and Socialist elements is found to rest very firmly on the former, and thus the function of Anglican education was to provide a source of integration for each social class rather than undermining the basis on which classes were formed. A similar concern with sectional interests is shown in the Order of Ethiopia which, as Wright demonstrates, was an offshoot of Methodism with specific black African aspirations which eventually attached itself – with a considerable degree of autonomy – to the Anglican Church in South Africa.

Rigby and Turner take the point made by sociologists like Peter Berger and Thomas Luckmann that institutionally based, market-research studies of traditional denominations are a field of decreasing significance in the sociology of religion. As evidence of a new form of religious collectivity they take a commune in Scotland and analyse its internal processes and beliefs. This is one of the few serious studies of communes ever to appear in recent sociological literature, and as far as I know there is very little published material even in the United States. While the number of people doing research on communes suggests an interesting potential output of work, the present article breaks new ground.

The article by Deacon and Hill on the 'female surplus' of the nineteenth century uses demographic data and contemporary sources to study the differential perceptions of a problem and the secular and religious alternatives presented as solutions. Parkin's article on the early social attitudes of the Salvation Army is similarly concerned with the perceptions of a problem and with the combination of traditional and novel approaches which William Booth and his fellow officers adopted. There is excellent documentation of Booth's gradual change of attitude towards poverty.

Campbell's analysis of cultic phenomena in terms of their *milieu* rather than their organizational features (to which, in any case, most writers are agreed in attributing great fluidity) is an important argument against 'cultural drift'. Troeltsch's category of 'mysticism' is much less formally defined than Becker's type of 'cult', and some of the analytical problems are solved by referring to Troeltsch.

For opponents of the argument that millennial movements only emerge among the poor and oppressed, the Catholic Apostolic Church has always been a powerful weapon. In his article, Jones indicates the well-heeled origins of this movement and its failure to make provision for any continuity of organization. A schismatic offshoot which did allow new appointments to the hierarchy shows an impressive contemporary membership in contrast to its parent body. Another type of decline is assessed by Bentley in his study of Anglican bishops between 1860 and 1960. The decline in quality of Anglican bishops (as perceived from within the church itself) is explained by reference to their restricted class of origin and their traditional attitude to other social groups. Because of this, they failed to see that the brand of national Christianity which they represented was substantially an expression of the interests of one particular class.

David Martin uses the type concepts of church and denomination to compare and contrast the political stances and the relationship to social change of Catholicism and Methodism. The differential responses to secularization are traced and future developments suggested.

Finally, there is another supplement to the bibliography of work in the sociology of British religion, which Bob Coles has very painstakingly assembled. The fact that it was constructed in this way rather than by the simple operation of a computer is sufficient indication that we have got no further in our pursuit of data-collection in the sociology of religion which was mentioned in the last Yearbook. In defence, we can only say that we have been too busy doing research to begin listing it.

1 Charisma and Reason: Paradoxes and Tactics of Originality

R. G. Waddell

CONSIDERABLE confusion surrounds the concept of charisma. Traditionally this confusion has been attributed to ambiguities inherent in Weber's own treatment of the subject.[1] Departing from this approach, I shall argue here that this confusion has two sources: the widespread misinterpretation of Weber's notion of charisma and the paradoxical nature of the phenomenon to which the term refers.

Individual sociologists have been remarkably consistent in charging Weber with a psychological bias and have set themselves to the task of putting him straight.[2] Worsley, for example, has gone so far as to indict Weber for having set a bad precedent.[3] In the face of such piercing indictments the student of charisma is easily seduced into accepting these views as gospel and their advocates as models of scholarly heroism.

It is, however, by no means certain that Weber had a psychological bias. I shall argue here that built into Weber's definition of charisma are two elements – (1) originality and (2) its recognition – and that the second of these effectively precludes the sort of psychologizing with which Weber has been charged. Weber's critics have built themselves a straw man; habitually they impute to Weber an excessive emphasis on the element of originality and busy themselves extracting this allegedly overlooked element of recognition. The entire exercise has not only cast a distorting light on Weber but, more importantly, has created a distracting, mythical obstacle in the way of attempts to develop a broader theoretical perspective on the notion of charisma.

It is only right that Gerth and Mills[4] should be held responsible for this pernicious critical trend. It is thanks largely to them that the dichotomy between charisma and routine is widely interpreted as being parallel to that between, for example, the psychological and the sociological, or originality and non-originality. But the simple fact is that charisma, as Weber defines it, is not parallel to terms in either of these dichotomies. Critics of Weber have persistently misread him as implying such parallels and on this basis have denounced him for having led us astray.

It is well to resist being overly generous in casting blame on Gerth and Mills. Equal emphasis ought to be given to the fact that much thinking today is plagued by a most persuasive Promethean myth regarding the nature of charisma, as well as that of originality, innovation, and creativity – members of the more general class of phenomena to which charisma belongs. It is apparent that Weber, too, was disturbed by this myth that agents of originality are isolated creatures, unfettered by tradition, history, or social structure; the concept of charisma is a very clear attempt to rise above this naïve view. Weber was specifically interested in coming to terms with the structural factors of social orders which permit certain individuals (and their ideas) to rise to positions of revolutionary eminence – a task to which the Promethean myth is clearly ill-suited as a model. It is remarkable that this myth, in one form or another, still permeates thinking about creativity, originality, innovation, and charisma. Psychologists have, on the whole, embraced this myth as their working model.[5] But there is no greater testimony to the power of the myth than the current attempts to reinstate it in Weber's work.

In the discussion which follows I shall attempt to demonstrate that the psychological bias with which Weber has been charged arises from a misinterpretation of charisma, and to indicate the paradoxical nature of the phenomenon to which the term 'charisma' refers. I shall concentrate on four themes: (*a*) the relation between charisma and originality, (*b*) the relation between recognition and charisma, (*c*) the roles of person and product in charisma, and (*d*) the sources and patterns of legitimacy. To this end, I shall present a framework within which Weber's notion of charisma, these four themes, and Weber's putatively psychological bias may be viewed. I offer this framework as a rather tentative first step towards taking up the challenge of Bendix's[6] suggestion that Weber has offered us the beginnings of a 'Sociology of Innovation'.

Weber's definition of charisma[7] consists in two elements: that of being different and that of recognition. Considering first the element of being different, Weber's entire discussion presupposes the ability of potential consumers of charisma to distinguish the ordinary from the extraordinary, or the non-original from the original. Since this is fundamental, we must consider what the distinction involves.

Any distinction between originality and non-originality arises from an evaluation of relative differences. Just as it is useless to speak of change without designating that which has changed, so too are we led astray by the notion of originality unless we can isolate the standard by which it is measured. To attribute a person or product with originality is to contrast that person or product with some expectation, habit, convention, or tradition.

Originality and the variables which determine its degree are best viewed on a continuum. Pure originality and non-originality are at opposite poles. The two are distinguished by assessing the influence of two variables: that of difference and that of responsiveness or relevance. Pure originality is viewed as something thoroughly different from tradition and is thought to be in no way responsive and relevant to tradition. Non-originality is viewed as in no way diverging from tradition and by virtue of this is seen as thoroughly relevant to tradition. At best non-originality validates tradition. Pure originality – and this is crucial – neither validates nor invalidates tradition. The ability of originality (an original person or product) to invalidate tradition varies inversely to the degree of its 'purity'.

There is another sort of originality – recognized originality – which lies somewhere between pure originality and non-originality; it has qualities of each. Implicit in Weber's notion of charisma is the view that recognition of this sort of originality involves something more than an evaluation of relative difference; implicit is some relevance to tradition. Thus recognition of originality implies two sorts of evaluation: an evaluation of the relative difference of a person or product and an evaluation of the *responsiveness* or relevance of that person or product to problems raised by convention. Weber's notion of charisma is quite clearly a special case of recognized originality; it partakes (by definition) of this balance between difference and responsiveness.

This raises some important points. First, charisma is not parallel to pure originality; charisma as recognized originality bridges the gap between pure originality and non-originality. If it is admitted that charisma simply does not exist apart from recognition, the concept of charisma is simply not subject to psychologizing. Second, there is a paradox here; this paradox stems not from Weber but rather from the phenomenon which 'charisma' describes. Weber tells us that persistence (i.e. becoming a routine with or without transformative consequences) depends on recognition; and recognition depends on some balance between difference and responsiveness. Originality pays a price for persistence: the gradual loss of its originality or uniqueness. Conversely, that which is original but not recognized remains original but at the expense of any historical efficacy. We are left with a paradox: to say that persisting originality is recognized originality is to suggest that perhaps the original person or product was not all that original in the first place. To study charisma is to study the structural factors which will permit and sustain such a paradox. The concepts of creativity and originality need not necessarily imply recognition. Weber's notion of charisma is unique in that it is defined so as to include this element. The demands of recognition and persistence progressively limit the degree to which originality can depart from its social context.[8] Pure originality is at best a nuisance; it involves too complete a departure from collective concerns and thus offers no challenge to tradition or history.

In a most important passage, Weber suggests that charisma is not the only form of recognized originality one might observe.

> In traditionally stereotyped periods, charisma is the greatest revolutionary force. The equally revolutionary force of 'reason' works from without by altering the situations of action, and hence its problems, finally in this way changing men's attitudes toward them; or it intellectualizes the individual. Charisma, on the other hand, may involve a subjective or internal reorientation born out of suffering, conflicts, or enthusiasm. It may result in a radical alteration of the central system of attitudes and directions of action with a completely new orientation of all attitudes toward the different problems and structures of the 'world'. [T. Parsons suggests here that the reference is to this-worldly as against other-worldly concerns.] In pre-rationalistic periods, tradition and charisma between them have almost exhausted the whole of the orientation of action.[9]

From this it would seem that Weber had in mind (at least) two sorts of recognized originality: charisma and rational originality. Charisma proceeds by effecting a subjective, affectual reorientation. Rational originality proceeds by effecting an objective, substantive, as opposed to a 'formal' or 'instrumental' reorientation.

Rational originality involves gaining leverage of the 'substantive' orientation of others; the charismatic attempts to gain leverage on the emotional tone of those around him.[10]

Weber observed that charisma and traditionalism have an affinity for each other; the passage above suggests that he saw a similar affinity of rational originality for rational societies. Rationalism and traditionalism are forms of routine control.[11] Charisma and rational originality emerge from, later merge with, and yet oppose these. What is the basis for this affinity?

All recognized originality consists in two elements: that of person and that of product (e.g. message). Charisma and rational originality differ not in content or in aim, but rather in tactics – in the extent to which recognition is facilitated by accentuation of person or of product. Charisma emphasizes the element of person. There is, of course, a product or message, but this (from a tactical point of view) is secondary in the process of recognition and gains importance only in the process of routinization. The charismatic product is present but not recognized in its own right; it is recognized and commands obedience only as expressed by the individual(s) bearing the product or message. In both its preconditions and consequences, the affinity of charisma for traditionalism lies in the fact that, in both, products (ideas, rules, messages, and the like) attach themselves to persons. Obedience is to persons and not directly to objective, impersonal rules or messages themselves.[12] Weber viewed both charisma and traditionalism as irrational (although he thought the latter somewhat more rational than the former). They are irrational specifically because they personalize products.[13]

The relative emphasis on person or product in recognition of originality is a specifically tactical matter. In any form of recognized originality the elements of person and product can be discerned; the point here is that built into the repertoire of tactics and strategies of charismatics is the knowledge (intuitive or otherwise) that in a traditional setting the value of the message is judged by the personal qualities of the bearer. Thus it is through image-making and accentuation of personal qualities that the charismatic obtains a lever on the public and facilitates his recognition.

In rational societies, built into the tactics of the original individual is the knowledge that it is the product and not the personality which sells.[14] (The very possession of such knowledge, of course, testifies to the close relation between the bearer of recognized originality and the social setting.) The affinity of rational originality for rational societies lies in the fact that they both impersonalize things, including (perhaps especially) things revolutionary and original. The rationality here, in the Weberian sense, lies in the fact that products are depersonalized and judged independently of the personality traits of the bearer. (The originality of, for example, Einstein, Marx, or Freud is ordinarily evaluated independently of the question as to whether they did or did not have endearing personalities.[15])

The contrast between charisma and rational originality is perhaps best illustrated by contrasting their very different claims: the charismatic claims, 'It is written ... but I say unto you' while rational originality claims, 'It is written ... but reason/observation tells us ...'. Evaluations as to the relative difference and responsiveness of charisma and rational originality rest on very different bases. The evaluation of the charismatic, in traditional settings, proceeds indirectly and *vis-à-vis* the charismatic person. Since affectual states are very often a reflection of the social order in which they appear, the charismatic (initially, at least) addresses himself rather indirectly to problems (e.g. affectual states) raised by convention or tradition. The evaluation of rational originality, from the start, is impersonal and direct; the product is judged on its own terms. The evaluation rests on the substantive appeal of the product. In sum, then, the charismatic gains his hearing by accentuating the persuasive power of his personality whereas the bearer of rational originality gains his hearing by accentuating the persuasive power of his message; persuasive people are more likely to find an audience in traditional settings while persuasive arguments are more likely to find their audience in rationalized settings. As Weber is understood here, the element of difference in both charisma and rationalized originality lies specifically in the attempt to transcend and supplant established criteria of legitimacy.[16] In this respect charisma and rational originality are alike; they differ only in the strategies and tactics employed to this end.

In this final section I shall attempt to bring the ideas derived from Weber and presented here to bear on some of the more important indictments of Weber contained in recent writing.

Firstly, it should be observed that the dichotomy between originality and non-originality *is* parallel to that between the forces of personality and those of society. The point to be emphasized here is that charisma, as a form of recognized originality, constitutes a connecting link between the purely personal and the purely social. To this extent, Friedland[17] tells us little we did not already know. Weber's concept of charisma does not ask that we oppose psychological and sociological forces. Quite the contrary. It seems clear that the concept, as Weber defines it, implies both the elements of responsiveness or relevance and differentness or originality. Recognition, and hence relevance, is implicit in the notion of charisma. Thus we must conclude that Friedland and all those charging Weber with a psychological bias have missed the point.

There have been efforts to discredit Weber's views on the social location of the charismatic individual. These efforts are part of the broader tendency to impute some psychological bias to Weber. It has been observed that the charismatic individual cannot be too far outside the centres of society or their area of influence; too much distance is likely to deprive the message of responsiveness. On the other hand, if the individual is too immersed in established ways of thinking this is likely to deprive him of any claim to originality. Charisma, in balancing responsiveness and difference, clearly must also balance distance from tradition with total immersion in it.

It is well known that Weber's researches led him to confirm the view that the Israelite prophets did not emerge from the ranks of the established priesthood. Less well known is his explanation of this fact: charisma depends on the capacity to be 'astounded'; that capacity is likely to be fostered where the individual stands outside the established centres of society.[18] Berger[19] has pointed out that recent biblical scholarship contradicts Weber's findings: the prophets are now thought to have arisen through the ranks of the established priesthood. In response to Berger, it should be noted that Weber's empirical findings are only part of the legacy left us, and impressive though the range of data may be, they constitute by no means the most important part. Far more important are his explanations: if these can survive, even be enhanced by, continuing empirical research, he has convincingly succeeded.

The important thing left by Weber in this case is the notion that charisma depends on the capacity to be 'astounded' and recognized for this. Weber's empirical data are meant to demonstrate for us the conditions under which this capacity is fostered; it is a matter for empirical demonstration as to whether in a particular case this capacity was fostered by physical or spiritual distance from established institutional centres.[20] It does seem, as Berger suggests, that recognition is even more likely where an individual has used his position in the established structure as a lever.

There has been a definite trend towards emphasizing the element of product (or message) in charisma and viewing the element of person (or agent) as superfluous.[21] The significance of personalization and the accentuation of personal qualities is a specifically tactical point; to minimize the importance of these personal qualities is to turn one's back on the element of strategy, on the factors which facilitate recognition. In overlooking the matter of strategy one also overlooks the continuities between strategies, their settings, and recognition. This, of course, makes it impossible to distinguish charisma from other sorts of recognized originality.

Friedrich[22] and Marcus[23] in particular address themselves to the problem of difference. Friedrich and those who would confine the notion of charisma to the religious sphere not only miss the underlying themes of power, domination, and transformation in charisma, but also miss the fact that the significance of charisma lies in its transcendence of established criterion of legitimacy, making these illegitimate in view of some superior, transcendent criterion. Whether this attempt is couched in religious terms or not, it seems to me, is quite irrelevant to matters apart from those of strategy.[24] This I take to be the general point of Marcus' paper.

In conclusion, I have not attempted here to review all the sorts of criticism reflected in recent writing. Least of all have I attempted to conduct a survey of the variety of ways in which current approaches diverge from the scheme presented here;[25] neither have I attempted to catalogue the varieties of abuse to which 'charisma' has been subjected.[26] Apart from the brief comments and notes here, I must let the interpretation of Weber presented here stand for itself.

I have attempted to shed light on some of the confusion surrounding the concept of charisma. Rather than follow the invitation of Worsley and attribute this confusion to ambiguities inherent in Weber's own thinking, I have, by placing the concept of charisma in a broader framework, suggested that certain of these ambiguities are imagined and that others stem from the paradoxical nature of the phenomenon. I have emphasized in particular the misunderstandings arising from the tendency to equate the dichotomy between charisma and routine with those between personality and society, and between originality and non-originality. I take issue with Gerth and Mills in so far as I think it clear that Weber's notion of charisma is an attempt to rise above these dichotomies. It is, in my estimation, a striking peculiarity of Weber's followers (many disciples and critics alike) that they have busied themselves hewing and chipping at his theory in order to *reinstate* this old dichotomy between personality and society – some, it would seem, out of a sense of ancestor-worship, but most for purposes of target practice.

NOTES

1. See, for example, P. M. Worsley, *The Trumpet Shall Sound*, MacGibbon & Kee 1968, p.323.
2. See especially ibid., pp.293, 315; H. Gerth and C. W. Mills, *From Max Weber: Essays*, OUP, NY 1946, pp.52-3; W. H. Friedland, 'For a Sociological concept of Charisma', *Social Forces*, 43 (1964), pp.18-26; K. J. Ratnam, 'Charisma and Political Leadership', *Political Studies*, 12 (1964), pp.341-54.
3. Worsley, op. cit., p.315.
4. Gerth and Mills, op. cit.
5. Those who charge Weber with a psychological bias would do well to examine psychological literature on creativity and originality. By contrast, Weber's approach is unspeakably radical in so far as he considers the social order as an important factor not only in the recognition but in the definition of originality.
6. R. Bendix, *Max Weber: An Intellectual Portrait*, Methuen 1962.
7. Max Weber, *Theory of Social and Economic Organization* (T. Parsons, ed.), Free Press, NY 1947, p.358; 'The term "charisma" will be applied to a certain quality of an individual personality by virtue of which he is set apart from ordinary men and treated as endowed with supernatural, super-human, or at least specifically exceptional powers or qualities.'
8. The point here is that *at no time* are ideas viewed as completely autonomous. The notion of 'elective affinity' applies as much to the recognition of originality as to its institutionalization.
9. Weber, op. cit., p.363.
10. Reference here is to Weber's discussion of the 'types of social action'. See Weber, op. cit., p.115. For an interesting discussion of the relation between Weber's types of social action and types of domination see R. Aron, *Main Currents in Sociological Thought*, Vol. 2, Penguin 1967, pp.241-2.
11. Weber, op. cit., p.361.
12. Weber, op. cit., pp.231-342.
13. Thus, for example, one might expect a traditional society to defend itself against charismatic threats by attacking the charismatic person rather than his ideas,

14. It is ironic that one of the effects of such depersonalization is to deflect attention from the structural factors which permit certain people to rise to positions of revolutionary eminence. The tendency to focus on the product makes it too easy to overlook the patterns of stratification which permit certain individuals to find themselves (or rather, their products) in a position to be recognized. Moreover it tends to add fuel to the functionalist view of stratification. To follow a somewhat different thread, the reader is referred to J. C. Davies, 'Charisma in the 1952 Campaign', *The American Political Science Review*, 48 (1954), 1083-1102, for his discussion of personality versus issues in voting patterns.

15. As these examples suggest, the sciences provide the very best examples of rational originality. See, for example, T. Kuhn, *The Structure of Scientific Revolutions*, Chicago University Press 1962. Moving from a cognitive to a social level, the current attempts to revolutionize science (i.e. to make it answerable first to its social consequences and only secondly to its cognitive consequences) provides another example of rational originality as defined here.

16. For a very good description of this phenomenon, see T. Parsons, *The Social System*, Routledge and Kegan Paul 1951, p.355.

17. Friedland, op. cit. See also Gerth and Mills, op. cit., pp.52-3; P. Worsley, op. cit., p.315; K. J. Ratnam, op. cit. Also note brief reference in C. J. Friedrich, 'Political Leadership and the Problem of Charismatic Power', *The Journal of Politics*, 23 (1961), pp.3-24.

18. Weber, *Ancient Judaism*, Free Press, NY 1952, pp.206-7.

19. P. L. Berger, 'Charisma, Religious Innovation and the Israelite Prophecy', *American Sociological Review*, 28 (1963) pp.940-50.

20. On the social location of charismatic persons see E. Shils, 'Charisma', *International Encyclopedia of the Social Sciences*, vol. 2, 1968, pp.386-90, D. Apter, *Ghana in Transition*, NY 1963; Eisenstadt (ed.) 'Introduction' to *Max Weber: On Charisma and Institution Building*, Chicago University Press 1968. Most of what passes in this literature as 'charisma' I should prefer to term 'originality'.

21. See, for example, Friedland, op. cit.; Worsley, op. cit., pp.285-345; Y. Talmon, 'The Pursuit of the Millennium: The Relation Between Religion and Social Change', *Archives Européens de Sociologie*, III, 1, 1962, pp.149-164. For a slightly different perspective see Davies, op. cit.

22. Friedrich op. cit.

23. J. T. Marcus, 'Transcendence and Charisma', *The Western Political Quarterly*, 14 (1961), pp.236-41.

24. For a very good discussion see Talmon, art. cit.

25. It is with regret that I must admit that even Weber's work seems to have suffered from his failure to fully explore the themes emerging from the passage quoted above in the text.

26. Particularly persistent failures to distinguish between charisma and other types of recognized originality may be found in Shils (1968), art. cit.; Eisenstadt, op. cit.; A. Etzioni, *A Comparative Analysis of Complex Organizations*, Free Press, NY 1961.

2 The Embryonic Stage of a Religious Sect's Development: The Jehovah's Witnesses

James A. Beckford

Brief history

THE founder of the evangelistic agency from which the modern group of Jehovah's Witnesses traces its descent was Charles Taze Russell, a moderately successful haberdasher from Pittsburgh. In his early twenties, Russell had organized a small Bible study group among some close acquaintances and had eventually undertaken to publish a Second Adventist journal of scriptural exposition called *Zion's Watch Tower and Herald of Christ's Presence.* Subscribers to the journal formed themselves into study classes in North America and in Europe in order to deepen their understanding of scriptural material and to share their experiences with like-minded people. Russell took the opportunity from 1881 onwards to make use of these local Bible study classes by arranging for the participants to act as promoters and salesmen of the growing volume of his exegetical writings.

In spite of several attempts by local class leaders to resist Russell's attempts to rationalize and maximize the evangelical productivity of the people who subscribed to his journal, the Zion's Watch Tower Tract Society (as the publishing organization was known after 1884) continued to increase its output of literature until the beginning of the First World War. The period 1914-18 proved traumatic in at least three aspects: (*a*) the widely held belief that the Battle or Armageddon heralding the imminent millennial upheaval would occur in 1914 was disconfirmed; (*b*) in some areas of the world the Society was legally forbidden to pursue its evangelistic goals, and (*c*) Russell's death in 1916 led to an unseemly struggle within the Society for the vacant presidency.

Joseph Franklyn Rutherford succeeded to Russell's position as President of Zion's Watch Tower Tract Society, but only at the expense of antagonizing a large proportion of the *Watch Tower*'s subscribers. Nevertheless, he persisted in moulding the Society to suit his own programme of activist evangelism under systematic central control, and he succeeded in creating the administrative structure of the present-day sect of Jehovah's Witnesses. Between 1919 and 1939 Rutherford occupied himself with shaping an efficient and dedicated band of administrators, salesmen and evangelists. While there can be no doubt that Rutherford attained most of his objectives in an impressive fashion, it is equally certain that he also precipitated a long series of acrimonious legal struggles in the USA and was largely responsible for creating the Jehovah's Witnesses' unpopular public image.

The Society survived the Second World War with fewer traumas than it had suffered in the First and it emerged under a new President, Nathan Homer Knorr, who had taken office smoothly following Rutherford's death in 1942. The new President promptly inaugurated a programme designed to improve the general intellectual level of Jehovah's Witnesses and to remove some of the group's more rebarbative features. Since the 1950s the number of Jehovah's Witnesses has continued to grow steadily, although in the western democracies the rate of growth is generally lower than in some of the developing areas of the world.

The problem

While it is difficult in the present state of sociological knowledge about the structure and dynamics of religious organizations to state hard and fast empirical generalizations to which no sociologist would object, there does appear now to be some agreement about the typical process by which new religious groups emerge and achieve organizational stability. In the case of the group founded by C. T. Russell, therefore, we would expect it to fit into the patterns described by Bryan Wilson as follows:

> Broadly, there are five distinct ways in which sects may be said to originate:
>
> 1 They may arise when a charismatic figure presents a new teaching, and recruits from any or all other religious movements, and from the population generally. The charismatic figure may be a new prophet, a man or woman who offers a new interpretation or who seeks to restore an old one, who, in short, tells men what they shall do to be saved.
>
> 2 Sects may also begin as a consequence of internal schism within existing sects.

3   They may arise more or less spontaneously by the coming together of a group of 'seekers' who evolve, as a group-experience, new patterns of worship and new statements of belief.

4   They may arise from the attempts to revitalize the beliefs and practices within a major religious movement, as old groups are called to intensify their commitment, or new groups called to express it for the first time. These developments may be associated with attempts to de-institutionalise and de-ritualise church organisation and practice.

5   Non-denominational revivalism may, as an unintended consequence, bring new sects into being, as those who undergo similar enthusiastic conversion find assimilation into existing denominations difficult.[1]

Many sociologists have echoed Wilson's propositions and have discovered confirmation of them in the historical development of religious groups. Much evidence is also available to show that, in the case of new religious groups which emerge around a leader with personal charismatic qualities, the process of 'translating' his authority into a stable basis for the development of a viable organization presents the group with a major administrative and moral problem.

The emergence of Russell's movement does not, however, approximate to any one of the patterns outlined by Wilson, although it must be said that aspects of all five methods are apparent in its early years. It is the purpose of this paper to investigate firstly the reasons why Russellism did not develop along the lines followed by so many other religious sects, and secondly the factors which might explain its unusual evolution. The latter include (*a*) the founder's original authority of office, (*b*) relations between the Society's centre and periphery and (*c*) its highly specific and visible goals.

The millenarian milieu

The early success of Russell's publishing venture must be placed in the context of popular American religious styles. Throughout the nineteenth century, evangelists of many persuasions had made a living out of publishing religious literature, organizing revival meetings and travelling widely to preach their particular message. Sufficient evidence exists about the most famous evangelists such as Alexander Campbell, William Miller, Finney, Moodey, Torrey and Billy Sunday to permit historians to construct a composite picture of the popular religious milieu. Furthermore, it would not be unjustified to assume that an equally large number of evangelists never managed to achieve fame, and have already receded into the inscrutable past. Nevertheless, the picture is clear enough to indicate that revival campaigns, camp meetings, millennialist 'scares' and evangelical magazines constituted some of the principal features of religious life in all but the most prosperous strata of American society. W. S. Hudson, for example, quotes Albert Barnes, minister of the First Presbyterian Church of Philadelphia, as claiming in the middle of the nineteenth century that there was seldom 'a city or town or peaceful hamlet that has not been hallowed by revivals of religion'.[2] The ascendancy of this religious style was most marked in rural areas, although urban revivalist campaigns were far from uncommon.

After the Millerite 'scare' of the mid-nineteenth century, the predominantly Arminian, moralistic theology of 'circuit evangelists' came to oust the millennialists from their former prominence, but a strong undercurrent of millenarian sympathy continued to make itself felt. Millenarianism persisted most successfully in urban areas where access to occasional visiting preachers and to millenarian literature was possible. While it is true that millenarianism had ceased to occupy a place of prominence in American popular religion towards the end of the nineteenth century, it is also the case that some evangelists continued to provide for the spiritual and intellectual needs of those people who maintained faith in a millenarian view of history. The most efficient and widespread means of ministering to these people was the written word, and a wide variety of magazines and tracts was in circulation at all times in the nineteenth century. Most of the magazines were short-lived and relatively weak in terms of the influence that they wielded over people's lives, but the market for them was such that a continuous succession of more or less successful magazines ensured the unbroken persistence of the millenarian tradition in America.

Given the millenarian tradition in American popular religion in the nineteenth century, it would be unwise to consider the enthusiastic support for C. T. Russell's own publishing enterprise as spontaneous. It is not true that Russell's writings stimulated the religious consciousness of *Zion's Watch Tower*'s first readers; they were already subscribers to an earlier journal, the *Herald of the Morning*, and were presumably convinced in large measure of the essential correctness of a millenarian *Weltanschauung*. It is also likely that there was a 'floating population' of people in America whose sympathies with millenarianism were sufficiently pronounced to make them susceptible to a new evangelist, and whose commitments to particular religious bodies were sufficiently weak to allow them to take up Russell's cause. His intervention in millenarian circles would be more accurately conceived of as a mildly innovatory contribution to a tradition with long-established roots in some sections of American society. His innovations were both doctrinal and organizational, but their innovatory character took time to develop and was certainly not visible in the early days of *Zion's Watch Tower*. There is some evidence, for example, that Russell conceived of his earliest contribution to religious publishing as nothing more than a means of complementing the available literature and thereby satisfying a growing demand. An article in the *Bible Student* of September 1923 reprints a letter from Russell showing that, while he was still an associate editor of the *Herald of the Morning*, he managed to insert a notice in the copy for February 1879 inviting subscribers to support his own monthly journal which would complement the *Herald* by appearing cheaply two weeks after that magazine's publication date. It is important to bear in mind, therefore, that Russell first of all played the role of a religious impresario and was originally content to supervise and provide financial backing for the promotion of someone else's religious ideas. The motivation to produce a publication of his own undoubtedly owed something to the entrepreneurial desire to maximize productivity and to develop new markets.

The publishing enterprise

One specifically novel and significant feature of the Watch Tower Society's development was its origins in a commercially sophisticated publishing enterprise. When C. T. Russell began publishing *Zion's Watch Tower and Herald of Christ's Presence*, he had already achieved considerable success in the world of trade, and he had collaborated with N. H. Barbour, whose experience in the field of Second Adventist publishing was to prove invaluable. Russell's business acumen and financial daring were sufficient to ensure the success of his journalism, and the secular growth of the magazine's circulation figures testifies to its 'professional' production and promotion. Within its first year of publication, for example, *Zion's*

Watch Tower was selling in greater numbers than was *The Christa-delphian* after twenty-five years in circulation.[3]

It is unlikely that Russell had had more than a fleeting acquaint-ance with religious publishing before launching *Zion's Watch Tower* in 1879, but he did have the initial advantage of access to the subscription list of N. H. Barbour's own journal, the *Herald of the Morning*. Since he was thus spared the task of seeking a large number of prospective subscribers, the very first editions were easily disposed of among the readership of Barbour's works. The scant information which we have about the initial publishing ventures indicates that tracts and pamphlets were being produced for distribution in hundreds of thousands within only four years of the magazine's appearance. The phenomenal success of Russell's volumes of *Millennial Dawn*[4] (published between 1886–1904) testi-fies to his flair for articulating a special brand of religious propa-ganda, for which there was a ready market. Moreover, his early success convinced Russell that the Lord had called him for this kind of work and that publishing was the appropriate means of giving expression to his religious feelings and convictions.

If Russell's original idea was to serve God through writing and disseminating literature, then the letter of that idea has been pre-served by successive generations of Bible students and Jehovah's Witnesses. The spirit of his vision, however, has gradually under-gone so many revisions that very little of the original conception is visible in today's Watch Tower Society. Nevertheless, it must be said that official statements continue to argue that the Watch Tower Society is still nothing but a publishing organization. Even during Russell's lifetime, the Society began to encourage Bible students to follow various schemes for creating local study groups and evangelical agencies, and after his death, the Society engaged in massive programmes to promote conventions and public meet-ings, to tighten up the organizational arrangements in local groups, to promote foreign outreaches and to centralize the administration, not only of publishing activities, but also of the local provisions for worship and study. During this time the headquarters staff increased in size in order to supervise and direct the Society's extra-publishing activities.

In fact, one of the most striking consequences of the Society's origins as a publishing firm is the prominence which has been attributed to the headquarters staff and the factory workers. Russell lost no time in gathering a small 'family' of co-workers around him in Allegheny, and the institution of a Bethel 'home' for full-time Watch Tower staff (begun in 1909) has persisted to the present day. Many articles in the magazines have described the detailed life within Bethel, and the 'family' has clearly functioned as a normative reference-group for more distant followers of Russell's ideas. For instance, it became the practice from 1909 onwards for the Watch Tower to carry information about the prayers, hymns and readings which constituted Bethel's own programme of worship. The pattern of worship in Bethel eventually attained the status of recommended practice in all Bible student groups, and today it constitutes the obligatory scheme of worship and study in all congregations of Jehovah's Witnesses. Bethel has also exercised the less formal and less precise function of setting and outwardly maintaining certain standards of orderly living, productive work and organizational loyalty. Today, it is still very common for Jehovah's Witnesses to pay occasional visits to their nearest Bethel in order to observe the work in progress and speak with the 'family' there. In the first two decades of the twentieth century, then, the Watch Tower Society ceased to be a purely publishing enterprise and assumed the functions of a fully-fledged religious sect. The nature of this evolution, as we have described it, does not conform entirely with Bryan Wilson's analysis of the Society's early transformations;

> Les Témoins de Jéhovah ... offrent l'aspect d'une transformation progressive de la direction charismatique en une autorité bureaucratique destinée à la propagation plus efficace des croyances des Témoins.[5]

It is hoped that the following pages will justify our departure from his views.

Centre and periphery

One of the most important consequences of the Society's evolution from a publishing house to a sect has been the undiminishing sense of dependence which local groups have felt towards the central organ. The Society began as a disseminator of literature serving its subscribers; even when local ecclesias came to play an important role for subscribers, the sense of the Society's overriding precedence could never be ignored. Consequently, initiatives have invariably come from the centre and have been dictated to the dependent groups. The Society has never acted as a federation of more or less autonomous ecclesias (as was the case with Christadelphianism and Brethrenism), but has always functioned as an indispensable source of life-blood to its dependent outlets. It remains the case today that each group must be in communication with a source of material for evangelism and must, therefore, remain dependent on the Watch Tower Society. The same considerations clearly apply to the hypothetically autonomous individual Bible student. The contrast with Christadelphianism could hardly be more striking. Christadelphian ecclesias have invariably, but with varying degrees of urgency, protested their absolute autonomy. It was only after a long time that the Birmingham Temperance Hall ecclesia and the editorial office of *The Christadelphian* began issuing material to help other ecclesias in their evangelical work.

The First World War imposed circumstances on individual Bible students and on the Watch Tower Society which appear to be paradoxical in some respects. On the one hand, progressive mobilization of the British and American adult male populations served to polarize Bible students by making a clear distinction between conformists and conscientious objectors. The need to make a personal decision on this issue must have contributed greatly to a heightened awareness of identity among the Bible students who registered as conscientious objectors, and must have strengthened their resolve to remain faithful to the Society's principles in all eventualities. In this respect, mobilization may have contributed to the Society's ability to survive severe persecution. On the other hand, the war indirectly brought official condemnation of the Society in the USA and in other parts of the world, and entailed the suspension of publishing activities for a short period of time. It is difficult to say on balance whether the trial, imprisonment and subsequent release of the Society's leaders proved favourable or unfavourable to their programme of comprehensive evangelizing. Even if it were considered that the effects of that period were largely unfavourable for the evangelization programme, it must not be overlooked that the suspension of activities almost coincided with, and brought an end to, the most tempestuous era in the Society's internal affairs. It could plausibly be argued that Rutherford, for example, returned from prison in 1919 in something like a martyr's guise and was immediately able to impose his will on a fellowship of Bible students which no longer contained his most acid critics. In a long-term perspective, the First World War might have contributed to the Society's survival and subsequent revival in an even more highly centralized form than its ante-bellum condition. Certainly, pressure on local ecclesias to conform to headquarters' initiatives was much stronger after 1918, and the bureaucracy increased in complexity at the same time. Yet, there is unmistakable evidence that the bureaucracy was already a significant feature of the Watch Tower Society in its earliest years, and this is nowhere better illustrated than in the chain of events which culminated in the Society's unofficial acceptance of responsibility for the administration of Bible student ecclesias.

Ecclesial formation and transformation

As a corollary of Russell's insistence that the Watch Tower Society should not compromise its status as a publishing enterprise by becoming just one more Christian sect, he was cautious about the formation of local groups of Bible students. Initially, he discouraged such groups completely, but he later came to appreciate their necessity and their usefulness in promoting sales of Watch Tower literature. The normative power of the *Watch Tower* magazine was consistently orientated towards checking the possibility that local group leaders would exercise priestly functions. Personal initiatives were conspicuously scorned, and stringent bounds were set upon the leaders' freedom of manoeuvre. As soon as the local congregations appeared to be achieving even a small degree of autonomy in the decade preceding 1914, Russell devised schemes for practical evangelism which necessitated closer liaison between individuals and the editorial office. Consequently, 'organization men' (as opposed to 'locals') began to exercise important functions in administering the distribution of tracts, public meetings, visits from Pilgrims and arrangements for conventions. In this way, the traditional leadership structure of Elders and Deacons was bypassed by the institution of 'pioneer captains' with the result that, after 1914 especially, the Watch Tower Society was able to exercise a much closer form of control over its dependent ecclesias. Even the stimulus to numerical expansion came from headquarters and found expression in officially organized and approved schemes. The evidence of administrative changes which took place during Russell's lifetime points to the inaccuracy of some interpretations of the Watch Tower Society's organizational development. Alan

Rogerson, for example, dates the change in style of the Society's organization from Rutherford's accession to power in 1917:

> Rutherford believed God was using the Watch Tower Society as His one and only channel of communication and therefore if anyone remained independent of God's organization it could only mean that they were not faithful Christians. These and other lines of argument were used by Rutherford to start the long campaign somehow or other to dominate the ecclesias.[6]

But, as we have already argued, this campaign had been mounted by Russell: Rutherford pursued to their conclusion policies that were slowly achieving definition towards the end of his predecessor's regime. W. Schnell[7] and W. C. Stevenson[8] have also tried to create the erroneous impression that it was only with Rutherford's accession to presidential power that significant changes began to occur in the movement's administrative policies. Their accounts are strongly coloured by personal prejudices and must be treated with extreme caution.

If it is hypothesized that the organizational and administrative changes effected by Rutherford were in many respects a continuation of trends instigated by Russell, then it is easier to understand how Rutherford was able to make such apparently serious changes without provoking a massive defection from the Watch Tower Society. Admittedly, many followers of Russell did cease subscribing to the *Watch Tower*, and some joined rival organizations, but the majority of subscribers remained loyal to the Watch Tower Society. What is more, the loyal subscribers must have taken up Rutherford's organizational and evangelical innovations with considerable enthusiasm, since subscription figures rose steeply after 1918. At the Magdeburg convention of 1925 there was a rough indication that 50% of the audience had been recruited to the Society since 1922.[9] Moreover, A. H. MacMillan had found in the previous year that of 349 Bible students who replied to a short questionnaire at the Chicago convention, only 35 had shown interest in the work of the Society as a result of parental influence.[10] We feel fairly confident, therefore, in arguing that the rapid numerical expansion of the Society's supporters after 1918 was not a reflection of efficient internal recruitment, but was due in large part to the implementation of new, Rutherford-style methods of evangelism. Yet these striking indications of success would be almost inconceivable if it were seriously maintained that Rutherford had begun to introduce radically new and unprecedented methods of organization and proselytization in 1917. On the other hand, if it were hypothesized that Rutherford was simply adding the finishing touches to schemes which had already been adumbrated within the Society under the previous presidency, then the success of the recruiting programme becomes more credible. In this respect, it might also be fruitful to examine later the ways in which Rutherford sought to 'borrow' some of Russell's official authority for his personal schemes.

Organizational dilemmas

The path of the Watch Tower Society's organizational evolution during Russell's lifetime indicates that he was continually performing a balancing act on a tightrope with, on one side the Scylla of excessively rational and impersonal evangelism, and on the other side the Charybdis of excessively autonomous local companies of Bible students. This view of the dilemmas facing Russell is supported by Theodor Sprague's analysis of the distribution of authority in the Society around 1940.[11] Sprague considered the 'organizing forces or common threads' in the Society as (*a*) social and (*b*) individualistic, sentiments. While the present analysis is not always in agreement with Sprague's, at least the basic dilemma forms a point of common agreement.

Russell's dilemma is a variant of what T. O'Dea has termed 'the dilemma of power; conversion versus coercion'.[12] While O'Dea concentrated on the problems of a religious body of deciding between optimal 'coverage' of the population and maintenance of stringent screening standards for membership, we could add the further complication of a decision between optimal membership and maintenance of exclusively religious reasons for belonging. It was not so much that Russell feared the necessity of compromising his theology, but that he abhorred the possibility of people joining Bible student groups simply for the sake of participating in a warm, primary social group. He frequently elaborated on the theme by criticizing the tendency of contemporary American protestant churches to become what he called 'social club churches'.

Russell's original plan was to promote rationality in evangelism at all costs, but constant complaints from *Watch Tower* subscribers eventually persuaded him that the formation of local groups of subscribers would fulfill an equally important, but expressive (as distinct from instrumental) function. Thereafter, Russell devoted a large amount of editorial space to the problems of achieving and maintaining a satisfactory balance between the purely expressive and the purely instrumental functions of the local ecclesia. Towards the end of his life, he seemed to have reached the conclusion that the desired balance would only result from severe restrictions on the expressive function and closer central control over the instrumental function. The Watch Tower Society's organizational development from 1878–1914 can be considered in terms of a dialectical progression.

(*a*) The initial phase was characterized by the emphasis given to the instrumental function of publishing and distributing millennialist literature. The purely instrumental phase lasted for about fifteen years.

(*b*) The second phase was characterized by a relaxation of the prohibition on forming groups of Bible students and by a willingness to offer advice on how each group should be constituted and administered. The reasons for relaxing the prohibition were undoubtedly complex and varied, but one can hypothesize such considerations as the fear of losing subscribers if they lacked social support for their ideas; the financial advantages accruing from group involvement in evangelism and sales of literature; the greater ease of checking doctrinal dissent if believers were grouped together for study and discussion; and the likelihood of greater commercial stability if the subscribers became a kind of permanent membership. This phase lasted for about ten years.

(*c*) The third phase opened around 1905 and can be considered both as a reaction against the previous phase and as a synthesis of the two earlier phases. The dangers of allowing local ecclesias to assume unrestricted expressive functions were reflected in the members' reluctance to remain committed to evangelism rather than to worship and study. The desirability of revamping the pristine image of a straightforward publishing concern was tempered by the realization that the expressive functions had become institutionalized and could no longer be ignored. The attempted resolution of the problems took the form of heightened central control over all aspects of the local companies. The Society even began dictating officially acceptable ways and means of fulfilling expressive functions.

Visible and specific goals

Both the notion of an unqualified publishing business and the notion of a loose federation of independent companies of Bible students were submerged under the influx of innovations dating from around 1905. Traces of the earlier character of the Watch Tower Society persisted in the new arrangements and, of course, Russell was still the visible head of the organization. Yet it is clear that the Society's structure and goals underwent very important changes in the years immediately preceding 1914.

It would be misleading to imply that Russell had consciously implemented a detailed plan for enlarging the scope of the Watch Tower Society's activities to include the close supervision of affairs in Bible student classes, for the Society's actual development bears greater resemblance to a concatenation of *ad hoc* adjustments to new situations. In the first place, the Society pursued the goal of supplying evangelistic materials and advice to independent Bible students. These people, in turn, pursued the goal of ensuring their personal salvation by a combined method of character development and public witnessing. While both the Society and the individual subscribers to Watch Tower literature were initially content to pursue their distinct yet interdependent goals without establishing more affective rapport, it soon became obvious that a need had been created among the Bible students for closer contact with the Society and with other Bible students. After early resistance, Russell eventually conceded the advisability of forming local classes where Watch Tower literature would be discussed. At this point he also saw an opportunity to increase the efficiency of the literature distribution by instigating formal, direct relations between *groups* of Bible students and the Society in the hope of finding even wider markets for Watch Tower books, tracts and magazines. He then seemed to achieve at one stroke the satisfaction of individual Bible students' needs and the improvement of collective productivity. These achievements, however, entailed further problems to which Russell was forced to find solutions which began to impose quite new and unforeseen goals on Bible students and on the Society.

As soon as the Watch Tower office accepted the desirability of dealing directly with classes of Bible students, it indirectly assumed responsibility for their organization and continuity. In addition, the Society came to rely on the continued orderly functioning of local classes as a guarantee of its own markets and literature-out-lets. Since it could hardly afford to condone lax administration of the classes or the possibility of collective deviation from Watch Tower doctrinal standards, the Society's leaders found themselves increasingly concerned with matters of guidance, administration and arbitration at the local level. But before order and continuity could be assured in all classes, a source of authority had to be identified and legitimated. Not surprisingly, the leaders began to claim legitimation for the Society's authority over the classes of Bible students in terms of its peculiar mission to the world and of the Bible students' collective responsibility to ensure that its divinely-ordained aims were attained. The earliest goal of litera-ture production and promotion was, therefore, eclipsed by the higher, prophetic goal of gathering together the body of people chosen by God to live as princes in heaven during the imminent millennial reign of Christ on earth.

At the same time, the individual Bible students' goal of character development and salvation-assurance gave way to a new goal of spreading the news of the Watch Tower Society's divine commis-sion as widely as possible. The new goal naturally entailed recog-nition of the Society's authority and was largely successful in sustaining the Bible students' orderly pursuit of its collective goals, but there were still many difficult obstacles to be overcome before perfect integration of personal and collective goals could be achieved. This represents perhaps J. F. Rutherford's most outstand-ing contribution to the re-organization of Russell's movement be-tween 1919–39.

To some extent, then, administrative reorganization and doctrinal revisions in the Watch Tower movement between 1890 and 1910 can be attributed to Russell's pragmatic attempts to solve prob-lems stemming from the original strain between collective and personal goals. As remedial measures were implemented, so fur-ther strains developed and necessitated still further departure from the organizational and doctrinal starting-points.

The distribution of authority

In comparing the organizational evolution of the Watch Tower Society with that of other religious sects, the most important point to emerge from its history is that its most persistent and characteristic form was that of a publishing enterprise. The consequences of this dominant characteristic have many ramifications for the Society's subsequent development. It has meant that, amongst other things, the editor of the *Watch Tower* has always exercised the most potent kind of control over the Society's following.[13] Even when schemes for evangelizing had been adopted which had nothing to do with the *Watch Tower*, the editor has still had the greatest power to influence decisions, advertise the schemes and stimulate support among the subscribers. During the presidencies of Russell and Rutherford, there was surprisingly little opposition to their simultaneous fulfilment of editorial and presidential functions, and one assumes that the present President has no small amount of control over the editorial policy of the magazine.

In the case of Russell, there can be little doubt that the subscribers to the *Watch Tower* legitimated his power in terms of both personal charisma as a preacher and institutional charisma as editor of the magazine. A. H. MacMillan was making essentially the same point when he wrote: 'Throughout his life, Russell had been "the Society". We had no real organization. There had been no need of it.'[14] It would have been more accurate to say that there had always been an underlying bureaucratic structure, but that in addition Russell had acquired so much personal, charismatic authority in the Society that very few people objected to his manipulation of the bureaucratic structure. For instance, the law of America demanded that there should be a Board of Directors to run the incorporated Zion's Watch Tower Society and that they should be elected annually. The Society ostensibly observed the legal requirements, but it was still the case that Russell nominated the prospective Directors himself, and his preferences were invariably respected. The exercise of informal pressure within a nominally formal organization ensured that Russell's authority within the Society (charismatic and rational-legal) could hardly be challenged. Not even accusations of immorality combined with the scandal of legal separation from his wife could undermine his power to influence the committed *Watch Tower* subscribers. In exercising leadership over the Watch Tower Society Russell was continually taking not only routine decisions about day-to-day business but also what Selznick has termed 'critical' decisions.[15] A critical decision involves, in addition to the routine task of adjusting means to ends, defining new ends and new means for their achievement. It is the kind of creative action which can be pursued only at the highest levels of a bureaucratic structure and which, to some extent, may entail procedures normally considered antithetical to the routine process of decision-making. The leader whose authority rests partly on claims to charismatic legitimacy is in the best position to make critical decisions, because he possesses the necessary independence to stand 'outside' the structure and to define or redefine the institution's goals and values. In this respect, Russell was peculiarly well qualified to make critical decisions affecting the administration and the policy of the Watch Tower Society.

From the evidence available on the Society's history, it seems clear that, in addition to fulfilling the function of the magazine's editor Russell personally made most, if not all, decisions affecting doctrine, teaching methods, missionary strategy and administration. In the words of a close collaborator: 'Russell had learned through many hurtsome experiences that few men could be trusted with serious responsibility.'[16] Allowing for the strong possibility that MacMillan may have been rationalizing Russell's unwillingness to delegate responsibility, it remains the case that his leadership within a nominally bureaucratic structure was intensely personal, creative and critical. A further aspect of Russell's critical leadership was his devotion to defending the Watch Tower Society's 'integrity'. Once again, we follow Selznick's usage of the term:

> The integrity of an enterprise goes beyond efficiency, beyond organizational form and procedures, even beyond group cohesion. Integrity combines organization and policy. It is the unity that emerges when a particular orientation becomes so firmly a part of group life that it colors and directs a wide variety of attitudes, decisions, and forms of organization and does so at many levels of experience.[17]

The notion of 'integrity' is especially apt with regard to the Watch Tower Society since, as we have seen elsewhere, Russell was quick to promote an image of the Society as the institutional embodiment of peculiarly sacred purposes. He defined the Society's integrity in such a way that no Bible student could easily divorce devotion to God from commitment to the Watch Tower Society, and he defended that integrity in the face of public opprobrium with basically similar arguments. It is no small mark of his salience and critical importance in the Society, therefore, that the institution became known as Russellism, and the committed followed as Russellites.

What is more, for some Bible students the Society's integrity was inextricably bound up with the person of Russell, and they found it impossible to consider the Society as integral in the absence of his personal leadership. One of the more obvious consequences of Russell's personal style of critical leadership was that many kinds of serious problems developed when a second President attempted to fulfil the leadership function.

We have already described the source of Russell's authority in the Society as two-fold: (*a*) as the editor of the magazine and of many books and pamphlets, and later (*b*) as the beloved nominal 'Pastor' of most Bible student groups. The distinction between these two kinds of authority is made for purely analytical purposes, and it is not suggested that Russell's behaviour as President could be realistically categorized under two separate headings. On the contrary, his continued success probably depended largely on the subtle ways in which he managed (*a*) to conceal the two-fold source of his authority and (*b*) to confuse the two types in practice. Thus, he was able to highlight the two kinds of authority either separately or in combination. The subtle practice of this device can be seen at its most impressive in Russell's own explications of his role in the Society and in history.

In some cases Russell was content to claim that God had chosen to bless the work of the Watch Tower Society of which he happened to be President. He exercised authority, therefore, as a consequence of his position in the Society's bureaucratic structure. He extended this line of reasoning to include his role as editor of the magazine and as author of many books. That was his task, and God had decided to give him support in its execution. There are frequent hints that the Society's success as a publishing concern had come as something of a surprise, for example in *Zion's Watch Tower* of 15 November 1881 : 'The work has been so much greater than we had anticipated, and seemingly was impelled by an unseen hand and at such special times, too, that we cannot doubt that it is all of the Lord.' But the temptation to claim anything more than divine blessing was checked by Russell's earliest and most tolerant view of the distribution of truth in the world, which was expressed in *Zion's Watch Tower* of 15 August 1879 as follows: 'We are glad to believe that all parties [i.e. religious groups] have some truth, and that they defend their errors with sincerity.' Rutherford, of course, took up this argument in trying to justify his exercise of authority as President after Russell's death.

Indeed, Rutherford took steps to make it clear that he would not try to assume Russell's role as Pastor in the Society, but would simply assume the bureaucratic role of President.[18] Not only did Rutherford not 'borrow' Russell's personal charisma, but he also began systematically to undermine the personal nature of the ecclesias' relation with the Society. All elected officials were instructed to resign because they had held office in ecclesias over which Russell had been Pastor. (It was argued that their appointments could not be considered valid now that Russell was dead.) New officials were elected whose loyalty was proven to be to the Society and not necessarily to the memory of Russell. The nature of the link between ecclesia and Society was further rationalized along impersonal lines, and the Society began to exercise a more pervasive and immediate control over local affairs. While the Society had always possessed a bureaucratic structure, this feature came to the fore in the years following Russell's death. The rules governing every aspect of the work and organization of Bible students were formalized and publicized; distinct spheres of competence were outlined for each official; the hierarchy of offices achieved better definition; the analytical distinction between office and incumbent was emphasized; and official kinds of document replaced the formerly informal means of communication between Bible students and the Society.

When it became clear that the Watch Tower Society was developing into an unusually successful publishing and evangelizing agency, Russell seemed less inclined to claim legitimation for his power in the organization on purely rational-legal grounds. In fact, as the work progressed and expanded, so the Society's image of itself veered in the direction of a historically unique and peculiarly privileged institution. Instead of thinking of themselves merely as propagators of the Truth, Bible students began to consider their group's role in history as unprecedentedly significant for the impending Millennial Age. It is doubtful whether this apocalyptic and exclusive image was common to Bible students in the earliest years of their associational existence, but one can detect hints of such an idea as early as 1882 when Russell wrote:

> Our work will not be one of destruction but of salvation.... We shall rule as kings.... We, the promised seed of Abraham, through whom all

the families of the earth shall be blessed, shall go forth a royal priesthood.[19]

At about this time, tolerant references to other religious groups appeared in the *Watch Tower* with distinctly lower frequency than did uncharitable remarks about them. The 1880s and 1890s were clearly a period of doctrinal hardening and of institutional entrenchment. Russell's image of himself and his image in the Society underwent such extensive revision during the period of entrenchment that he emerged around 1900 cast in a radically different role. From that time onwards, he flirted with the notion that he had been personally selected by God to lead the propagation of exclusive truth on earth. It may be more than coincidence that the transformation of his image began to take place at roughly the same time as the first volumes in the *Millennial Dawn* series began to appear. He was no longer just an editor of a magazine; he had evolved into an influential author in his own right. Significantly, it was also towards the close of this period that some Bible students objected to Russell's autocratic methods of running the Society and ruling the Bible House at Allegheny. This episode could be interpreted as evidence of resistance towards Russell's assumption of powers which were not strictly related to his position in the bureaucratic structure.

Russell's personal charisma also arose from, and in turn reinforced, the pastoral function which he exercised over a large number of ecclesias. (Rutherford referred to this as Russell's 'peculiar relationship to the church' in *Zion's Watch Tower* of 15 January 1917.) Since the emotional attachment of the majority of Bible students to Russell was extremely strong, it is not at all surprising that his death should have precipitated such a traumatic succession crisis. For while Rutherford was partially able to inherit the charisma of Russell's office, he was completely unable to inherit his predecessor's personal charisma. Given what we know about the 'few ambitious ones at headquarters [who] were holding caucases here and there,'[20] it was almost inevitable that a successor to Russell who lacked his personal charisma would face severe difficulty in justifying his claims to power in the Society. In the event, Rutherford adopted the tactics of undermining the very idea of personal charisma in order to establish his own authority on the only acceptable base, i.e. on rational-legal grounds.

As we have already shown, the bureaucratic structure of the

Watch Tower Society was strengthened in its third phase of development. The strengthening process was pursued with renewed vigour under the presidency of Rutherford, and a contributory factor in his successful bid for power was the decision to restore immediate, concrete aims to the Society. He stimulated a resurgence of evangelical fervour among Bible students by giving them specific tasks on specific days, organizing co-ordinated sales campaigns, appointing Service Directors to administer evangelism in local ecclesias and publishing a magazine which was geared towards the recruitment of new workers for the Watch Tower cause. After the disappointment of prophetical disconfirmation in 1914, the trauma of Russell's death in 1916, the disturbance caused by a succession crisis in 1917, and the demoralization caused by legal obstructions to publishing work in 1918, Rutherford chose to re-vitalize the movement by imposing specific tasks and setting stringent standards of loyalty and enthusiasm. In the process, of course, he alienated a large number of people but he at least had the satisfaction of knowing that those who were still keen to work with him in the 1920s were deeply committed to his ideals. If Rutherford was unable to inherit Russell's personal charismatic authority, he more than compensated by justifying the distribution of official power on the grounds of rationality and expediency. The change in Presidents was accompanied, then, by a change in the ways in which the new President justified the distribution of power within the Society. The change in grounds for claiming legitimation of authority did not, however, represent a complete break with previous practice, for, as we have repeatedly stressed, Russell's original claim to authority rested partly on his position within the bureaucracy of a publishing firm. In his case, it would be wrong to argue that personal charisma had undergone routinization; rather, his original charisma of office gave rise to, and came to be complemented by, personal charisma. Corresponding changes also took place in the sect's organizational structure and in the order of priority among its beliefs.

Conclusion

The early organizational development of Zion's Watch Tower Tract Society, from which the sect of Jehovah's Witnesses is descended, does not conform with any of the available sociological models of religious group formation and evolution. Rather, an idiosyncratic combination of features from several models can be said to characterize this particular group's history. A full understanding of its development must include consideration, not only of the role of a charismatic founder, of schism and of organized revival as circumstances determining the organization's emergence, but also of the founder's position as editor of the magazine, President of the publishing enterprise and nominal 'Pastor' of the majority of Bible student classes in the USA. The sole fact that the publishing function preceded the establishment of study groups accounts very largely for Russell's ability to exercise so much personal control over the way in which they were organized. His position as editor of the only medium of communication among far-flung groups of people sharing his special brand of Second Adventism also facilitated his eventual monopolization of authority within the Society. Finally, his subtle but significant alterations to the focal doctrines of the Watch Tower Society served to clothe his authority and the precise arrangements of his organization with an air of divine sanction. In consequence, the Watch Tower Society emerged from the position of being nothing more than an evangelistic publishing concern to assume the functions of an hierarchically organized, exclusivist body of evangelists claiming for themselves divine commission and protection. It seems unlikely that this pattern of development would have been forthcoming if the group had emerged from one of the sets of circumstances more commonly associated with the rise of religious sects. In large measure, its departure from the expected pattern of events can be used to explain the precise ways in which Jehovah's Witnesses nowadays differ in respect of organization and activities from apparently similar sects.

NOTES

1. Bryan R. Wilson in his Introduction to *Patterns of Sectarianism*, ed. Bryan R. Wilson, Heinemann 1967, pp.17-18.

2. W. S. Hudson, *American Protestantism*, University of Chicago Press 1961, pp.103-4.

3. Bryan R. Wilson reports that there were less than 5,000 subscribers to *The Christadelphian* in 1893. *Sects and Society*, Heinemann 1961, p.250.

4. *Millennial Dawn* was the original title of a series of books whose separate titles and dates of publication are as follows:

1886   *The Divine Plan of the Ages*
1889   *The Time is at Hand*
1891   *Thy Kingdom Come*
1897   *The Battle of Armageddon*
1899   *The Atonement between God and Man*
1904   *The New Creation*

The collective title was changed in 1904 to *Studies in the Scriptures.*

5. Bryan R. Wilson, 'Apparition et persistance des sectes dans un milieu social en evolution', *Archives de Sociologie des Religions*, 5, 1958, p.144.

6. Alan Rogerson, *Millions Now Living Will Never Die. A Study of Jehovah's Witnesses*, Constable 1969, p.50.

7. William J. Schnell, *Thirty Years a Watch Tower Slave*, Marshall, Morgan and Scott 1957.

8. W. C. Stevenson, *Year of Doom, 1975*, Hutchinson 1967, p. 146.

9. *The Watch Tower*, 15 November 1925.

10. Ibid., 15 March 1924.

11. Theodore Sprague, 'Some notable features in the authority structure of a sect', *Social Forces*, XXI, 1943, pp.344-50.

12. Thomas O'Dea, 'Sociological dilemmas: the paradoxes of institutionalization' in *Sociological Theory, Values and Socio-Cultural Change: Essays in Honor of Pitrim Sorokin*, ed. E. A. Tiryakian, Free Press of Glencoe 1963, p.84.

13. I am indebted to Dr B. R. Wilson for drawing my attention to two instructive cases for comparison. In Christian Science, the Trustees of the Publishing House were engaged in a bitter struggle for power with the Directors of the Mother Church between 1919 and 1920, and in Christadelphianism the editorship of the sect's magazine has always conferred strong informal leadership on the incumbent.

14. A. H. MacMillan, *Faith on the March*, New Jersey, Prentice-Hall 1967, pp.61-2.

15. P. Selznick, *Leadership in Administration*, Harper & Row 1957, p. 56.

16. A. H. MacMillan, op. cit., p.62.

17. P. Selznick, op. cit., p.138.

18. *Zion's Watch Tower*, 15 January 1917.

19. Ibid., November 1882.

20. A. H. MacMillan, op. cit., p.68.

3 The Secularized Sabbath: Formerly Sunday; Now the Weekend

W. S. F. Pickering

T H E way in which I intend to use the word secular does not contain the subtlety of implication that certain modern theologians have taken pleasure in adding to its meaning. Rather, I shall use the words secular and secularization as referring to an absence of religion or religious influences. And by religion I assume systems, values and actions related to a deity or superhuman being. The secular has meaning, therefore, only with reference to religion. It is its inverse correlate.

In encouraging Christians to attend worship on the first day of the week to commemorate the Resurrection of Christ, the leaders of the early church established a pattern of devotion which was to persist all down the ages. Loyalty to this practice has afforded a simple means of gauging the strength and following of the church. An examination of church attendance on a Sunday in an allegedly Christian society offers an indicator – admittedly one amongst many – of the level of religiosity, or obversely the level of secularization in that society. It is an indicator which has validity in terms of the present as well as the past. By this and other criteria it is hardly necessary to be reminded that contemporary western society is undergoing rapid secularization, which to some observers has increased notably over the past few years.

However, the degree of sacralization of Sunday, or its secularization, is not to be seen merely in terms of dominical worship. True, the early church viewed Sunday primarily with regard to the gathering of the faithful in order to take part in a worshipping service, generally the eucharist, which they had to attend before or after work. But as early as 306 at the Council of Elvira in Spain, Christians were called upon to abstain from work on Sundays, and this was confirmed at the Council of Laodicea in 380. In 321 Constantine, without reference to any Christian ideals, ordered Sunday to be a public holiday.[1] Such teaching and legislation in connection with Sunday forms a basically socio-religious component, which has its roots in Jewish Sabbatarian precepts, though a day each week free from work found its way into various parts of the Roman Empire before the time of Christ. It is interesting to note that the church begins to recognize Sunday as a day of rest at a time when the church itself was being given considerable status in society and was ceasing to be a sect. Sunday legislation thus appears when Christianity shows signs of becoming an established religion. The church applied Sabbath attitudes to Sunday because it feared idleness and vice would be rampant on a day free from work. The attempt of Christians from the early fourth century to apply the fourth commandment to Sunday has persisted with various interpretations right down to the present day. The point of controversy and reform has nearly always centred on the application of the ideals of the Sabbath to social behaviour on a Sunday. That it should be a day of worship has never been an issue of debate.

Sabbatarianism, as a movement calling for the careful regulation of social behaviour on a Sunday, first appeared in the advanced stages of the Reformation. England and Scotland alone sustained it. Later, in the light of Sabbath slackness, the Evangelical Movement revived interest in Sunday legislation – witness, for example, the Lord's Day Observance Act of 1780 drawn up by Porteus, the evangelical Bishop of London. The Act severely limited Sunday trade, and all places of entertainment which demanded payment of money were to be closed. Sabbatarianism came to the fore through the mid-Victorian upsurge of Puritanical ideals and was given expression in the Acts of 1854 and 1855 which closed public houses on a Sunday and prohibited trading in connection with newspapers, shaving, smoking, etc. The Factory Act of 1847, in guaranteeing at least a day's rest to almost the whole of society, encouraged the possible enactment of Sabbatarian ideals. The general habits of people on a Sunday in the middle and late nineteenth century, and further into the twentieth century, especially among the middle classes, are well known. They have been gleaned, if not from literature, then from stories of grandparents or great-grandparents. The norm of that strange phenomenon, the English Sunday, was based on attendance at church, once, twice, or thrice each Sunday, and might also have included attendance at Sunday school or the Bible class. Forbidden were trade, travel, games, and all activities which gave physical pleasure or caused paid work, and to cap it all people were expected to wear sombre clothes. To laugh on a Sunday was even thought to be sinful. Such was the English Sabbath – a Sabbath baptized in the name of Christianity and confirmed by the Church of England and the Nonconformist churches. A foreign observer wrote: 'I do not know for what unspeakable sin the Lord has sentenced England to the weekly punishment of her Sunday.'[2]

The norms established in the nineteenth century, it has been argued, were basically middle class. Quite apart from their religious justification they could be more readily carried out by the wealthier sections of society than the poorer. The precepts may have given little or no pleasure to their participants but they suited the middle classes because:

(*a*) The middle classes had the opportunity of enjoying themselves during the week, whereas working class folk could not do this by reason of the long hours they were forced to work during the week.

(*b*) The Sunday activities permitted by the Sabbatarians were home-based, that is, they were completely removed from public entertainment which was outlawed on a Sunday. The middle classes benefited from this because in their comfortable homes they could relax and marginally enjoy themselves. For the poor, their hovels afforded no such facilities and at the same time they were prevented from enjoying public amusements and so escaping from their wretched conditions.

(*c*) The wealthier sections of society could carry out the religious precepts of a Sunday only by employing servants to do necessary work on Sunday in their homes, such as lighting fires, preparing meals, and so on. They had little or no guilt feelings about employing servants in this way, though they prevented other people from working on a Sunday in ways which would have given the working classes a more enjoyable day of rest.

It seems reasonable to suggest that for the working classes Sunday during the nineteenth century and into the twentieth century was viewed above all else as a day of rest – above church-going, even above recreation. The hard toil of the week and the constant fight against poverty or near poverty gave to the working classes what they most needed – the opportunity to rest from their labours.

However it is necessary to add a *caveat*. Nineteenth-century Sabbatarianism was middle class in origin and ideology, but in the acceptance and carrying out the precepts there was no absolute division between the classes. Many working-class individuals, in particular skilled craftsmen, accepted Sabbatarian teaching and faithfully carried out its precepts.[3]

In attempting to analyse the level of religiosity or secularization of a Sunday, two components can thus be seen to exist.

Component A   that which relates to attendance at public worship and other religious services – the religious component.

Component B   that which relates to activities outside public worship which are social in form but which are justified according to religious precepts – the socio-religious component.

From this it can be deduced that secularization is at a maximum when components A and B, according to some determined scale of measurement, are at a minimum; and similarly Sunday religiosity is at a maximum when the two components are maximized. Such reasoning would indicate that the Puritan Sunday or the English Sunday was more sacralized than the Mediaeval or Continental Sunday.

I want to examine the two components with regard to contemporary society in England. Some of the propositions that are advanced are difficult to substantiate empirically: they arise out of personal observation and a general awareness of what is believed to be happening in society at the present time. Again, some are subject to variations according to region, age, or class, and by and large these variations have not been incorporated. Moreover, the propositions are descriptive rather than analytical and they apply with certain reservations to European countries and to North America, indeed to the western world itself. (The terms middle class and working class are used in a wide sense which are held to be adequate for the purposes in hand.)

A   *Factors relating to the religious component*

1. Church-going has at the present time been reduced to the order of what is believed to be about or slightly more than 10% of the adult population. This is an overall figure for England which

includes people of all denominations and which varies relatively little in the matter of regions. The level may rise to something like 15% on Easter Day but the signs are that the figures on a normal Sunday as well as on festivals are declining. It is probably true to say that the number of people who are fairly regular in attending church, that is once a month or more frequently, is double the number who would be found in the churches on a normal Sunday.

2. The proportion of those who attend church twice on a Sunday also appears to be diminishing. What thin statistical evidence there is points in this direction. The pious, and perhaps the not-so pious in Victorian times and afterwards, were in the habit of attending church more than once on a Sunday. This is no longer the case. Certainly in the Anglican church, anyone attending church regularly once a Sunday is given high marks! It must also be recalled that choirs are no longer as popular as they used to be; at least those who were choir members frequently went to church twice on a Sunday.

3. The relative sizes of morning and evening attendances have changed, and in part this has been due to a decline in the number of people attending twice on a Sunday. Regional and denominational factors are probably still important in considering this. In the Anglican Church, changes in ecclesiastical teaching, particularly that associated with the Parish and People Movement, which is basically theological in origin, have placed great emphasis on regular morning worship at the eucharist. The teaching has conceded the point that evening worship is optional which, coupled with other social pressures to be mentioned later, has encouraged the serious decline in such congregations. This seems to be very much the case in working-class areas where even twenty years ago the evening congregation was generally much larger than the morning congregation. The position is now reversed: the morning congregation, usually centred round the parish communion, has become much larger than the evening congregation which in many cases has virtually dwindled away. Evening congregations probably remain much stronger than morning congregations in many Anglican churches in rural areas, though probably not in those which have a parish communion. It is interesting that in some Methodist churches which used to have larger congregations in the evening

than in the morning, the position is now reversed.[4] Evening congregations have fallen away and worshippers are encouraged to come in the morning. There is no attempt to justify this change theologically; it has been adopted on grounds of expediency in relation to changing social habits.

It ought to be mentioned that evening services as public acts of worship in churches where morning services have already taken place, constitute in the main an essentially British phenomenon. The phenomenon has its roots first of all in the Prayer Book service of Evening Prayer which according to the rubrics has to be said each Sunday and on weekdays as well, in every church or place of public worship. Another root is to be found in the development of the Methodist churches which initiated evening services in the late eighteenth century. When working class folk went to church in this period and later, the general practice was that they attended an afternoon or evening service; the wealthier classes went as a rule in the morning. However, on the Continent, in both protestant and catholic churches, evening services have either never been held or else held in low regard. They have had a status equivalent to that of a daily service, that is, a service intended for a minority. Some of the dislike by Sabbatarians of the continental Sunday is often expressed by the fact that the churches on the continent do not hold services on a Sunday evening. (The recent practice of having mass on a Sunday evening is considered further on.)

4. It is hardly necessary to document the very great decline that has taken place in Sunday schools. During the nineteenth century and up to the Second World War, Sunday schools had a prominent place in the British Sunday. Meetings for children were held in the morning and, as in the case of the Anglican Church, particularly in the afternoon. Morning and afternoon meetings were very common in the Free Churches, often involving a number of adults. But with the passing of years, especially since the turn of the century, no facet of church practice has shown more signs of decline than the Sunday schools and this has occurred in all the denominations, not least the Free Churches, where they were formerly so prominent. The reasons for the change are complex. In part, the cause is to be found in the changed social habits of parents, to be mentioned later on. In the Anglican Church, the

growth of parish communion has meant that children are now brought into the adult service, though perhaps given special lessons during part of it, and this has helped to bring about the general decline of Sunday schools as activities in their own right. In Methodist churches, with the emphasis on morning family worship, the afternoon Sunday schools have virtually disappeared but the morning Sunday schools parallel to the adult services continue to be held.

B *Factors relating to the socio-religious component*

In dealing with factors associated with the socio-religious component of Sunday, I want to consider a number of propositions not so much from the standpoint of Sabbatarian legislation as from the attitude of people today towards Sunday. In other words, I wish to start from the secular rather than the religious side of this component, and I have no intention of trying to demonstrate the weakening of Sabbatarian legislation.

It is difficult to talk in general terms about the social characteristics of contemporary Sunday activity or the overall attitude of people towards Sunday. There are probably as many attitudes as there are people. On the one hand, it is necessary to avoid the obvious; on the other, there is the danger that generalizations cannot be empirically substantiated and that serious variations exist with reference to region or class. However I wish to hazard a few propositions about what might be called the *Zeitgeist* of Sunday which I hope will avoid these dangers.

1. Sunday is viewed by the society at large as a day free from work and as a day of pleasure and relaxation.

This general attitude is given expression through legal formulation and it is an attitude that is widely held and given considerable prominence. It might be argued that most people would admit that Sunday is a day that they deserve – that they are entitled to – in the light of the work that they have undertaken during the week. Further, society gives them great freedom in spending it very much as they wish to. This basic attitude over Sunday can be seen in terms of (*a*) rest from work; (*b*) as a corollary – relaxation and pleasure. The first of these attitudes might be seen to stem from the fourth commandment, and as we have had occasion to mention, the church has propagated the norm that Sunday is a day of rest. The issues that have dogged Sabbatarianism have been both the question of rest from work *and* the issue of relaxation and pleasure. The later Reformers in starting Sabbatarianism did so in reaction to people working on a Sunday and enjoying too much frivolity that went with Sunday past-times, as is witnessed by Nicholas Bound's *True Doctrine of the Sabbath* (1595). It was the Factory Act of 1847 that guaranteed one and a half day's rest to all those in paid employment: it was done in order to allow those working long hours in heavy work to have necessary rest. The famous Report on Mines of 1842 said that women and girls were so exhausted from their work that they had to sleep all day Sunday. Sabbath breaking by the physically stronger was for one purpose only, to make ends meet. Manchester dockers are said to refer to Sunday wages as the 'Golden Nugget'.

The attitude among the working classes that Sunday is essentially a day of rest has persisted and it is still seen as a day to stay in bed, to mill around the house in a relaxed manner, to be with the family, and to be able to do what one likes. A letter, written to the *Daily Mirror* in the 1950s said:

> At ten every Sunday I take my husband up his breakfast, prop him up with the papers and don't see him again till 11.30. Then he gets up and goes out till 2.30. He comes back, has his dinner and goes back to bed, and we don't see him till next day. We're all very happy too ... [!]

This letter is almost identical in pattern to that derived from the well-known descriptions given by Charles Booth in his *Life and Labour of the People of London*,[5] when he talks about the way the working classes spend their Sundays.

These working-class norms were widely accepted beyond class lines and the notion that Sunday is primarily a day for relaxation has been increasingly strengthened by the popularity of TV. In a Gallup Poll of 1958 published later in connection with the Crathorne Report (1964), the most widely subscribed Sunday activity from a given list was watching television – 51% of the people said they watched, and that was 14 years ago! The general acceptance of watching television on Sunday has meant that Sunday is seen as a day of relaxation in terms of pleasure and entertainment. It is no different from any other day and 'frontal visions' occur as much on Sunday night as on a Saturday night! Television has probably been one of the most effective means of smashing the Sabbath anathema against people enjoying physical or sensual pleasure on a Sunday.

2. The second proposition is that alongside the secularization of the Sabbath, people have found increased relaxation and pleasure in being able to travel.

The National Sunday League which was founded in 1875 was an organization, working-class in ideology, which was set up to oppose the British Sunday, undergirded as that Sunday was by the Lord's Day Observance Society.[6] In particular, the League wanted working-class people to enjoy their well-earned day of relaxation. Not having the facilities of the middle classes, this involved agitation for the use on Sundays of community amenities such as public houses and museums. The League actually organized railway excursions and in 1896 museums and art galleries were opened on Sundays. At the same time, irrespective of laws relating to Sunday employment and the closure of public buildings, railways, trams, bicycles, theatres and later cinemas were becoming increasingly available to the populace. Educational classes, day trips to the seaside, popular concerts and so forth, held during the week and in some cases on a Sunday, were also welcomed. During the latter part of the nineteenth century there emerges an enormous development of voluntary societies and entertainment facilities for large sections of the population.

Little wonder then that the clergy from the 1850s onwards either lamented or attacked the habit that all sections of society, but especially the working classes, were going out on Sundays for day-excursions instead of attending church and, it was argued, that such facilities were instrumental in bringing about a decline of church-going. From those ministers more puritanical in outlook emerged fears that people at large were embarking on Sunday pleasures which were bordering on the sensual. Sometimes the clergy blamed the upper classes for giving a lead in encouraging Sunday amusements and by their actions it was becoming a day when the dominant questions were: 'What shall we eat? How shall we be amused?'[7]

What has happened subsequently is all too obvious: a continued and increased use of public facilities, the opening of cinemas, theatres and public houses on Sundays and now the emergence of professional sport. And what of course is particularly interesting is that the middle classes or more accurately those in the middle range of occupations, have readily accepted and used these facilities.

The greatest change in Sunday leisure activity is the extended use of the motor car, formerly only to be found amongst the well-off middle classes, but now universal among the working classes. This in some measure is a great novelty to those in lower income groups. It is the new toy, the status machine, the great escape. Every working-class street, every council estate, has its many or endless cars parked outside houses where before, even ten years ago, there were none. Witness also the traffic jams on a Sunday which are frequently more serious than those on a weekday and the fact that on Whit Sunday in 1964 it was estimated that nine million cars were on the roads.[8] The dramatic attempts of the railways to compete with the cars for people's leisure-time activities is but another aspect of the same issue.

Sundays are therefore becoming increasingly days of mobility – days to get away from it all. It also means that these activities have something of a family connotation, for trips in the car have an appeal to the father, the mother and the kids – they all appear to enjoy it. Teenagers also become fascinated by cars and seek to have their own.

It also means that Sunday is a day of visiting. It always has been so in certain quarters, but with families more dispersed and kinship connections extending over wider areas, Sunday has become the day to meet members of the family and to visit relatives, usually by car. It has to be realized that mobility does not only relate to people's place of residence or place of work, but to their leisure activities as well. Today vast numbers are prepared to search out, with the aid of their own transport, the pleasures they seek. The car makes them mobile; it allows a high level of differentiation or, as some would prefer to call it, independence.

It has often been said that mobility is the very enemy of church life. For the weakly motivated and the not so weakly motivated, a change of residence may mean the end of an association with a church, especially if the distance of the move is fairly great. The church nearby may not have the same power of attraction the former church had and as a result no fresh links are forged. Sunday mobility, as distinct from residence mobility, has also been viewed as detrimental to active church affiliation. A trip to the countryside or a trip to the church are considered as exclusive alternatives in some people's minds. There are probably good empirical grounds for maintaining the truth of this analysis. It also seems to be the case that trips in the car on a Sunday afternoon which involve the children have had an adverse effect on attendance at Sunday school, and incidentally in Methodist churches this is often stated as the reason why afternoon Sunday schools have radically declined and why parents and children are encouraged to attend in the morning.

Despite all the control mechanisms that exist in the Roman Catholic Church in maintaining attendance at mass on a Sunday, Sunday mobility is more than likely having an adverse effect on church attendance. In order to combat people's escape from church on a Sunday in central European countries, the churches, both Catholic and Protestant, have set up joint notices outside each town or village often in the form of a cross on which are stated the times of church services. In France the words 'Ton Dimanche' appear on the reverse side. Whether Sunday travellers are per-suaded by these signs is something open to investigation. Perhaps the notices are maintained as an act of witness rather than a direct means of encouraging travellers to attend church.

3. The third proposition is that Sunday has given way to the weekend.

When we examine Sunday we are not really looking at one day but at the second half of two days. People no longer think of having Sunday off but having the weekend off. Indeed the French have coined the word *Le Weekend* and speak of 'the week with two Sundays'. Sunday has been so frequently thought of as a dull and boring day – compare for example the evidence of that some-what limited but entertaining book *Meet Yourself on Sunday*.[9] And it might be added that whereas Sunday in so many people's eyes was associated with that which was uninteresting and cheer-less, by contrast the weekend is exciting and promising.

Since the end of the Second World War there has been constant agitation for a five-day working week and in fact it is becoming increasingly accepted. Those conservative institutions, the banks, no longer open on Saturdays and many offices and administrative bodies have ceased to open on Saturdays at all. Instead of keeping open late on Saturday nights as was often the case in working-class England, shops now close earlier than on weekdays and it is said that it is difficult to get staff for jobs which involve Saturday work. Pressure for a 40-hour week is maintained and this means that in many occupations involving those in lower income groups as well as in higher ones Saturday is or will shortly be a day off work. Grigor McLelland, a fellow of Balliol College, Oxford, and head of a grocery chain said: 'The retail trade ought to be looking forward to the era of the seven-day trading week coupled with a four-day working week.'[10] Sunday is no longer inviolable.

The extensive growth of shift work has also challenged the sacredness of Sunday as a fixed day of rest. More and more people work on Sunday and have a day off during the week, thus undermining the uniqueness of Sunday itself. Sunday work in the twentieth century first became sanctioned in munitions factories in the First World War when employees were offered double pay. In 1964 it was estimated that 12% of all workers were employed on a Sunday[11], and with increasing automative processes relatively more people will find themselves on shift work with no option of having Sunday off, irrespective of double pay on that day. Sunday work which was once frowned on by church leaders is accepted, even in cases where such work may be said to be optional. In short, clergy and laity have found themselves forced to bow to an inevitable situation which has violated the day they have always held to be so important.

The overall social pattern that is now emerging in Europe has in part been set by the United States, where the basic term of reference is the weekend rather than Sunday. In North America the car is an even greater means to pleasure and mobility than it is in Europe. The sprawling suburbs to be escaped from, the wide open spaces calling the casual tourist as well as the speed maniac, the weekend cottage by the lake or the sea, or up in the hills, all beckon the motorist and his family to be up and going. But this has its cost. There is the impossible task of getting back to the suburbs on a Sunday evening in the summer by reason of the endless traffic queues which may be, and indeed are, worse at weekends than they are from Mondays to Fridays.

One way in which the churches in Europe and in North America, but it seems not in England, have tried to cope with the weekend situation and still retain the basically religious character of Sunday is to encourage adherents to attend services during the week. Thus, in Canada some churches hold what are literally called 'Sunday-on-Thursday' or 'Sunday-on-Monday' services, usually timed for the evening, which are much the same kind of services worshippers would expect on a Sunday. In Canada and the United States some excuse for this practice is legitimate as in the summer those who take weekends at summer cottages are perhaps 50 miles from a place of worship. In many European countries, mass is said on a Saturday night which counts as a Sunday mass and frequently people attend this and do not trouble to attend mass on a Sunday, though they may remain in the parish. The Sunday evening service is usually a said mass which is intended to attract those who have not been before during the weekend. One way of trying to deal with the situation in the United States is by means of drive-in churches which operate in a similar fashion to drive-in cinemas and in some people's eyes may perform the same function!

4. The fourth proposition is that the general attitude of society towards Sunday as a day of rest, recreation and pleasure is to be found within church congregations as well as in the populace at large.

The churches do not exist in isolation. Boundaries are hard to draw between the churches and other institutions in society. Even those who attend church regularly and who spend an hour, or two hours, or three hours a week in church are also members of the larger society and they are subject to the values and norms propagated by that society. In other words, even the most devout spend much of their time – indeed, the greater part of their time – 'in the world'. They may try not to be 'of it' but secular ideas propagated by mass communications inevitably enforce values that are very much 'of the world'. References to the ways the churches have attempted to meet social changes have been deliberately introduced in order to demonstrate that the churches themselves are aware of what is going on in society. That the churches try to meet new general attitudes with regard to Sunday and the weekend is at the same time to confess that the church people are subject to the pressures and values of society which tend to lead them away from their Sunday devotions rather than towards them.

I have argued elsewhere that even within the churches themselves there emerged in the nineteenth century elements which by their nature encouraged people to think of church attendance in terms of a leisure-time activity.[12] The churches, in particular the Free churches, stimulated worshippers to find pleasure in what they were doing – in the singing of hymns, in listening to self-confirming sermons, in hearing organ voluntaries, solo singing and choral works. Members were encouraged to dress in their Sunday best and to enjoy simple pleasures espoused by Sabbatarianism. But the churches, in the light of their failure to win over the new working-classes, attempted to provide other forms of entertainment in order to attract the outsider into chapel and church, hence the Pleasant Sunday Afternoons, the musical concerts, the popular lectures. If people could not be herded into the churches for 'religious' reasons, the attractions of the concert platform had to be tried. And of course these encouragements came at the right time, for with more leisure and money in the working classes, people were athirst for public entertainment. Later secular, fully-fledged, gospel-less entertainments were offered outside the churches and those who had originally found the churches attractive drifted away from them and in other cases the heirs of the faithful went straight to secular sources. The churches found themselves in a very difficult position. Amusements fostered and enjoyed on a Sunday were seen by them to be a counter attraction to church-going and to empty the pews. On the other hand, if the churches introduced something of the leisure-amusement factor into their services they lowered their flag of religion[13] and reduced it to a leisure and pleasure-time pursuit.

What of church-goers today? Those who faithfully attend church also accept Sunday as a day of rest and relaxation. They enjoy the opportunity of a trip to the coast or to relations, of an evening watching television or entertaining friends. Like the rest of society, they are glad to escape for a weekend by the sea or in the country. They are the faithful in so far as they attend church – once a Sunday, once a fortnight, once a month – but Sunday is as much a holiday to them as it is to others.

The propositions that have been put forward raise a number of issues about the future of Sunday. It has been replaced by the week-end and is increasingly seen as a day of rest, and particularly one of relaxation and pleasure. At the same time Sunday and the weekend may not have much of a future as days set apart for the *whole of society*. A greater demand for public facilities on Sunday and a continuing growth of shift work mean that for increasing numbers of people other days will become 'Sundays' and 'weekends'. For society at large the changes call for a certain amount of social re-adjustment. But for the churches larger issues are at stake. Perhaps church leaders will be forced to give greater prominence to week-day services. Looking back over recent years and in the light of working-class norms, it might well be asked if the churches were in fact right in trying to establish worship almost exclusively in the morning rather than in encouraging it in the evening. On the other hand, the rise of Sunday evening television viewing as an unpredicted factor might suggest the church did the right thing in pressing for morning attendance. For those who feel that Christians should make a greater stand than they do at present, Sunday might be seen as a day *par excellence* for worship and witness. Should it not be given wholly to the church for a host of activities, from attendance at the eucharist to repairing the church roof, from teaching the young to holding parish council meetings? Such neo-sabbatarianism, however, is likely to appeal only to those who feel the church must attempt to stand against the stream, irrespective of whether this means becoming sectarian in outlook.

NOTES

1. Willy Rordorf, *Sunday*, SCM Press 1968, pp.154ff.
2. See J. A. R. Pimlott, 'Farewell to the British Sunday', *New Society*, 22 October 1964.
3 See Roger Homan, 'Sunday Observance and Social Class', *A Sociological Yearbook in Britain 3*, ed. David Martin and Michael Hill, SCM Press 1970.
4. K. G. Greet, *The Sunday Question*, Denholm House Press 1970, p.87.
5. Charles Booth, *Life and Labour of the People of London*, final volume, Macmillan 1903, pp.47ff.
6. See Homan, art. cit.
7. Booth, op. cit., p.49.
8. See Pimlott, art. cit.
9. Naldrett Press 1949.
10. See Pimlott, art. cit.
11. Report of the Departmental Committee on the Law of Sunday Observance (Crathorne Report), Parliamentary Papers 1964-5, Vol. 13.
12. W. S. F. Pickering, 'Religion – a Leisure-time Pursuit?', *A Sociological Yearbook of Religion in Britain 1*, ed. David Martin, SCM Press 1968.
13. Booth, op. cit., p.55.

4 F. D. Maurice and the Educational Role of the National Church

Michalina Vaughan and
Margaret Scotford Archer

UNTIL the beginning of the nineteenth century, Anglican domination over educational institutions from primary to university level was justified mainly through the appropriateness of an established church dispensing instruction to the elite of the nation as well as to the people. This argument was not part of any specifically Anglican educational philosophy. Indeed the plurality of theological interpretations coexisting within the church from its origin was a deterrent to the formulation of any theories likely to prove divisive or to uncover existing divisions in its midst. The essence of Anglican compromise was to leave unspoken the assumptions which, if expressed, might turn out not to be shared. Such an approach was facilitated by the absence of controversy on the educational role of the church, since no other group endeavoured to compete with the clergy as providers of national instruction. The challenge to clerical domination in this sphere came from dissenters and utilitarians who propounded alternatives (either denominational or secularist) to Anglican education and endeavoured to create competing establishments, so far as their financial resources and the constraints of legislative provisions permitted. The rise of the manufacturing middle class – from among whom their adepts and supporters were mainly drawn – altered the distribution of wealth in society during the Industrial Revolution and the balance of forces in parliament after the First Reform Bill. Threats to the privileges of establishment and criticisms of clerical supremacy in education stimulated a reassessment of the earlier assumptions by which they had been legitimated.

Characteristically, this defence of religious education was not the expression of one mainstream of Anglicanism, but reflected the

major trends which divided Anglican opinion at the time. The
parties which coexisted and competed within the church not only
differed on theological issues; they also upheld divergent educational philosophies. Their views on the church's mission in the
world and the clergy's role in society led to assigning unidentical
aims to religious instruction and imparting differential priorities to
some types of education over others. Thus Newman's *Idea of the
University*, though his first work as a convert to Roman Catholicism, was still impregnated with the philosophy of the Oxford
Movement, with the antimony it posited between faith and reason,
with its intellectual classicism, its political conservatism and its
social exclusiveness. On the other hand, Thomas Arnold's educational writings and practice stemmed from the Broad Church
party's concentration on Christ's example rather than church
membership and from its attempt to integrate denominations within a common ethical system. The emphasis placed at Rugby on
character training and the utilization of classical learning as a
means to a moralistic end were in direct contrast with Newman's
disbelief in the morally formative power of intellectual tuition and
the value he attached to knowledge for its own sake. The principle
of religious education was thus defended on different grounds in
each case,[1] since Newman saw in the church the guardian of
revealed truth – in accordance with the doctrine of apostolic
succession – while Arnold considered it as the bulwark of social
morality. Yet despite these fundamental divergences Newman and
Arnold were equally concerned with the instruction given to the
members of the upper classes rather than to the community as a
whole. Newman relied on college tutors to render the elite polished,
while only the church could make them virtuous. Arnold expected
the public school to prepare its pupils for the performance of their
duties as Christian leaders. Neither dealt with the elementary
schooling of the lower orders or with technical and business training – except to stress the distance which separated them from the
liberal education.

It was within the Christian Socialist group of Anglicans that a
commitment to national education under religious auspices crystallized and in the writings of F. D. Maurice that it found its most
articulate expression. This approach was rooted in religious and
social ideals distinct from and in some respects incompatible with
those of the other parties in the church. As propagandists within

the Anglican communion, the Christian Socialists held a similar position towards dissent as the Tractarians did towards Rome. While Tractarians shared with Roman Catholics the desire to strengthen hierarchy in the church and authority in the clergy, the Christian Socialists shared with the sects the wish to increase the role of the congregation and to reduce the power of establishment. Whereas the social implications of Tractarianism were aristocratic and its political overtones authoritarian, the Christian Socialists derived their name from their political ideal and considered co-operation as its social counterpart. Unlike the sharp contrast between these opposite poles of Anglican thought, differences in relation to the Broad Church party were less marked. Indeed, the Christian Socialists laid a similar stress on the paramount importance of the scriptures and consequently also advocated a reduction in the theological role of the clergy – as distinct from a pragmatically defined social role. Both parties held that the more minimal the part of dogma in the church, the greater the role of Christianity in the community. Sectarian divisions did not widen the Christian appeal, they merely softened its impact by acting against social cohesion. Ecumenicalism – to the exclusion of Roman Catholics – was therefore a common platform of the Broad and Low Church. However, the means proposed by the two parties to achieve this end reflected divergences less in their views of Christianity than in their attitudes towards the secular society. While to the Broad Church any rapprochement between the Christian and the citizen had to be sought for in the context of a *status quo*, the Christian Socialists reversed the problem and sought those changes in the political and social structure which would lead to the identification of citizenship and Christianity. Thus to Arnold, Christian citizenship was a necessary condition for political reform; to Maurice, social change was an indispensable precondition of citizenship.

In their opposition to both 'unsocial Christians' and 'unchristian Socialists', Maurice and his followers endeavoured to demonstrate that the Bible, 'instead of being a book to keep the poor in order ... is a book, from beginning to end, written to keep the rich in order'.[2] The assumption of Christian equality before God had to be translated into the temporal world. It was a religious duty to engage in political action in order to promote social equality and to stimulate co-operation in order to develop economic equality. To recognize the divine sovereignty in the spiritual world was not enough; it was the responsibility of the believer to work for its acknowledgment in the temporal sphere. Christian Socialism was based on the dual postulates of the equality of men and the supremacy of God. Since the supreme relationship is between man and God, religion must dominate all human activities. Since the nation is the main political unit, national life must be religious. Therefore to the Christian Socialists, worship in a national church was an aspect of patriotism and their concern for ecumenicalism was prompted by a desire for national unity.

One of the main responsibilities of a national church was to educate men for Christian citizenship. This task could not be undertaken by the state, since secular schooling would accentuate class differences instead of promoting social solidarity and the integration of all individuals into an organic community. Only a national church could be disinterested enough to define and provide an education which would promote social order without this being tantamount to preserving the *status quo*. Only a national religion could detach individuals from narrow group allegiances and replace the barriers of exclusive prejudice by bonds of social integration. Only a religious education could form men, citizens and patriots, instead of merely training for trades, professions or positions. The Christian Socialists relied on education to overcome the divisive effects of information. Like all socialists, they faced the problem of intellectual inequality as a source of stratification and endeavoured to devise a system of schooling to minimize this effect. While secular Socialists have proposed comprehensive schools as a solution, the Christian Socialists relied on religion not to eradicate intellectual differences, but to render them socially unimportant and nationally useful.

In the religious philosophy of Frederick Denison Maurice, the main educationist of the Christian Socialist party, the fundamental concept was the goodness of God, of which the incarnation provided a proof. As a former Unitarian, Maurice limited his acceptance of dogma to those tenets which could be deduced from his initial assumption of divine love. In this scheme the idea of the fall of man and of literal damnation played no part. Therefore the incarnation was interpreted less as atonement for original sin than as a pledge of divine rule in the world. To assume divine rule in temporal matters was to posit a rational order in the universe

which men's intellect can comprehend. Maurice was less concerned with the exemplary aspects of Christ's life than with the
evidence that his incarnation gave of a rational plan for the universe. He remained close to his Unitarian origins in equating God
with reason and in positing that scientific discoveries, far from
destroying faith, could only increase knowledge of the divine
design for the world. All the intellectual needs of man can be satisfied by religion under the guidance of the church. Thus, unlike
other parties in Anglicanism, Christian Socialism gave the church
neither an emotional, nor an exemplary, but a teaching role.

The knowledge of a divine plan implied the existence of a Christian ideal for society. To Maurice, human behaviour could acceler-
ate or hinder the evolution towards this social order; any agency
dividing men against each other necessarily hampered it. The main
types of divisive forces were sectarian practices in the religious
sphere and status divisions based on prejudice in the secular
society. His support of Anglicanism was based on the hope that it
could transcend sectarianism. Maurice 'remained a Nonconformist
in disguise. He never became an Anglican in the sectarian sense;
in fact he only joined the "Great Sect" in order to undermine its
sectarian character and transform it into what it had always refused to be – a truly national church.'[3] He accused sects of destroying national unity and of accentuating class divisions. The member
of a sect 'excommunicates the rest of his countrymen; not from
ignorance, but on principle'.[4] Thus not only is religious unity
divided, but also national sentiments are dissociated thereby from
religion and lose much of their cohesive force. 'Thus, what spiritual
feelings they (sectarians) have are wholly limited and narrow;
what comprehensive feelings they have are almost wholly secular.'[5]
The church alone can strengthen national unity by appealing to
Christians of all classes. Maurice believed – a questionable assumption – that Anglican ministers were drawn from all sections of
society and could therefore speak to all regardless of social division.
For the established church to become the only and hence truly
national church would eradicate the class divisions fostered by
sectarianism. Only a unitary church could ensure that the nation's
policy would aim at 'the gradual unfolding of God's purpose for
mankind and the universe'.[6] In England, 'nationalism was not to
be distinguished from protestantism'[7] or citizenship from church-
manship.

This religious ideal of protestant unity was paralleled in the temporal world by a desire for the 'organic' society, in which the individual achieves his true identity through integration with the group. Maurice contrasted unfavourably the French philosophy of natural rights with the view of the English Revival that education should subdue or change nature, not follow it. Far from believing in the spontaneous development of innate human qualities, he was convinced that man depends on society to subdue his selfish impulses and stimulate his spirit of co-operation. The connection between the good man and the good citizen arose from this basic tenet that man cannot be good unless he is a member of society. Moral betterment is the product of associating in groups and is furthered by the widening of these associations. Consequently the highest human qualities will flourish when the ideal of the integrated nation-state has been implemented, ending the fragmentation of social life by class dissensions.

'In every stage of our own history, the class which has been within the circle of the people or the citizens has shown a desire that those who lay without it might be kept in a fragmentary condition.'[8] These attempts to retain political rights as an exclusive prerogative and to enforce social control over the lower orders prevented the development of solidarity in their midst and discouraged them from becoming organic groups. The gradual and long-delayed emancipation of each social class depended upon its capacity to render some distinctive service to the whole of society – whereby it achieved cohesiveness and bargaining power. Within the feudal system the free men in towns achieved this position and, with the industrial revolution, the middle class became enfranchised. The working class was the only group still left in a fragmentary condition and aspiring to full participation in society. 'Those who are capitalists have exhibited the same disinclination to gratify that longing which the English patricians exhibited when their class established itself in guilds and corporations, and then became represented in the legislature.'[9] Maurice held that the cause of the middle class was identified in history with the democratic principle and hoped to see that of the working class associated instead with Christianity. Thus, while deploring the position of workers in society, he did not advocate militancy as a solution. Social integration could not be realized by means, such as strikes, which were essentially divisive. He advocated peaceful industrial relations and the extension of co-operation among workers in order to recapture the spirit of the mediaeval guilds. To Maurice, the first stage in achieving national unity was the attachment of every individual to an organic group, the second stage being the co-operation between the groups.

The overriding aim of Maurice's social philosophy was to achieve co-operation between classes. The goal of his socialism was to integrate all classes, not to defend the interests of one. Thus, although he sympathized with the position of the working class, he disapproved of any violent attempts to gain political participation. He was unprepared to trust the people while they were concerned with their rights rather than their duty to God. 'The horror of democracy which you impute to me is a horror in the interests of the people ... if they grasp at any power merely as a power, I believe the voice of Demos will be the devil's voice and not God's.'[10] Indeed, the pursuit of power for its own sake or even to assert genuine rights is inefficacious, since it will perpetuate or promote divisions in society. The class struggle is a product of godlessness, since it is prompted by self interest, uninformed by a spirit of co-operation and incompatible with a Christian sense of duty. Unlike many Socialists, Maurice did not strive for social uniformity – he did not wish to abolish classes, merely to change the relations between them. His goal was national and religious unity in the midst of social diversity.

Maurice rejected the theory whereby the possession of property was the only index of responsibility and the criterion for enfranchisement. As a Socialist, he recognized this as a policy derived from self-interest; as a Christian, he could only measure responsibility by moral standards. He would have wished to limit the suffrage to those who had a moral stake in the country and demonstrated it by dutifully fulfilling their obligations. Though acknowledging that the working class had not yet shown its suitability for enfranchisement by turning itself into an organic group, he looked forward to corporate representation when workers' solidarity prevailed. Meanwhile the working class should await reform rather than seek revolution. Nevertheless Maurice was aware of the revolutionary potential of Chartism which he viewed as deplorable precisely because it had some chances of success. Only a new religious reformation could act as an antidote to this form of social disruption, as the Wesleyan revival had counteracted Jacobinism in eighteenth-century England. There was no hope of political reform through state intervention divorced from moral awakening. It was only through education that the people could be morally regenerated, bound in an organic unity and enabled to participate in the political life of the country. 'The end of Education itself ... is to form a nation of living orderly men.'[11] By increasing sympathy between classes, such an education would fit the workers for political responsibilities and train all citizens to place the national good before their own sectional interests. To achieve these ends, the instruction given would have to be religious since Christianity provides the only common denominator between classes and is therefore the true basis of citizenship. Undenominational schools organized by the state would yield the same results as sectarian schools: they would maximize differences within the population. Maurice condemned state education not only as Godless, but as socially divisive.

Unlike Newman, he refused to recognize education as good in itself. It is only valuable in so far as it contributes towards an organic society. And it can only do so when it is religious. 'It was not so much that he considered all education should be religious but rather that he felt any education worth the name inevitably was religious.'[12] Indeed, for instruction to be truly formative, its paramount object must not consist in the mere imparting of information. 'Ecclesiastical Education ... is information not of a specific quality, but that which belongs to man; here is development, not of some particular faculties, but of that which is universal in men; here is not a Spartan, not an Athenian, not a modern Education, but a Christian Education, which comprehends and reconciles them all.'[13] This educational ecumenicalism would yield the same consequences as its religious counterpart, namely promote unity on the basis of a common denominator. For learning not to prove socially divisive, it must have a minimal intellectual content which can be inculcated to all in order to have a maximal integrative force:

> There must be a portion of the information which the higher class has leisure to receive, which the middle class has not leisure to receive, and a portion which the middle class has leisure to receive, which the lower class has not leisure to receive; and that which is communicated to all, the higher class will have leisure to receive well, the middle class indifferently, the poor class very ill. Here then, Education, which we want as

the great bond to connect classes together; which we want as the means of building up a nation becomes the very instrument of dividing us.[14]

Maurice was fully aware that educational opportunities were widely different for the various classes and that as a result intellectual barriers were erected between them. It was on these grounds that he rejected secular instruction as a mere training for future occupations and advocated religious education, based on character formation and on the perpetuation of national culture. Unlike the state, the national church could train for Christian citizenship, since it would emphasize morality, and not only knowledge. Unike secular teachers, clergymen could speak equally freely and authoritatively to all groups and extend to all subjects the light of religious knowledge – emphasizing the difference between the material and the spiritual world, between facts and values.

Maurice envisaged religious education at all levels as aiming at the production of Christian citizens. While this goal was compatible with a wide diversity of curricula, it required that all should give access to a general cultivation indispensible for turning all classes into members of an integrated nation. Yet privileged social groups endeavoured to exclude others from the institutions in which their own members were educated and provided no alternative means of acquiring culture rather than mere training:

> The whole body of our tradesmen and yeomen, as well as all beneath them, are excluded from our schools and universities, except upon the condition of their becoming something else than tradesmen and yeomen. We are disposed to separate our different professions and no longer to regard the cultivation of a general humanity as essential to them.[15]

The middle class, however, sought entry to the universities and its lower echelons to secondary schools, not only to imitate their social superiors, but in search of a wider culture that vocational establishments failed to provide. Maurice stressed the historical widening of university intake: 'Lastly came in the commercial men who had risen into importance by their wealth. They came confessing that their wealth was not of itself sufficient to make them citizens. They begged to be reckoned among those whose business it is not to deal with things but with men.'[16] Not only was there a need for more general education, there was a desire for it as a prerequisite for full citizenship.

Having demonstrated that each social class ought to be and

wanted to be better educated, Maurice outlined proposals for the extension and reform of schooling under the auspices of the church. 'Someone must be felt as the chief mover of Education, who has not the children only, but the parents under his influence – not the poor only, but the middle class – not the middle class only, but the rich.'[17] Social solidarity would be ensured by the religious content of instruction, but did not imply or require uniformity in the treatment of different social classes. Each class should be given an education adapted to its function in the community and related to its role in English history. This emphasis on historical tradition may be conducive to patriotism, but while it stimulates national integration, it perpetuates social inequalities. This apparent contradiction was resolved by Maurice's assumption that, if patriotism is strong enough, co-operation will replace competition between classes. In such a context, inequalities between the types of learning imparted to different classes would not reflect degrees of privilege, but only differences of responsibility. For the upper class and the professions, Maurice was satisfied with a predominantly classical education:

> Our knights connected us with the whole of Christendom.... That character, for the sake of the nation, we would like to see (the Aristocracy) retain, and for this end we would give them a large Catholic cultivation, training them along with professional men in the two most Catholic languages (Latin and Greek). But the members of the middle class gave us the feeling of our distinct English position ... not using a common Christendom language, but speaking a homely native tongue, – Saxons not Latins, islanders not Europeans.... The central point in their intellectual cultivation should be the study of their own tongue in its vigour and purity.[18]

Thus the education of the middle class should be centred upon the English language and history because this class 'has or ought to have a peculiarly national character'.[19] To reinforce this character, members of the middle class should be taught Anglo-Saxon, 'a study which they could call their own'.[20] Finally, the education of the working class should form men rather than train workers. Not only the national language and history, but also the national religion would provide a general culture rather than a minimal literacy. 'All these will make him (the worker) more human ... awake in him feelings of reverence and awe ... make him more humble.'[21] Thus education was to make the aristocracy more cultivated, the middle class more patriotic and the working class more Christian.

This educational plan dealt with each class separately in order to respect its distinctive character. Thus it would be fitted for greater political participation without any reduction of its organic unity. The working class would be prepared for enfranchisement, while the religious content of the instruction given would discourage any disruptive political agitation. Education would only further change in order to strengthen national unity, not to increase social mobility. Religion both determined the limits of change by defining society's ideal as a theocracy and through the provision of differentiated instruction regulated the pace of this change.

The Christian Socialist defence of Anglican education was thus founded on the national character of the established church, on its vocation to provide a common denominator between groups, on its unifying and integrating potential. To demarcate between the instruction which only the church could give and the inferior substitutes dispensed by secular agencies, Newman had invoked revealed truth, and Arnold, Christian morality; Maurice concentrated on social solidarity. It was collective as well as individual salvation that religious education was to achieve. According to Newman, the church as educator sought to engineer a complementarity between the cultivation of the gentleman and the obligation of the Catholic, or at least to prevent the two from remaining unacquainted. According to Arnold, it trained the Christian gentleman in the practice of the virtues essential to the performance of his individual and social duties. According to Maurice, it was to develop the moral attitudes and inculcate the type and degree of knowledge which would further a sense of pride within each class and of co-operation between classes. His concern was less with individual fulfilment than with national harmony—in fact he would have denied the possibility of such fulfilment outside group membership.

Like Arnold, Maurice emphasized the essential contribution of Christian morality to responsible citizenship—but he widened this concept to include the unenfranchised. While he foresaw and desired political change, he repudiated violent means and relied on the church to further gradualism through education. Though ultimately the diffusion of learning was to facilitate what he considered the inevitable evolution towards a more democratic polity and a more co-operative society, his plan of differentiated instruction for each social class perpetuated the acceptance of station in life as divinely appointed. His recognition of preordained divisions into groups for whom upward mobility through education was subordinated to the requirements of the division of labour contradicted the egalitarian assumptions of Christian Socialism. The rich and the privileged were to be 'kept in order' – but to retain their rank and prerogatives, including educational ones. This respect for social hierarchies which Maurice shared with other supporters of Anglican education shows that in his thought Socialism was ultimately subordinated to Christianity.

NOTES

1. On the educational philosophies of J. H. Newman and T. Arnold, see M. Vaughan and M. S. Archer, *Social Conflict and Educational Change in England and France, 1789-1848*, CUP 1971.

2. Kingsley, quoted by R. B. Martin, *The Dust of Combat. A Life of C. Kingsley*, Faber & Faber 1959, p.241.

3. Lord Altrincham, 'F. D. Maurice and Christian Socialism' in *Two Anglican Essays*, Secker & Warburg 1958, p.87.

4. F. D. Maurice, *Has the Church, or the State, Power to educate the Nation?*, 1839, p.223.

5. Ibid., loc. cit.

6. Lord Altrincham, op. cit., p.90.

7. Ibid., p.93.

8. F. D. Maurice, 'The Workman and Franchise' in *English History on the Representation and Education of the People*, 1866, p.213.

9. Ibid., p.215.

10. Ibid., p.215.

11. F. D. Maurice, '*Has the Church ...*', p.51.

12. Lord Altrincham, op. cit., p.36.

13. F. D. Maurice, '*Has the Church ...*', p.29.

14. Ibid., p.32-3.

15. Ibid., p.193.

16. Ibid., p.185.

17. Ibid., p.255.

18. Ibid., p.207.

19. Ibid., loc. cit.

20. Ibid., p.218.

21. Ibid., p.279.

5 The Sect that Became an Order: The Order of Ethiopia[1]

Beryl Wright

IN the last quarter of the nineteenth century the military and social situation in South Africa was very unstable.[2] Inter-tribal warfare, followed by conflict between African tribes and settlers of European descent had disrupted the traditional economic life of the peoples, and with the shattering of the political power of the chiefs social cohesion began to crumble. By the 1870s, however, Christianity was well spread throughout the sub-continent and by its potential to draw together the disparate tribes with their varying languages it provided an ideal – indeed the only – medium through which unity and the legitimation of African leadership might be achieved. Furthermore, South Africans had long been aware of the religious implications of politics and the political implications of religion in their land: even as far back as 1818 Makana, a powerful Xhosa witchdoctor, used religious belief and fervour to raise his people against the government of the Cape Colony. Yet even in the church problems of inter-racial tension arose, as many who sought power through the church found themselves thwarted by what they saw as white domination. The result was schism.[3]

This paper concerns itself with schism from the mission churches, in particular with the revolt against European guidance which came to be called the 'Ethiopian Movement'.[4]

One of these schismatic groups is particularly interesting as a case illustration of church-sect models, since it not only broke from the Methodist Church, but subsequently joined itself to another multi-racial church, becoming the Order of Ethiopia in the Church of the Province of South Africa (Anglican Church). The history of this group also provides a good case study for a sociological theory of schism.

Dissatisfaction within the mission churches was fairly general.

The Paris Evangelical Mission in Basutoland (French Protestants) split in 1872. In a major schism from the Methodist Church, the Rev. Nehemiah Tile established the Tembu National Church, in 1884.[5] A further split took place in 1892 when the Rev. Mangena Mokone, 'a powerful preacher', resigned from the Methodist Church and formed the 'Ethiopian Church'. Where Tile's church was and has remained mono-tribal, Mokone's was not, being situated in the Transvaal goldfields where men from many tribes were living. The Ethiopian Church was consciously racial, as Mokone's resignation report to the Methodist Synod clearly shows.[6] According to Sündkler, Mokone interpreted texts such as Ps. 68.31 ('Ethiopia shall soon stretch out her hands unto God'[7]) and Acts 8.26–34 as a prophecy of self-government of the African church under African leaders.[8]

Thus an important aspect of this schism was its appeal to African nationalism: to unify and to indigenize, and the choice of name is likely to be closely related to such an appeal. The slogan of this new movement was 'Africa for Africans'. According to Sündkler the name of the new church was of great significance, having 'a programme in the very name'.[9] The ancient Church of Ethiopia, of some seven or eight million African Christians, traces its origins back to the fourth century AD, is part of the group of five churches forming the Oriental Orthodox Church of between sixteen and seventeen million Christians, and lays claim to being the only indigenous African Church. The Church of Ethiopia is also a model of a united church that has endured pressures and persecutions over fifteen centuries without significant schisms. There is a further element of legitimacy given by the 'Ethiopian' whom the Apostle Philip baptized according to Acts 8.26–34. A united, indigenous church was very attractive to Mokone and his followers, and later plans regarding missions to Rhodesia, the Sudan and Egypt indicate clearly that such thoughts were in the minds of some leaders of the schismatic South African churches.

The young Ethiopian Church in South Africa received a significant boost when in 1894 another Methodist minister, the Rev. James Mata Dwane, and his followers joined it. Dwane was the son of a clan chief of the Gaika Tribe, and thus he was already in some respects a traditional leader and could claim traditional legitimacy, even if he had little authority. His reasons for resigning from the Methodist Church took a different form from Mokone's but were basically similar in their tenor. Dwane had become a minister in 1881, was very successful and twelve years later was sent to England to raise funds. He had his own Mission at Mount Coke in the Xhosa-speaking area and had visions of establishing an institution for higher learning there. The vision of academic and industrial education caught the imaginations of his audiences and he raised a large sum. But the Methodist Synod had other plans for the money and insisted it be paid to general funds. Dwane gave in and resigned.

Dwane's strong personality and ambition, and the way he imposed his ideas on his people, are important factors in the subsequent history of the Ethiopian Church.[10] Mokone welcomed him. He was a great success and was soon a challenge to Mokone's popularity. His leadership combined charismatic and traditional claims. However, he did not feel secure in his position, and possibly under the influence of 'Ethiopianism' wanted to make quite sure of the legitimacy of the Ethiopian Church as the authentic national Church of South Africa, descended from the apostles.

Then Mokone heard about the African Methodist Episcopal Church in the United States, through the parents of a girl who was studying at the all-Negro Wilberforce University, and he wrote to them. The AME was an all-Negro church resulting from a schism in the Methodist Episcopal Church over racial discrimination. One of the ministers had been ordained by an Anglican bishop, and this was cited as proof of valid apostolic succession. If the Ethiopian Church could claim true apostolic succession the legitimacy of its future leaders would be assured, so Mokone called a conference of the Ethiopian Church in 1896 to discuss the possibility of joining the AME.[11] Dwane played a leading part and the upshot was that he went to America to investigate possibilities of joining the African Methodist Episcopal Church to obtain valid succession. In America he again raised large sums of money and assured his audiences that the Africans would never allow the white man to ride roughshod over their country, that the Africans were 'rapidly imbibing civilized habits' and would soon be able to run great civilized governments. Then they would say to the European nations, 'Hands off!' His orientation to a western, rather than African, political form is clear, plus his call for independence. At home he received a cooler reception, some members feeling he had gone too far. The AME appointed him Superintendent of

African work, and thus absorbed rather than united with the Ethiopian Church, though no one seemed to realize this until later.

The South African AME received official recognition from the Transvaal government and planned missions in Rhodesia, and funds for sending missionaries to King Menelik of Abyssinia to spread the activities of the church to the Sudan and Egypt. An American bishop, H. M. Turner, ordained sixty-five elders and made Dwane vicar-bishop in 1898. Through Turner's visit membership more than doubled to over 10,000, drawn mainly from the affiliation of 'malcontent groups and congregations from mission churches'.[12] The Ethiopian dream seemed within reach.

However, certain bishops of the American church had not accepted Dwane's ordination, and since valid orders meant a great deal to the Ethiopians one of Dwane's reasons for going to America again in 1899 was to have his ordination ratified. He was hoping, apparently, to be raised to the status of a full bishop. He certainly did not want Africa to be subordinate to America any more than to the white man. He came back fearing the Americans' desire to have matters under their own supervision, and unsure whether he was a proper bishop. He approached an Anglican rector, the Rev. Julius Gordon, about the latter problem, and Gordon, a whole-hearted Tractarian, suggested he approach the Anglican Archbishop of Cape Town if he wished 'to exercise a ministry in accordance with catholic and apostolic teaching and belief'. This Dwane did want to do, but he wanted to take his people with him as a separate group, and not to submerge their identity in the institutional structure of Anglicanism. He wanted valid orders, but separate identity. In sociological terms he wanted his group to become a fully legitimated church organization, while retaining the independence of a 'sect': a kind of hybrid very difficult to incorporate into organizational life, as subsequent history showed.

The Archbishop favoured the idea, and thus the embryonic notion of an Order of Ethiopia, within the Anglican Church, was formed. Many people criticized the bishops of the Anglican Church for having any truck with 'Ethiopianism', since informed liberal opinion had favoured total apartheid for some time. One famous missionary, Dr Philip, had been in trouble with the colonial government for supporting apartheid, his aim being to protect the African culture against being overwhelmed by European culture. However, by the 1890s westernization had gone too far for 'pristine African culture' to be redeemed. Tribes were breaking up, or had already done so, a money economy was becoming established with the development of the gold mines, and mission schools were producing men like Jabavu who edited the first African newspaper.

According to Verryn, the upshot of negotiations was that Dwane rather impetuously, but as a token of good faith with the Anglicans, informed the AME of what was happening and lost their support before negotiations with the Anglicans were finalized, thus curtailing expansion by withdrawal of resources. According to Sündkler, Dwane did not succeed in carrying the majority of the Ethiopians with him, the main stream of the Ethiopian movement continuing in the channels of the AME church or of other independent groups that sprang up during and after the Anglo-Boer war. In 1908 the adherents of the Order of Ethiopia were only some 3,500.[13]

All Dwane asked for was valid ministerial orders. As a postscript to his first letter he suggested as 'a compromise, if absolutely necessary' that the Ethiopians become some sort of missionary order within the church. The Superior of such an order was presumed to be a bishop. Most of the Anglicans in conference favoured creating an order within the church for priests and catechists only, the rest of the people to be absorbed into the 'ordinary' (multi-racial) church. Had this been done the order would have fitted the sociological definition of an 'order' very well. But the Ethiopians wanted a complete, parallel, but racially segregated church, not governed by a diocesan bishop (who at that time was invariably a white man). Most of the Ethiopians were as anxious as Dwane about the importance of valid ministerial orders. According to Verryn, a small minority, led by Mokone, returned to the AME church and the rest put the following proposition to the Anglicans:

> 1. That having regard to the great importance of Christian unity, and being convinced that the scriptural and historical safeguard of the same is the Catholic Episcopate, this Conference resolves to petition His Grace the Archbishop of Cape Town and other Bishops of the Church of the Province of South Africa to give our body a valid Episcopate and priesthood and to make such arrangements as may be found possible to include our body within the fold of the Catholic Church on the lines indicated in our Superintendent's letters to the Archbishop of Cape Town.
> 2. That this Conference accepts and embraces the Doctrine, Sacraments and Discipline of Christ as the same are contained and commanded in Holy Scripture according as the Church of England has set forth the same in its standards of faith and doctrine.

It is clear that the Ethiopians were not concerned with a return

to a state of distinct theological purity, as a characteristically sectarian group might have been.

The Anglicans were most anxious to incorporate this remarkable
body of Christians into their church, but they had the serious
administrative problem, which would not have arisen had the new
order been a true 'Order' or a Third Order, of fitting the Ethiopians
into an existing diocesan and parochial structure, yet allowing them
a separate identity. A 'compact', or temporary document, was drawn
up to get things going and to allow time for experiment and further
deliberation, and at a special ceremony on Sunday, 26 August 1900,
the Archbishop of Cape Town confirmed Dwane and appointed
him Provincial of the Order of Ethiopia. Later that year Dwane
was ordained deacon. In their pastoral letter the bishops pointed
out that the formation of the order was a step of 'much gravity,
and one which may entail demands upon the forbearance and good
will of parish clergy and mission priests within whose charges
order churches fall'. They also pleaded for 'brotherly love, patient
wisdom and readiness to impart and receive new modes of thought
and activity'.

The order certainly was peculiar in that the church had an assistant bishop ministering to one section of one race in a number of
different dioceses, not specifically because there was too much work
for each diocesan bishop, but because part of one race within the
diocese wanted its 'own' bishop. As Verryn puts it, 'this does not
seem to be the type of "glue" for binding Christians together which
St Cyprian pictured'. There were serious teething troubles, particularly over the authority of the Provincial as against that of the
church regarding the ordination of deacons and staffing of missions.
In 1905 Dwane and his followers nearly seceded, but by remarkable
diplomacy on both sides they were reconciled, and in 1909 the Provincial Synod endorsed the Constitution of the Order of Ethiopia,
retaining its extra-parochial character. After this Synod Dwane
was ordained priest, at the age of sixty-one. He died four years
later.[14]

The history of the Order of Ethiopia provides a good illustration
for a sociological model of the process of schism, as well as an
interesting example for the application of the church-sect typology
to an empirical case. Analysis of Mokone's resignation report and
consideration of the social conditions prevailing in the Methodist
church at the time of the schisms reveals the presence of almost all

the 'necessary and sufficient conditions for the occurrence of schism' isolated by Neil Smelser, as discussed and developed by John Wilson.[15]

In the Ethiopians' case structural strain seems to be the key concept comprising a disjuncture between norms and values, or between roles and norms – more precisely, racial discrimination and the brotherhood of man. Such strain is augmented where members on both sides have different interests, motives and life styles. In the context under study life-style was clearly a critical factor. According to Smelser a schismatic group originates in a dispute over norms, alleging that the main group has departed from those norms implicated in the values of the original movement. So the conflict escalates to one over values, not to result in an attempt to overthrow the existing authority in the group, but to result in withdrawal from the group. Withdrawal may be by secession or offshoot. In the Methodist schisms in Britain the latter were genuinely 'revivalist in emphasis' and developed a following from the unchurched masses with only a very few ex-Wesleyans at the top, while the secessionist groups were 'almost entirely composed of ex-Wesleyans and did little recruiting in the outside world'.[16] As Verryn indicates in his narrative, the Ethiopians were very largely secessionist, a good example of this being the mass transfer of Dwane's own tribe from the Methodists to the Ethiopians. Dwane's father, a sub-chief of the Gaika Tribe, had quarrelled with the chief and moved away to become a councillor of Chief Kama of Amaqgunukebe. 'Most of this tribe became members of the Order of Ethiopia. They had a Christian tradition extending back for three generations, the grandfather of the chief in Dwane's day having been converted by the first Methodist missionaries in that part'.[17]

Although values stand high as legitimators of normative patterns, they are general, and are always vague enough to permit a debate which nobody can win as to what is the right form of association. There is thus always a fund of issues over which conflict can legitimately take place, and it is not enough to point to doctrinal disputes or underlying social differences, as Wilson points out. In an analysis of schism within the Plymouth Brethren the argument was advanced that members probably entered the movement with different assumptions about just what normative patterns were implied by the set of values on which they all agreed. Most certainly this was the case with the Ethiopians, who differed from the remaining ministers of the Methodist Church in the interpretation of the Christian value of the brotherhood of man, and possibly on other values too.

Structural strain, however, is hardly a sufficient factor for schism, since many organizations show strain without schism. The Methodist-Ethiopian schism included several more factors adding up to a virtual 'blueprint' for schism. Kinship and community obligations competed with the Methodist Church to the degree that Dwane's whole tribal unit resigned from the Methodists to join the Ethiopians, and Tile's church remained identified with the Tembu people. The legitimation of authority is a further important aspect. Schism seems to be more likely where the legitimation of authority depends entirely on an ideology than where an organization is held together by a charismatic leader. The former is capable of more than one interpretation, where the latter subsumes all competing interpretations under his own. The authority in the Methodist Church certainly depended entirely on an ideology, while the schismatic group had in Mokone, and even more so in Dwane, a strong charismatic leader whose interpretation of the ideology was fully accepted.

Yet, paradoxically, the same people subsequently joined and remained within the Anglican Church. By maintaining the extra-parochial character of the order, structural strain was doubtless reduced considerably and the personal need of the charismatic leader to legitimate his position and that of his successors-in-office was also a strong factor in preventing schism. But there are other factors in this case which predisposed the group towards schism from the Methodists and against schism from the Anglicans, the most important being the degree of 'sacredness' of the organization itself. Unlike the Methodist Church, the Anglican Church could be seen as carrying the sacred apostolic succession which became so important to the Ethiopians. Where the organization itself is in some way sacred, schism is less likely than the serious attempt to reform from within. It would seem that in this particular situation the 'sacredness' of the organization was an over-riding factor in preventing schism.

Preparedness for and ability to resolve conflict is another factor apparently present in the Ethiopian schism. It can be suggested that the nineteenth-century Anglicans had a 'fuzzy' way of referring matters to committees and postponing decisions,[18] which may have been less schismatic than the Methodists' personal confrontation in Synod. The manner in which the Anglicans negotiated with the Ethiopians in the near-split of 1905 may also be related to this. Schism is further likely where communication channels are absent or blocked. Mokone clearly stated that there was discrimination in hearings and that certain African men, whom he named, were still dissatisfied that 'all is not heard'.[19] Diplomatic ability in the individuals involved is another important part of communication and the Archbishop of Cape Town is reputed to have handled the crisis of 1905 extremely well.

A minor extension to Wilson's condition of 'structural conduciveness' to schism might be the structure of the formal organization itself. Where there is an arbitrator, equally acceptable to both sides, and whose authority is accepted by both sides, within the organization, schism is less likely to occur then where no such position exists. In the office of Pope the Roman Catholic Church has such an arbitrator, who has acted as such at different times. Neither the Anglican nor the Methodist Churches had such a status in their organizations to help resolve the Ethiopian disputes, leaving them entirely vulnerable to the caprice of individual personalities.

The precipitating factor that Smelser regards as necessary to crystallize the issues and stimulate people to action is not known in the Ethiopians' case, though it might be guessed. Important, too, is the role of a leader as 'mobilizing agent' to organize the dissident group and define its belief system. Outstanding figures frequently play an important role in turning a conflict group into a schismatic group, and Tile, Mokone, Dwane, and doubtless others were clearly mobilizing agents in the Ethiopian schism. Conversely, such figures may also play a role in resolving conflict, as did the Archbishop of Cape Town in the difficulties of 1905. The Order of Ethiopia has grown in the years since 1909, but it has remained concentrated in the Xhosa-speaking group, and has been no more successful in converting the heathen than have diocesan missions in the same areas. Still within the Anglican Church, they have their own synods and finance themselves. They accept Anglican doctrine and the authority of the bishops of the Anglican Church. Where there is no order church communicants attend the diocesan church quite faithfully, and vice versa, though often there are two churches within a few yards of each other. Verryn concludes his history with an appeal for an end to 'this apartness so fiercely maintained'.

APPENDIX

Report of the Rev. Mangena Mokone to the Synod of the Methodist Church[20]

'The reasons caused me to resign from the Wesleyan Ministry. I pray you, sir, to accept these following reasons in order to see how and what things you must do to the native ministers in the future to those who are still in your ministry. For I know if you do to them and their teachers they will leave your work one by one. I am sure that there is no native minister nor teacher who are content with your treatments. If you neglect to take notice in these things you won't get on so well with them. And also there must make known to every superintendent who has a native man as a teacher, etc.

I   The District Meetings

1. It has been separated from the English in 1886 without a cause and reason. Perhaps the native must not learn the proper names[21] of the District Meeting, or perhaps they must not have an right of voting for any thing in the Meeting, for all the natives are on trial or probationers and only one full minister and one is the interpreter of the Meeting.

2. Native District Meeting is just like the boys in the office or before the Landdrost[22] for the passes. All what white minister said is infallible and all natives are found guilty. Hans Aappie, Mag. Lotie, Klass Olifant, Samuel Mabhobatha. (You can't mend the bad feelings among these two District Meetings. Natives' cases are heard fully and not Others, fellow labourer and all is not known.)

II   Native Ministers and their Wives and Children

The native minister has no allowns for his wife and children from the Society. the reason of that we don't know perhaps might be separation of the District Meeting and that Native Ministers must not learn to know better about the rights of others.

2. The native minister although is ordained is good for nothing for he won't put in place of honour but the English probationers will set over black full minister as a superintendent. There is no reason of that only the colour.'

In clauses 3 and 4 he complains that native men and teachers' salaries are not enough, of discrimination in the use of wagons for fetching families, and about housing. He ends with a declaration that they are overworked, not consulted and, 'Well for all this I don't see any *justice, brotherly love, union*'. Unlike the sectarian, Mokone was perfectly happy with the way the doctrine of the church was presented, since he closes his report: 'Your doctrines are correct and I sincerely believe them, and I will in future preach the same as usual. Only one thing you neglect to do to your fellow labourers the Native working men and ministers. Take my word for a truth and beside what I have said above is nothing wrong with you. Believe me your most obedient and humble servant, Mangena Maaba Mokone.'

The Synod flatly denied all Mokone's points and confirmed the agreement of the other native ministers with the Synod.

NOTES

1. The history of the Order of Ethiopia is taken from T. D. Verryn, *A History of the Order of Ethiopia*, unpublished dissertation, the Archives of the Methodist Missionary Society, London, and S. M. Mokitimi, 'African Religion', in E. Hellmann (ed.), *Handbook of Race Relations in South Africa*, OUP, Cape Town 1949.

2. In 1860 the Colonial Governor, Sir George Grey, sent a dispatch advocating closer union between the Cape Colony and the independent Boer republics for protection against the African people who were banding together, and in 1877 the Ninth Kaffir War broke out in the Eastern Cape. In 1884 John Tengu Jabavu established the first Xhosa newspaper, *Imvo Zaba Ntsundu* (Opinions of the Brown People), financed by European politicians.

3. Schism as a result of thwarted power-seeking was not limited to the multi-racial mission churches. The schismatic African bodies themselves fragmented into the 1,000 sects described by Mokitimi. However, racial discrimination in the society at large was the ultimate driving force in most schisms since it blocked opportunities for black people to assume leadership in other areas of social life, making expressions of leadership through the church especially important.

4. B. Sündkler, *Bantu Prophets in South Africa*, Lutterworth Press 1948, pp.38ff.

5. For further discussion of the African separatist church movement in South Africa, see L. A. Hewson, *An Introduction to South African Methodists*, Standard Press, Cape Town 1951.

6. See Appendix for full report.

7. According to Mokitimi this text was emblazoned on the church's banner.

8. Sündkler, op. cit., p.39.

9. Ibid., p. 39.

10. An important factor in most of the schisms: see Mokitimi, art. cit., p.570.

11. Sündkler says (p.40) that all 'independent' church leaders were there. If this is so, it must be one of the first serious attempts to unite the African sects under common leadership.

12. Sündkler, op. cit., p.41.

13. Sündkler, op. cit., p.42.

14. According to Sündkler, six years later, in 1915.

15. J. Wilson, 'The Sociology of Schism', *A Sociological Yearbook of Religion in Britain 4*, ed. Michael Hill, SCM Press 1971.

16. R. Currie, *Methodism Divided*, Faber & Faber 1968, p.54.

17. Quoted by Verryn from 'Grahamstown Occasional Papers', January 1896—October 1903, p.239, Grahamstown Diocesan Library, Grahamstown, South Africa.

18. The nineteenth-century Convocation debates, with their often studious avoidance of open conflict, suggest this.

19. See Mokone's report to the Methodist Synod, appended.

20. Extract from the Minutes of the Transvaal and Swaziland Synod,

January 1893, by courtesy of the Methodist Missionary Society Archives, London.

21. Proper names: secrets, important things. A name is sacred, almost as in the Old Testament.

22. Landdrost: magistrate.

6 Findhorn Community, Centre of Light: A Sociological Study of New Forms of Religion

Andrew Rigby and Bryan S. Turner

A T a time when institutional Christianity is in decline, it appears that interest in religion is abundant: this paradox has already approached the commonplace in recent discussions in the sociology of religion. The commonplace is not trivial since it points to a fundamental reorientation in the sociological interpretation of religion. The fact that, especially in the West, 'religion' can no longer be comfortably equated with 'the church' has deep implications not only for the study of religion but for society as such. While the origins of cultural pluralism – of which the emergence of non-institutionalized religion is simply one aspect – must be located in the nineteenth century and earlier, the significance of the new religious situation for sociology of religion was not driven home for sociologists until the middle sixties. In particular, 1963–64 saw the publication of two major and, in retrospect, highly liberating articles, namely Peter Berger and Thomas Luckmann's 'Sociology of Religion and Sociology of Knowledge' and Robert Bellah's 'Religious Evolution'.[1] The reorientation of sociology of religion brought about by these and other authors has made certain types of research and perspective irrelevant or, more charitably, misleading.[2] As a preface to this study of modern religious phenomena, it will be useful to consider some aspects of the new perspective in sociology of religion.[3]

One major target of contemporary criticism has been empirical research into 'church-affiliated religiosity', especially characteristic of both American sociology and Catholic parish sociology. Research into Christian institutions and the characteristics of church members lends itself to the mechanical application of positivist research techniques. More importantly, 'it avoids questions that go beyond the immediate pragmatic concerns of the employer (since such questions are not amendable to treatment by the methods utilized) ...[4] The consequence of such narrowly defined research interests has been to rob sociology of religion of its proper position as a discipline central to the interests of sociology itself. While for Weber and Durkheim 'religion' was the very essence of the 'social' the sociology of institutionalized religion can be conveniently relegated to a minor part of the sociology of organizations. The approach of Berger and Luckmann can be seen, therefore, as an attempt to restore sociology of religion to theoretical significance. The restoration is to be achieved, on the one hand, by the comparative study of Christian and non-Christian religions and, on the other, by viewing religion as a major vehicle in the construction of social reality. Within the perspective of the sociology of knowledge, the major task of sociology of religion is

> to analyze the cognitive and normative apparatus by which a socially constituted universe (that is, 'knowledge' about it) is legitimated. Quite naturally, this task will include the analysis of both the institutionalized and the non-institutionalized aspects of this apparatus.[5]

Approaching the subject from a vastly different angle, Robert Bellah has arrived at noticeably similar conclusions. But, whereas Berger and Luckmann have argued that the sociology of religious institutions in the narrow sense is an illegitimate offspring of the Weber–Durkheim traditions, Bellah's position is that traditional forms of sociology of religion are inappropriate in understanding the new forms of religion. The complexity and flexibility in emergent systems of religious symbols requires at once both a new metatheoretical position and a new set of research interests. Bellah has severely criticized such traditional metatheories as consequential reductionism (the reduction of religion to its social consequences) and symbolic reductionism (the reduction of religion to the Oedipus complex or to society itself). By contrast, Bellah has argued for symbolic realism which involves treating 'religion' as 'a reality *sui generis*', that is, treating religious symbols as 'real'.[6] Given the pluralism of modern symbols and a stand on symbolic realism, Bellah claimed that

> To concentrate on the church in a discussion of the modern religious situation is already misleading, for it is precisely the characteristic of the new situation that the great problem of religion as I have defined it, the symbolization of man's relation to the ultimate conditions of his exist-

ence, is no longer the monopoly of any groups explicitly labelled religious.[7]

Again, given the emergent divorce between religion and institutionalized Christianity, the task of sociology of religion is the analysis of symbolization (Bellah) or the analysis of socially constructed reality (Berger and Luckmann).

So far the reorientation in the theoretical approach to religion is too young to have borne fruit in the area of empirical research: only time can tell whether appropriate methodology and appropriate research can back up the theoretical advances already achieved. There have, of course, been other types of reward. Harry Hiller has noted a distinctive convergence between the interests of the new sociology of religion and the new theology. Just as sociologists like Berger and Luckmann have been pointing out the religious quality of all socially constructed universes of meaning which are no longer the monopoly of the churches so 'the secular theological response to the tendency towards reification is the flight to the extreme opposite as expressed in "the church incognito" or "the underground church".'[8] This convergence of interest between theology, phenomenology and sociology is, of course, being manifested in the growth of departments of religious studies, but the translation from convergent theoretical interests to specific research interests is still a major task. Until this is achieved, church-oriented sociologists may feel a certain unease but their largely positivist and narrow approach to religion will be in practice unchallenged.[9]

The following study of a non-Christian, de-institutionalized commune may be thus legitimately conceived as one attempt to begin the reorientation of sociology of religion at the research level. In short, it is a descriptive attempt to fill in some gaps in our understanding of the progress of churchless religion in Britain. In a more theoretical vein, the study will illustrate the essentially flexible, open and synthetic nature of contemporary developments in symbolization. The guideline for focussing on symbolic flexibility is taken from Bellah's observation that

> Private voluntary religious association in the West achieved full legitimation in the early modern situation, but in the early stages especially, discipline and control within these groups was very intense. The tendency in more recent periods has been to continue the basic pattern but with a much more open and flexible pattern of membership.[10]

If Bellah's view about the increasing flexibility in religious adher-ence within protestantism is correct, we may expect even greater flexibility within communitarianism, the 'underground church' and other movements. As a final introductory comment, any attempt to fit the commune into the church-sect typology or its variants has been eschewed. There are a number of reasons for this decision which may be noted briefly. The typology does not allow for rigorous re-search because it is never clear how the researcher is to cope with 'deviant' cases: with the resulting proliferation of types and sub-types, the original clarity of the typology is obscured.[11] Further-more, the typology was specifically designed for the analysis of religious organizations within a Christian social context; it is, as a result, a typology which is restricted both to certain historical periods and to certain organizations.[12] The application of this typology, especially in some mechanical fashion, to a non-Chris-tian, inchoate, religious group would be misleading. Instead, atten-tion will be focussed on the socially constructed and maintained 'sacred cosmos' of a modern commune.

Since in our view the Findhorn community does not fit neatly into existing sociological categories which have been developed predominantly in the context of major, organized religions, it is highly appropriate to start by giving the community's own account of its origins and nature. In May 1969, the community published a brief statement of its beliefs and history:

> The community at Findhorn consists of a group of people pioneering a new way of living. There are no blueprints. . . . My wife Eileen hears the still small voice within and receives detailed guidance which we have followed with astonishing results. . . . We are living a way of life which is undenominational and therefore cannot be labelled . . . Our aim is to bring down the Kingdom of Heaven on earth AND THEREFORE EVERYTHING MUST BE AS NEAR PERFECT AS POSSIBLE, perfect to meet the need for which it is sought. To do this we have had to go ahead and do the seemingly impossible. . . . Each of us has come along a different spiritual path and people of all religions are welcome at Findhorn, for this is a totally new conception of living. We are pioneering a new way for the New Age which is gradually unfolding and will require a new type of man.[13]

The statement also recalls how in 1962 the Caddy family and Dorothy Maclean settled at Findhorn Bay Caravan Park to seek a new form of life. After failing to find employment, Peter Caddy started work on a garden at the caravan site and

> Then started the expansion, step by step, under God's guidance. We

had to learn the laws of manifestation, for each one of us had given up all and were now entirely dependent upon God's limitless supply to meet our needs. As we became aware of a need, together we would ask that the need be met. We learnt that our united thought and our act of asking were both important to manifest our needs, and we gave thanks immediately knowing in complete faith that they would be manifested.[14]

Through the laws of manifestation, the community has been able to acquire numerous caravans, bungalows and a community centre.

Findhorn, then, is a community pioneering a way of life into the New Age. Like other 'frontier' situations, its membership is composed of people who have travelled along different spiritual paths and from different backgrounds. The members consist of the young and old, middle and lower class, the 'hippies' and the 'straights'. The recent history of Findhorn mirrors, in some respects, the history of certain mystical cults. Until 1968–69, the membership at Findhorn was largely composed of middle-aged, middle-class people, but during the last three years they have been joined by an increasing number of young 'hippies' and people associated with the 'underground'.[15] This development can be associated with the overlap that exists between certain aspects of the Findhorn belief system and drug culture. The goals of drug-taking have been frequently phrased in terms of 'expanding the consciousness', a phrase which is constantly used by the members at Findhorn. Moreover, many 'heads' give a central focus to the development of one's inner psychic state with the implicit, and occasionally explicit, devaluation of active involvement with the material world. Again, the sense of deep personal relationship with fellow 'trippers' is mirrored in the sense of community and group consciousness at Findhorn.

The conception of the Divine held by members of the community has a noticeably mystical component. At Findhorn, the term 'God' is usually employed as a short-hand for the richer terminology of 'universal mind', 'infinite truth' and the 'universal energy source'. Thus, 'God' is a word used to refer to a 'universal presence', an energy force which is acting throughout the world, on all planes of existence and which is within us and without:

The Being 'outside' is the Being 'within'.
There is only that which is and has always been.[16]

It is through the 'living Force' that is immanent in all things that the essential oneness of all things is to be found:

I AM always there like the breath that keeps your body alive.
Become aware of ME all the time.
I AM the Living Force within your being.
I AM life.[17]

Unlike certain mystical traditions which develop a distinction between, as Weber termed them, the virtuosi and the mass, Findhorn
quite specifically rejects a

spiritual elite. The answers lie within each and everyone.... You need no
teacher, no guru. All you need is an expansion of consciousness so that
you can accept these truths. They are there for all mankind to accept
when mankind is ready to do so.[18]

There is, then, no mandate within the belief system for any type of
organization or for any particular method of religious development. On the contrary, it is said that each individual must find his
own path and form of spirituality:

Try to understand there are hundreds and hundreds of different paths
but they all lead to the same goal. That is why every soul must learn to
do its own seeking and never try to follow someone else's path unless it
is inspired to do so from deep within.[19]

While there is this stress on individuality, there is also an injunction to subordinate the self completely to the inner dictates that
stem from the 'divine presence'. Since there is no one way to inner
perfection, there is no 'model' of development which members
must accept if they are to remain with the community. However,
there are certain limits within which development must take place.
It is recognized that the things of the spirit must be placed before
all else. Eileen Caddy, whose spiritual name is Elixer, received the
following message couched in biblical terms:

First things have to be put first in every soul for it to find true satisfaction in this life. You cannot serve Me and mammon, the choice lies
before every soul. He who has much in the way of the world's goods will
not find it easy, for all that he has to be given second place and at times
has to be given up completely...[20]

Furthermore, the spiritual life comes first, but it must be made
relevant in daily existence. In the message received by Elixer, there
is the repeated emphasis on the importance of individual exemplary
action in this world, since, as one member reported, 'It is not much
use talking about faith if you do not demonstrate what faith really
means to you by living it.' One's actions in this world must be char-

acterized by the spirit of purest love and the New Age is to be built on the foundations of love. This Tolstoyan emphasis on the power of love is accompanied by a similar emphasis on the power of non-violence, with the Christian injunction 'Resist not evil but overcome evil with good.'[21] Linked with the notion of doing everything in the spirit of love, there is a stress on the need to look for the best in everything, to 'dwell on the things of the light and ignore anything of the dark'. There is the belief that if attention is paid to the voice within, then everything will fall into place. Finding the right attitude to life and people is seen to be vitally important, for it is the 'power of positive thinking' that will make a significant contribution to the coming of the New Age. One should not hesitate when one hears the voice within, or dwell on past mistakes:

> there is a silver lining to every cloud, no matter how dark it may appear at the time. Therefore look for the silver lining and never rest content until you have found it.[22]

So far our description of Findhorn beliefs may have suggested that Findhorn is simply another example of a cult working on themes borrowed from traditional Christian mysticism. Indeed, the Findhorn emphasis on the 'light within' could suggest that it is a proto-introversionist sect, but the Findhorn belief system contains many other themes which in terms of existing typologies are contradictory. On the one hand Findhorn has developed beliefs which are quite common among introversionists but, on the other, it has specifically adventist notions.[23] The purpose of Findhorn as a centre of light is none other than that of bringing down the kingdom of heaven on earth. The function of Findhorn is to demonstrate in practice the workings of the divine laws so that those who are willing to learn can see and recognize. Furthermore, this adventism is expressed in almost Zoroastrian terminology. Findhorn is seen as a centre from where the forces of light will emanate to counteract the forces of darkness. This battle between light and dark is fought out by Findhorn in two directions. One is that of demonstrating to the 'drop-outs' of the younger generation, who feel that they are of the New Age and have freed themselves from materialism, a positive way of moving towards the Age of Aquarius. The other is to demonstrate to the world how to work harmoniously with the inhabitants of the 'elemental world', the devas and nature spirits. It is this belief in the harmonious world of man, nature spirit and devas which makes any attempt to classify Findhorn according to typologies of traditional sociology of religion especially dubious. We can now turn profitably to Findhorn's 'coral gardens and their magic'.

Although Findhorn is sited on a sandy and wind-swept part of the Morayshire coastline, the commune members are to a large extent self-sufficient with regard to vegetable produce. The people at Findhorn explain the results revealed in their two acres of garden by stating simply that the produce has been made possible by the harmonious co-operation between the beings of the three kingdoms or planes of existence: man, the devas and nature spirits. Man, the organizer and practical creator of the garden is represented by Peter Caddy. He is not a sensitive and is unable to contact directly the other realms of existence inhabited by the devas and nature spirits. 'The devas are the angelic beings who wield the archetypal forces. There is one of these for every species of the plant kingdom and in addition there are devas of sound, colour, wind, etc.' Dorothy Maclean, whose spiritual nave is Divina, is able to communicate with these architects of the plant kingdom, to hear them as the voices within during spiritual meditation and to consult with them about the garden and the growth of plants.

Just as the devas provide the blueprint for the plant world, so the nature spirits are seen as carrying out the actual work. These nature spirits, under the leadership of Pan, the god of nature, communicate with the people at Findhorn through a sensitive known at the community as Roc. It is to Roc that Pan has manifested himself at Edinburgh, Iona, Findhorn and other places and has made clear the necessary task at Findhorn. Pan's teaching is that man must work in co-operation with the nature spirits and devas if the earth is to avoid an ecological disaster. To quote Sir George Trevelyan:

> The world of nature spirits is sick of the way man is treating the life forces. They (the devas and elementals) are working with God's Law in plant growth. Man is continually violating it. There is a real likelihood that they may even turn their back on man whom they sometimes consider to be a parasite on earth. This could mean a withdrawal of life force from the plant forms, with obviously devastating results.
>
> Yet their wish is to work in co-operation with man who has been given a divine task of tending the earth. For generations man has ignored them and even denied their existence. Now a group of men consciously invite them to their garden ... The delight in the deva world is apparently great. At last men have begun to wake up. Since the spiritual world is all one,

a great living unity, the news shoots around instantly and the devas throng in with joy to help.

They are literally demonstrating that the desert can blossom as the rose.[24]

If God's hand is seen at work in the garden, it is also seen manifested in other ways through what Findhorn members call the laws of manifestation. Although people who want to join the community on a permanent arrangement must provide their own caravan or bungalow for accommodation and pay their share of the rent, rates and electricity, many of those items that have required the expenditure of relatively large amounts of capital have been funded by voluntary donations from friends of the community. For example, the community centre and the sanctuary were acquired in this way. The decision to obtain new property or community equipment and the actual donations are all seen to be the results of the laws of manifestation. Briefly stated, the laws work as follows. Peter Caddy or one of the other members will have a sudden idea or hunch that something is needed for the community. The normal process is then to ask Eileen Caddy (Elixer) for a 'reading' on the matter. The ability of Eileen to contact the ultimate source of authority, God, for a reading or verdict on almost any matter means that one of the major practical problems of communal life – decision-making and authority – has been dealt with at Findhorn without to date causing dissent. Eileen generally receives confirmation that it is God's will that they go ahead and obtain the desired item or whatever it may be. The community members then feel utterly confident that their need will be satisfied by God working through human agencies – by means of well-timed gifts of money, the arrival at Findhorn at opportune moments of people with the required skills to complete jobs in hand.

As Festinger, MacIntyre and others have pointed out, belief systems are real and work for their adherents.[25] The growth of the garden, the increasing number of people who visit Findhorn and the impressive community centre, all attest to the validity of the laws of manifestation. Only one incidence of 'failure' has been brought to our attention. The need for a caravan for one particular member had been manifested but, having been promised, it failed to materialize. This apparent failure was explained as a consequence of the failure of the potential recipient to give thanks to God for answering her need. Like any belief system worth being termed such, Findhorn beliefs cover most, if not all, eventualities.

Reference has been made to the fact that many of the authority and decision-making problems normally associated with sectarianism have been avoided at Findhorn by the uniqueness of Elixer's role as a medium. However, there are a number of sensitives at Findhorn and one might expect that, for example, Roc's message from Pan could conflict with Elixer's reading of the light. To our knowledge, this has never happened. If such a conflict arose, then, from discussion with community members, we gather that the sensitives would have to go back to reconsider their interpretation. The day-to-day running and organization of the community is firmly in the hands of Peter Caddy who tends to allot the daily tasks among the members, deals with correspondence and escorts the visitor around the community. By virtue of his position as founder of the community, his relationship with Elixer and his undoubted organizational ability and personal charm, Peter Caddy's authority is rarely challenged. When a minor disagreement occurs at Findhorn, it is the diplomacy of Peter Caddy which restores the community to tranquillity. Given the flexibility of belief and the absence of formal criteria of membership, problems about general principles are minimized. The fact remains that Findhorn members have not given thought, at this stage, to the question of who, if anyone, should take over as sensitives or daily organizers when the present group is dead. There is little doubt that even raising such an issue at Findhorn would constitute a loss of confidence in the laws of manifestation.

Although Findhorn beliefs have enjoyed a luxuriant growth, there has been little accompanying development in terms of a specific ritual system. This absence does not indicate any puritan rejection of ritualism; Findhorners have not made any statement about the need for ritual, but it is likely that their implicit feeling is that the use of ritual is a personal decision according to the nature of specific spiritual paths. What ritual exists is of a fairly undemonstrative nature. There are, for example, the twice daily periods of meditation in the sanctuary. At the morning assembly Elixer's message from the light, received during the previous evening, will be read out to the members and this is followed by discussion and prayer. There is, however, no compulsion to define ritual in such narrow terms. Accepting Barth's more general definition of ritual as 'sets of acts, or aspects of acts, which carry and communicate meanings in contexts vested with particular value', we might see the regularized patterns of visiting and participation as a wider Findhorn ritual system.[26] These regularized rounds of activity are centred on communal mid-day and evening meals.

There is no simple method of counting the members of Findhorn community. Since it does not define its membership criteria, Findhorn has no recognized boundaries. However, there are approximately twenty full-time residents who have no intention, often because of age, of leaving Findhorn. In addition, there are at least six people who might be called 'permanent visitors'. These people are attracted by Findhorn and are living there to develop their spiritual talents – to 'charge their batteries', as Findhorners call the exercise. Permanent members of the community live in their individual caravans or bungalows, while visitors live more communally by sharing those caravans specifically reserved for visitors. This basic group of twenty-six people is greatly augmented during spring and summer by ever-increasing waves of visitors. In 1969, the community received about 600 visitors and this figure increased in 1970. In Durkheimian terms, the community is scattered during the winter season and then is drawn together again with the fine weather when 'collective representations' or 'collective batteries' are recharged.

Another interesting feature of the community is the absence of attempts to convert new members. Given Findhorn's rejection of spiritual elitism, one might expect community members to be engaged in spreading the message to society but, on the contrary, Findhorners make an effort to shield the exact nature of their existence from local inhabitants. They feel that any attempt to proselytize in the area would be wasted. It is their belief that all who are led to seek the light will be led to Findhorn at some stage and hence they refuse to involve themselves in any active attempt to convert the unbeliever. This attitude was clearly set out in a message received by Elixer in early 1968:

> This is but the beginning of tremendous happenings. It will have a chain reaction and nothing will be able to stop it ... Never try to justify Me or what I have said. Let each soul seek within and find the true interpretation of My prophecies ... Never try to convince any soul.[27]

Findhorn's millennialism and its rejection of the concept of an elect is not, therefore connected with any conversionist theme. The activities of the members at Findhorn concerned with spreading the light are confined to sending their literature on request and receiving visitors. They neither encourage nor discourage people from visiting them. Furthermore, they have no formal criteria of membership. This 'open-door' policy was expressed in another message received by Elixir in which she was told that

> You are living and creating something here which the many long for, but do not know how to achieve and they will want to know more and see more, so again I say to you be ready for anything. You will find seemingly very unlikely people will become really interested in all you are doing. Let them all come, see that they take part in what is going on, for only by taking part can they really find out. This is an action group living a life, not one that spends its time talking and doing nothing.[28]

It is only after a person has decided to stay at Findhorn that he is expected to contribute to the community in some practical way.

Towards the end of his life, Weber delivered a speech at Munich University in which he observed:

> What is hard for modern man, and especially for the younger generation, is to measure up to *workaday* existence. The ubiquitous chase for 'experience' stems from this weakness; for it is a weakness not to be able to countenance the stern seriousness of our fateful times.[29]

In Weber's view, the realities of workaday existence would finally subdue student romanticism as the charismatic qualities of life were submerged under increasing adherence to routine. Starting from different theoretical assumptions, Durkheim came to the conclusion that 'the old gods are growing old or already dead, and others are not yet born'.[30] By contrast, however, Durkheim envisaged not a thoroughly bureaucratized society of the future but one in which occupational communities and a new secular morality would control the tide of anomie. In our view, neither Weber nor Durkheim provides sociology with a reliable interpretation of the present religious situation. If Findhorn is typical of modern developments in religious symbolism and organization, then Weber's picture of disenchantment and Durkheim's idea of social morality are misleading.[31] Weber's attempt to argue student romanticism away has not proved particularly successful; Durkheim's brand of St Simonian socialism shows no sign of general acceptance.

If a sociological mooring is sought on which to anchor Findhorn religion, then our description of this community could be examined within Troeltsch's analysis of mysticism.[32] Although Troeltsch noted that valid predictions about the future of Christianity were impossible:

> Under these circumstances it is impossible to give a description of the present situation, and to deduce from it principles for the future

he sensed that mysticism or 'spiritual religion' would continue through the nineteenth into the twentieth century.[33] Troeltsch saw mysticism as an individualist, anti-hierarchical and emotive form of religiosity which was distinguishable from both church and sect types. Mystical fellowship was found, not on this earth, but in the invisible church. In so far as mystics formed groups, these were based on Philadelphianism:

> There was nothing rigid about these groups; they formed and re-formed naturally and easily, according to the situation in any given place.[34]

Clearly, Findhorn does operate on a form of Philadelphianism and also its ethic resembles protestant mysticism as stated by Troeltsch. Despite these resemblances, it is still difficult to situate Findhorn within the Troeltschian framework. Church, sect and mysticism were treated by Troeltsch as three main streams of religiosity flowing from the Christian gospel. While Findhorn draws on the mystical Christian theme, it also combines adventism (the Age of Aquarius), dualism (the light and the darkness), animism (the elementals) and aspects of the drug culture.

This synthetic, flexible religion of Findhorn is not the mysticism which Troeltsch thought the educated classes would come to adopt. For this reason and others discussed in our report on Findhorn, it appears that there are no firm sociological models against which this new religiosity can be satisfactorily located. In the absence of a well articulated theory of modern styles of non-institutionalized religion, the first objective must be to identify the problem and to describe the actor's own social reality. This discussion of the Findhorn community has been, therefore, an exercise in identification rather than explanation of modern forms of religion.

NOTES

1. Peter Berger and Thomas Luckmann, 'Sociology of Religion and Sociology of Knowledge', *Sociology and Social Research*, vol. 47, 1963, 417-27. Berger has developed this perspective in greater detail in *The Sacred Canopy*, Doubleday, NY 1967. Luckmann's separate contribution first appeared as *Das Problem der Religion in der modernen Gesellschaft*, Verlag Rombach, Freiberg 1963 (*The Invisible Religion*, Macmillan, NY 1967 is

a revised version). R. N. Bellah, 'Religious Evolution', *American Sociological Review*, vol. 29, 1964, 358-74.

2. We are not excluding our own previous research from this criticism.

3. In many ways, of course, the 'new perspective' is the traditional one, since it is an attempt to restate the theoretical centrality of sociology of religion, stemming from the research of Weber, Durkheim and Simmel.

4. Berger and Luckmann, op. cit., p.419.

5. Ibid., p.424. Luckmann went much further in equating 'social' and 'religious' in his study of the 'anthropological condition' of religion. For Berger's rejecton of this equation of 'religion' with the human *tout court*, cf. appendix one of *The Sacred Canopy*.

6. R. N. Bellah, 'Christianity and Symbolic Realism', *Journal for the Scientific Study of Religion*, vol. 9, no. 2, summer 1970, p.93.

7. Bellah, 'Religious Evolution', p.372.

8. Harry H. Hiller, 'The New Theology and the Sociology of Religion', *Canadian Review of Sociology and Anthropology*, vol. 6, no. 3, 1969, p.181.

9. For an example of the anxieties of parish sociology in the new climate of sociology of religion, cf. J. Dhooghe, 'Socio-religious research as a professional role in the institutional church', *Social Compass*, vol. 16, no. 2, 1969, 227-40.

10. Bellah, 'Religious Evolution', p.373.

11. For a thorough criticism, cf. Allan W. Eister, 'Toward a Radical Critique of Church-Sect Typologizing', *Journal for the Scientific Study of Religion*, vol. 6, no. 1, spring 1967, pp.85-90.

12. Troeltsch's own view was that his typology was limited historically to pre-eighteenth century Christendom.

13. Peter Caddy, *The Findhorn Story*, The Findhorn Trust 1969.

14. Ibid.

15. cf. T. Robbins, 'Eastern Mysticism and the Resocialization of Drug Users', *Journal for the Scientific Study of Religion*, vol. 8, no. 2, Fall 1969, 308-17.

16. David Spangler, *Limitless Love and Truth: Continued Revelation*, The Findhorn Trust and the Universal Foundation, part 1, August 1970, p.9.

17. Elixer, *God Spoke to Me*, The Findhorn Trust, January 1968, p.12.

18. Ibid., p.32.

19. *Findhorn News*, March 1969, p.11.

20. Ibid., p.12.

21. Elixer, op. cit., p.18.

22. Ibid., p.24.

23. The combination of millenarianism and introversionism within a single religious movement is not, of course, unknown. The Quakers were millenarians in the 1660s. On John Naylor's messianic entrance into Bristol, cf. William C. Braithwaite, *The Beginnings of Quakerism*, Macmillan 1912, ch. XI.

24. Sir George Trevelyan, *The Findhorn Garden*, The Findhorn Trust 1969, p.5.

25. L. Festinger et al, *When Prophecy Fails*, Harper and Row, NY 1956. Alasdair MacIntyre, 'Freudian and Christian Dogmas as Equally Unverifiable', in John Hick (ed.) *Faith and the Philosophers*, Macmillan 1966, pp.110-11.

26. F. Barth, *Nomads of South Persia*, Allen & Unwin 1964, p.63.

27. Spangler, op. cit., p.1.

28. *Findhorn News*, March 1969, p.5.

29. Max Weber, 'Science as a Vocation' in H. Gerth and C. Wright Mills (eds.) *From Max Weber: Essays in Sociology*, Routledge & Kegan Paul 1948, p.149. For a very useful statement on Weber's idea of the secular, cf. Richard K. Fenn, 'Max Weber on the Secular: A Typology', *Review of Religious Research*, vol. 10, no. 3, spring 1969, 1959-69.

30. Emile Durkheim, *The Elementary Forms of the Religious Life* (tr. J. W. Swain), Free Press, NY 1965, p.475.

31. Findhorn is one of the many communes studied by the senior author as part of a Ph.D. dissertation. In the 'Directory of Communes' of August 1970 (Commune Movement, 141 Westbourne Park Road, London, W.11) reference was made to over 50 communes then in existence in Britain, along with nearly 50 'Mystical/Spiritual/Esoteric London Groups'.

32. E. Troeltsch, *The Social Teaching of the Christian Churches* (tr. Olive Wyon), Allen & Unwin 1931, 2 vols.

33. Ibid., vol. 2, p.992.

34. Ibid., vol. 2, p.746.

7 The Problem of 'Surplus Women' in the Nineteenth Century: Secular and Religious Alternatives

Alan Deacon and Michael Hill

ANY catalogue of the social problems which confronted the conventional wisdom of mid-Victorian Britain would have to include that of the 'female surplus'. The first perceptions of the 'problem' seem to have occurred in the 1820s and the debate rumbled on into the last quarter of the nineteenth century; but the fulcrum can be identified fairly precisely with the Census of 1851. There is no difficulty either in defining the exact nature of the 'problem': in an age when the vocation of the middle-class woman was clearly designated as the acquisition of a husband and subordination to him, it was believed that large numbers of women – thought to be middle class – had been condemned by a marked demographic imbalance to a life of spinsterhood.

At the outset, it must be stressed that we are above all concerned with the *perception* of a problem and the solutions which were advanced as a means of coping with it. We will, of course, attempt to document the factual basis for these views and to show, among other things, that although the problem was interpreted (or at least presented) as predominantly one involving middle-class women, this was most probably not the case. However, our main interest is in the kind of definition which contemporary observers gave to the phenomenon and the consequent arguments they put forward as a remedy. This entails a certain lack of precision, since the attempt to identify a prevailing attitude rather than a more readily quantifiable factor cannot be altogether exact, and there is in this particular case a certain amount of interpenetration of ideas. Nevertheless, we think it is useful to approach the data using two axes—one of them contrasting secular and religious definitions and the other contrasting radical and conservative solutions. Finally, we will suggest how the competing definitions resolved themselves in the direction of one female role rather than others: here we will be concerned in particular with the role of nursing.

The background to the problem is a combination of demographic and social influences. While large surpluses of women over men had existed in earlier periods[1] the social problem of 'redundant women' was essentially a product of the changes brought about by industrialization. In feudal society there had existed a series of tasks which, falling within the province of woman, had helped to give her a fixed place in a marriage union based on mutual necessity. However, with the spread of mechanized mass-production and the growth of shops such tasks no longer required the labour of a wife. The prerequisite of this situation was of course a sufficiently high income, and so to keep one's wife in comfortable idleness became the chief hallmark of middle-class status. The employment of domestic servants by the middle classes and by those who aspired to middle-class status became synonymous with such 'respectability', until by the mid-nineteenth century the idleness of the wife was the most sensitive indicator of social standing. She became the means by which the income of the husband was translated into symbols of respectability. Indeed, the inanity of female existence within the prosperous Victorian home becomes comprehensible only when it is seen as being the wife's contribution to the social esteem enjoyed by the whole family.

The crucial distinction between lady and woman was defined in terms of work and non-work, and it followed that a true lady should know nothing of practical value. The education of the middle-class girl thus consisted entirely in the acquisition of fashionable accomplishments; chiefly piano-playing, languages and fancy-work. This, moreover, was in accordance with contemporary beliefs concerning the capacity of the female intellect. While they inherited rather than invented the notion of a God-given inferiority in the female mind, the Victorians succeeded in articulating a much more subtle rationalization of the distinction than had been hitherto achieved. The ultra-conservative *Saturday Review*, for example, carefully distinguished between the inductive intellect of man, which was capable of reason and serious thought, and the deductive intellect of woman, which had rather different properties:

They do not proceed by arriving at argumentative conclusions from clearly defined premises, but they throw out observations which they cannot tell how they came by but which give the discussion a new turn and open up new lines of thought.[2]

Thus if a woman was to do herself justice she simply required a superficial knowledge of the topics likely to arise in conversation – nothing serious or unpleasant would be discussed in her presence anyway – as well as her feminine accomplishments and her command of etiquette. We do not have space to give a full account of her 'syllabus', but a rough impression can be given by comparing the lack of importance attached to her daughter learning 'farthings and half-pennies' by one mother – 'She can have no use for it when she marries, her husband and housekeeper will do that' – with that set upon the ability to use a cream jug without letting the cream run down from the lip by the author of the *Young Ladies' Friend*:

> I knew of one very happy match which grew out of the admiration felt by the gentleman on seeing a young lady preside well at the tea table. Her graceful and dextrous movements first fixed his attentions upon her and led to further acquaintance.[4]

Having been thus taught that her prime duty in life would be to do nothing, and having been instilled with the virtues of chastity, temperance and – above all – submissiveness, the educated girl was well conditioned to her role as the animated ornament of the Victorian parlour. Not only did she appear incapable of reason, she was often unable to perform the simplest household tasks.

In such an environment the role of spinster became little more than pitiable. Having none of the advantages of the role she had occupied in the larger, more self-supporting households of former times, the spinster was driven (if she lacked independent means) either to desperate authorship or to the multitudinous ranks of the governesses.[5] Even if she had independent means she was condemned to a solitary life of utter futility. Stigmatized as a failure and trained for a life she could not lead, the middle-class spinster was the lamest of lame ducks. She received correspondingly little sympathy:

> Married life is woman's profession and to this life her training – that of dependency – is modelled. Of course by not getting a husband, or losing him, she may find that she is without resources. All that can be said of her is: she has failed in business and no social reform can prevent such failures.[6]

And so the task which confronted the middle-class mother was quite simply the capture of the best possible husband for her daughter. The greater the competition, the more earnest the training – and the more desperate the plight of the failures.

The fate of the spinster, and especially the middle-class spinster, was a theme which had been taken up as early as 1826 by the Rev. A. R. C. Dallas and was emphasized again in 1829 by Southey, who noted:

> Considering the condition of single women in the middle classes, it is not speaking too strongly to assert, that the establishment of protestant nunneries, upon a wise plan and liberal scale, would be the greatest benefit that could possibly be conferred upon these kingdoms.[7]

In a pamphlet of 1851 Florence Nightingale added her own highly characteristic comment on the fate of the unmarried, unoccupied woman:

> It has become of late the fashion, both of novel and of sermon writers, to cry up 'old maids', to inveigh against regarding marriage as the vocation of all women, to declare that a single life is as happy as a married one, if people would but think so. So is the air as good an element for fish as the water, if they did but know how to live in it. Show us *how* to be single, and we will agree. But hitherto we have not found that young English women have been convinced. And we must confess that, *in the present state of things*, their horror of being 'old maids' seems perfectly justified; it is not merely a foolish desire for the pomp and circumstance of marriage—a 'life without love, and an activity without an aim' is horrible in idea, and wearisome in reality.[8]

Against this background, it is not hard to appreciate the consternation aroused by the results of the 1851 Census of England and Wales (the first to ask questions about marital status). These seemed to indicate that many young women would find it impossible to secure a husband. Not only was society saddled with the present generation of spinsters but the assumptions which underpinned the education of women now began to be challenged. The Census in fact showed a crude excess in the numbers of women over the age of 20 over the corresponding numbers of men of around 405,000. The actual number of *unmarried* women, however, would clearly be much larger and a more accurate picture is afforded if the marital proportions of the Census are applied to the No. 3 Life Table for 1838–54.[9] This shows that 30% of the women between 20 and 44 in 1851 were unmarried, that is some, 1,129,000 single women.[10]

A large proportion of these women were believed by contem-

poraries to be middle class. Southey had emphasized the problem
of middle-class spinsters, and another commentator, Frances Power
Cobbe, wrote 'Now it is of educated women that the great body
of "Old Maids" consists, in the lower orders celibacy is rare.'[11]

Although the lack of sufficient data prevents precise measure·
ment, it is clear that this assumption was incorrect. The two major
causes of the surplus were the higher rate of emigration amongst
men, and the excess of male over female mortality rates. However,
whilst emigration was predominantly male it was also an over-
whelmingly working-class phenomenon.[12] Similarly, the differential
between male and female mortality was much greater within infant
mortality rates than for other age groups.[13] Infant mortality – for
obvious reasons – was very much concentrated in the working class.
Furthermore, the higher the infant mortality rate, the greater was
the excess in deaths of boys over girls.[14] Thus, the two main factors
creating the surplus of women were operative amongst the working
class far more than the middle class.

The belief that the surplus was composed predominantly of
'ladies' arose largely from an exaggeration by contemporaries of
the importance of a third set of factors generating the surplus, which
we may call the 'institutional' causes. The most significant of these
was the deferment or rejection of marriage by the middle-class male
due to the conventional necessity for him to have an income
sufficient to allow him to support a family without sacrificing the
enjoyment of luxury.[15] This meant that if he did finally marry it
was usually when he was over 30. His bride, however, would be in
her early 20s and so the relevant balance for the marriage market
was between women of 20–25 years and men some 10 years older.[16]
This was exclusive to the middle class as there were no such re-
straints on the poor; indeed, Brewer noted in a lecture delivered at
Queens College in 1854:

> Marriage is indispensable to a poor man, widowers constantly come
> into the workhouse, their homes are uncomfortable, they are robbed
> when they are out at work and there is no one to prepare meals for them.[17]

This and similar features – for example, the refusal of an offer
of marriage by a lady on the grounds that the match entailed a loss
of station – undoubtedly added to the surplus. The importance of
such factors overall was, however, slight – if only because the
income groups in which such situations would arise comprised only

a small part of the population.[18] Nevertheless, the fact remains that the surplus was seen at the time as being one of middle-class 'redundant women'.

We think it is useful to envisage the responses to this problem in terms of a four-part schema comprised of conservative/radical and secular/religious dichotomies. This perspective has certain limitations – for instance, ideas tended to be exchanged freely between the different areas of interest – and it must be emphasized that the orientations we refer to are *contextual*: thus, what are referred to as 'radical' solutions in a nineteenth-century context may appear much less so in terms of present values. Similarly, the reference to 'radical' religious solutions is to be seen against the background of the nineteenth-century Church of England. All the same, there was a notable degree of consistency in the way these attitudes were held, and the single most important common currency was the definition of the woman's role. To those who defined it in terms of a rigid obverse of the superior male role, the conservative solutions – both in society at large and in the Church of England – held a strong appeal. Those who saw women as capable of autonomous activity were more likely to welcome radical solutions. Thus conceived, the schema can be presented in the following way:

	Secular	*Religious*
Radical	Education and professions	Sisterhoods
Conservative	Emigration	Deaconesses

Secular conservatives

The conservatives, since they firmly held that the *raison d'être* of every woman's existence was the acquisition of a husband, could conceive of the surplus as being in the nature of an imperfect market. Their solution was to restore the natural balance between the sexes by encouraging the large-scale emigration of unmarried women to the colonies, where there also existed an imperfect market in the form of a male surplus. W. R. Greg, whose *Why Are Women Redundant?* was the classic exposition of this policy, recognized only two difficulties, the first of which was mechanical:

To transport the half a million from where they are redundant to where they are wanted, at an average rate of 50 passengers per ship would require 10,000 vessels or at least 10,000 voyages.[19]

Undaunted by such difficulties, a number of emigration societies had grown up, chief among which were the Female Middle Class Emigration Society, the British Ladies Female Emigration Society and the Family Colonization Loan Society. Despite their impressive titles they achieved remarkably little: the FMCES, for instance, succeeded in despatching only 158 women in the first eleven years of its existence.[20]

However, the more serious difficulty as far as Greg was concerned was that if, as most people believed, the majority of women involved were middle-class, then they might well prove unsuitable for the rigours of a colonial existence. Nevertheless, any reduction in the excess would be beneficial: 'Just as bleeding in the foot will relieve the head or the heart from distressing or perilous congestion.'[21]

Similarly, the solution to the problem posed by those women who, influenced by the 'morbid literature of the age', were prone to refusing a suitor if they considered his status to be inferior to their own, was to make the life of the spinster even less attractive and thereby render marriage a matter of 'cold philosophical choice'. The doctrine of individual responsibility could not yet be applied to the spinster with the severity with which it was applied to the able-bodied pauper, because whilst there was a job for all who wanted one, there was no such supply of husbands – hence the need for emigration. Nevertheless those who sought to improve the lot of the spinster were as misguided as those who wished to remove the punitive deterrent of the workhouse. They were both 'labouring not to make us go backward and go right, but to make it easier and smoother to persist in wrong.'[22]

Secular radicals

This contemptuous equation of women and merchandize was strongly attacked by the feminists and by those liberals whose consciences had been aroused by the plight of the governesses. They argued against the emigration solution by pointing out that the life of many colonial pioneers made it necessary for them to remain single, and a remarkable ally in their debate was provided by the Tory *Saturday Review*, which declared that the exported women would only become prostitutes.[23] The basis of the radical argument

was that women should have the alternative of working if they did
not marry, and Jessie Boucherett was one feminist who argued that
it was more sensible to double the rate of male emigration so as to
open up more possibilities on the home market for women:

> The plan, then, which I advocate for superflous women is that of allow-
> ing them to engage freely in all occupations suited to their strengh.[24]

For, as the feminists pointed out, women already *did* work, and
the appalling nature of the work they did was the result of lack of
opportunity to do anything more suitable. The 1851 Census had revealed 1,210,663 unmarried females who were industrially employed,
and Harriet Martineau, writing anonymously in the *Edinburgh Review*, presented a horrifying analysis of the nature, pay and conditions of women's work.[25] To the conservatives such statistics were
irrelevant since they almost invariably referred to working-class
women, whom nobody had suggested should not work (though even
Greg recognized that it tended to detract from the husband's comfort). Also, many of the women workers were domestic servants,
and this did not constitute a problem because it fitted very neatly
with conservative male definitions of the female role. Domestic service fulfilled 'both essentials of woman's being; they are supported
by and they minister to man.'[26]

The basic question remained one of whether or not women had
the intellectual capacity to perform responsible tasks, and on this
issue the conservative view was dogmatic and entrenched. The laws
of supply and demand prohibited feminine entry to the established
professions; and when Barbara Leigh Smith proposed that women
could be apprenticed to 10,000 watchmakers and 10,000 accountants
the *Saturday Review* was beside itself with scorn:

> There is something positively touching in the buoyant simplicity of
> this – in its airy way of disposing of earthy evils – in its sublime indiffer-
> ence to means and strong apprehension of ends ... we wish she would
> get one of the 10,000 good accountants to calculate what each of the
> 10,000 watchmakers would be ever likely to get per week.[27]

In this situation, feminists like Mrs Jameson who accurately diagnosed the fundamental weakness of a woman's position on the labour
market gave their support to the cause which they saw as most likely
to bring about change — that of female education:

> The education given to our women is merely calculated to render them
> ornamental and well-informed; but it does not train them, even those

who are so inclined and fitted by nature, to be effective instruments of social improvement. Whether men, without the assistance and sympathetic approval of well-educated women, are likely to improve and elevate the moral tone of society, or work out good in any especial sphere or profession, is, I think, hardly a question.[28]

Religious conservatives

Many of the broader issues contained in the secular debate percolated through into the controversy within the Church of England over what was the most appropriate role in the church's organization for women. Significantly, those who were advocating a conservative view of this role tended to use supplementary arguments drawn from the conservative wing of the secular debate. In this way, social definitions of the female role were combined with theological positions so as to give a dual legitimacy to particular attitudes. A clear example of this is given by the Evangelicals' support of the institution of deaconess as the most appropriate role for women in the Church of England.

One of the foremost proponents of deaconesses was Howson. He had published an article on this subject in the *Quarterly Review* of 1860 and in a pamphlet of 1862 he noted with some amusement that one of the least important points made in his 1860 article – that the preponderance of females in the British population made it necessary to find employment for women – had been magnified out of all proportion by reviewers. He agreed that the recently analysed Census statistics raised some serious questions, but '... it would be a great delusion to suppose that the establishment of a system of Deaconesses would redress the evils which, however keenly felt before, have now been clearly defined by help of the Census'.[29] While he was prepared to admit that a female surplus lent proof to the idea that there were some specific ministries providentially assigned to the female sex, he thought that the best solution in view of the scale of the problem was planned female emigration. This was also suggested by an extremist protestant pamphlet of 1872 which warned that the sex imbalance was attracting swarms of Jesuits to this country who had got wind of a vast horde of potential recruits to Roman Catholic convents.[30]

That Howson's advocacy of the role of deaconess was coupled with a conservative view of the female role in general can be seen by his description of the deaconesses function. He thought that woman's position in society was 'to help', and he gave the Greek equivalent of 'deaconess' as signifying 'helpful service'. In like vein, the Upper House of the Canterbury Convocation in 1885 heard the Bishop of Winchester describe the admission procedure for the office of deaconess and call for the establishment of a deaconess institution for training and occasional retirement. He thought this was necessary because 'women need more support than men'.[31] Another of the supporters of deaconesses, Cotton, had a firm notion of 'natural' distinctions between men and women and thought that the education of women should be moral education, of the *heart* and not of the head, because that was where the particular attributes of women lay.[32] All of the advocates of deaconesses were agreed on one thing – that each individual deaconess should work under the supervision and strict control of the parish priest.

Religious radicals

From the start, sisterhoods, were founded on the quite different principle that women were intellectually capable of administering their own organizations and of taking all major decisions themselves. If this meant altering the whole purpose for which the institution had been founded – as, for example, in the case of the Wantage sisterhood which had originally been founded by the Rev. W. J. Butler to do educational work but which, on the decision of the Mother Superior, turned to penitentiary work instead – this was preferable, in the opinions of most of the male founders, to interference in the work of the community. Pusey, perhaps the single most influential character in the growth of sisterhoods, maintained this view of women's autonomy from the beginning of the movement. In 1840 he wrote:

> We, who are admitted to the priesthood, are under vows; we devote ourselves for a whole life; why should not women also for their offices?[33]

Again, in 1865, he wrote:

> I think that it is a wrong ambition of men to wish to have the direction of the work of women. I should fear that it would be far the injury of both. Women ought to understand their own work, the education and care of young women; or they would not be fit for it at all.[34]

There were, of course, other than implicit feminist reasons behind Pusey's attitude. For one thing, he saw no possibility of establishing permanent orders of women if they were merely to be created and directed by enthusiastic ecclesiastical *entrepreneurs* among the parochial clergy. Centralization and a certain degree of autonomy were thus needed. Predictably, the contemporary innuendo attributed much of his attitude to the protection and advice he offered Priscilla Lydia Sellon, Superior of the Devonport community.

But there was a much more crucial notion underlying the Tractarian defence of sisterhoods, and this was the idea of celibacy as a matter of voluntary choice. Until the role of unmarried women could be defined in positive terms, as something to be adopted for reasons other than that of sheer failure to find a mate, there was a social stigma to any occupation or vocation composed of single women. Florence Nightingale also encountered this obstacle, and we will suggest that one way in which she overcame it was to use the sisterhoods as a useful source (though certainly not the only source) of redefinition of the nurse's role. A good example of the Tractarian criticism of contemporary ideas of women's role is provided by J. M. Neale – another community founder – who, in a sermon of 1857, drew a neat comparison between the status of women in pagan society and their status in Victorian England:

> ... woman was at best the plaything, at the worst the slave of man. All heathen ideas of woman's happiness lay in marriage; without that, hers was a wasted existence.[35]

Commentators on sisterhoods regarded the female surplus as a mixed blessing. Some, like Archdeacon Harris speaking at the Church Congress of 1866, were prepared to see the hand of divine providence behind the Registrar General's figures:

> The last two census (sic) have revealed a singular state of Christian society within our own country – namely, the immense preponderance of the female sex. The last census, I believe, showed a preponderance of something like half a million. This will lead to more female employment, some will say; but I view it as a remarkably providential feature of the present day, that when there is this anomalous state of society, God has created amongst us a high vocation, a high calling, a vocation in the highest sense of the word of God calling his servants to do a particular work for Him.[36]

The opposite view was given by Margaret Goodman, a strong but highly perceptive critic of sisterhoods:

> It would appear from the writings of some persons, who urge the multiplication of sisterhoods, that they think them desirable because calculated to prove a blessing to women who have nothing to do: a mode of existence for ladies who, after every effort on their part, from the supply not equalling the demand, are unable to find husbands; or a refuge for the

woe-worn, weary and disappointed. For neither of these three classes will
a sisterhood prove a home. The work is far too real to be performed by
lagging hands.[37]

One way in which the resolution of these conflicting ideas about
women's roles occurred took the form of a gradual adoption by
women of the occupational roles available in philanthropy and
nursing. Such occupations were 'transitional' in two ways: firstly
because they represented the first step away from the all-embracing
Victorian middle-class family in the direction of complete acceptance of women in the professions; and secondly, because widely-
held male conceptions of the role of women were only partially
challenged by these occupations.

The principal requirement if philanthropic work was to be accommodated within conventional role-definitions was for a strict demarcation between the work of the man and that of the woman.
Furthermore, it was necessary that this demarcation should leave
the responsibilities of organization and decision-making to men. An
excellent example of such a division of labour in the 'non-profes-
sional' sphere can be found in the attempts to improve the sanita-
tion of English cities as a result of the widespread fear of epidemics.
This work could conveniently be divided into the twin tasks of
planning and executing schemes of sanitary engineering – an exclusively male preserve – and that of inculcating the poor with the
habits of hygiene and improved infant care – clearly work for
women. The Ladies Sanitary Association was founded in 1857 to
pursue these aims through home visiting and the distribution of
tracts (some 138,000 by 1861).[38] It found an enthusiastic supporter
in the *Saturday Review*:

> In a society called the Ladies Sanitary Association we seem to have dis-
> covered just that which reason, and circumstances of the time, and the
> fitness of things require and suggest as woman's true work.[39]

An equally good example is the Workhouse Visiting Society
which was founded by Louisa Twinning in 1859. The early issues
of its journal were anxious to stress that the ladies in no way wished
to challenge the male organization of the institutions but merely
to bring the feminine touch to bestow 'sweetness and light'. An
indication of the nature of this 'sweetness and light' is given in a
letter from the Guardians of the City of London which appeared
in the 'City Press' of February 1860 and reported that:

> The ladies visiting the Workhouse read a portion of scripture and ex-

pand upon the same, distribute tracts, converse with the sick and other inmates and conduct a bible class for the young women on Sunday evenings.[40]

This kind of work, which had long been performed in the rural parish and the visiting societies, could easily command the approval of religious doctrine. St James was widely quoted: 'Pure religion and undefiled before God and the Father is this; to visit the fatherless and widows in their affliction.'[41]

Nursing represented a rather more substantial challenge to the traditional conception of woman's proper role, though even here there occurred a process of 'permeation' by conventional male definitions. It has been said that Florence Nightingale set out to redefine the concept of what a nurse was.[42] Originally, the work had been repellent and was carried out by women of low status: however, the need to improve nursing standards in hospitals meant that it was necessary to attract a more educated (therefore, higher status) group of recruits. The nursing sisterhoods were too closely linked with one theological party and also inculcated certain norms of vocation that were inimical to the growth of a salaried profession – the establishment of which was Miss Nightingale's main goal: hence the task of nursing reform could not be achieved primarily through these institutions.[43] On the other hand, the nursing sisterhoods already existed, contained trained personnel and above all were recruited from the strata of 'ladies'. By using these groups for the Crimean expedition, she was able to project an image of the new kind of nurse and thereby to popularize nursing as a potential occupation for educated spinsters. At this point, secular nursing began to acquire its own prestige and eventually the nursing sisterhoods became recipients rather than donors of public acceptance.

But the role of nurse was one which could very easily be defined in terms of women's 'natural' attributes. Veblen's argument that male tasks are defined as 'exploit' while females were expected to glory in 'drudgery' seems especially appropriate. Many nursing duties resembled simple domestic tasks, and even Florence Nightingale referred to the occupation as 'this coarse, repulsive, servile, noble work'.[44] Women's 'dependent' status was stressed by the fact that nurses had an ancillary role under the supervision of the (predominantly male) medical personnel. The struggle of a woman like Elizabeth Garrett Anderson to enter the medical profession presents an instructive contrast.

It is clear that the female surplus in Victorian society – however inaccurately it may have been diagnosed by contemporaries – gave an enormous impetus to the early growth of the social service and nursing professions in the mid-nineteenth century and left its indelible trace on their subsequent growth.[45] That influence can still be seen. The legacy of societal attitudes towards social work, for example, derived from its origins in the work of 'old maids' and 'parish women', may help to explain in part the relatively slower development of a consciousness of professional status among British social workers compared to their American counterparts.[46] It is by examining the secular and religious alternatives which were available to the mid-Victorian woman who was seeking an autonomous role outside the middle-class family that some of these influences emerge most clearly.

NOTES

1. V. Klein, *The Feminine Character*, Routledge & Kegan Paul 1946, p.21. Doctrines of female inferiority could always be traced back to the Bible: witness, for example, St Paul's directive to the Corinthinians that 'she that is married careth for the things of the world, how she may please her husband'.

2. *Saturday Review*, 8 October 1859.

3. Quoted in E. Wostenholme 'The Education of Girls', *Woman's Work and Woman's Culture*, ed. J. Butler, Macmillan 1869, p.296.

4. Reviewed in *Saturday Review*, 3 October 1863.

5. In 1861 Maria Rye told the Social Science Congress at Dublin of 810 applications for a post at £15 p.a. and 210 for one offering £12 p.a. The position of the governess became even more desperate if she survived to an age at which work was no longer possible, when her eventual destination was either the workhouse or the lunatic asylum. In the latter, governesses formed the largest single class on the female side (*Edinburgh Review*, April 1859, p.307). John Fowles' recent novel, *The French Lieutenant's Woman* (Panther Books 1971) is a brilliant work of *verstehen* in its treatment of the role of women, and especially the role of governess, in Victorian society.

6. Accredited to the *Saturday Review* by R. Strachey in *The Cause* (G. Bell 1928), p.92.

7. Robert Southey, *Sir Thomas More: or, Colloquies on the progress and prospects of Society*, London 1829, vol. 2, p.36.

8. Florence Nightingale, *The Institution of Kaiserwerth on the Rhine*, London 1851, pp. 6-7.

9. The application of a Life Table removes chance variations in both the numbers born in previous years and in the mortality suffered by the different cohorts represented in the table. For a discussion of the construction of such a table, and for the detailed calculations from which the figures in the text are derived, see 'The Social Position of the Unmarried Woman in the Mid-

Victorian Period and its Relationship to the Development of Philanthropy', A. Deacon, Unpublished Dissertation, University of London, 1969.

10. The proportion of unmarried women also exhibited wide regional variations, being nearly twice as high in Westmorland as in Staffordshire, for example (United Kingdom, Census of 1851, *Census Report*, p. xxxii).

11. *Essays on the Pursuits of Women*, Emily Faithful 1863, p.74.

12. N. Carrier and J. Jeffery, *External Migration: A Study of the Available Statistics*, HMSO 1953, p.57.

13. 'Mortality in England and Wales from 1948 to 1947', W. P. D. Logan, *Population Studies*, vol. 4, no. 2, esp. p.146.

14. See W. Farr, 'Vital Statistics (edited by N. Humphreys for the Sanitary Institute of Great Britain, 1885), esp. pp.184ff., and *First Report of the Commissioners for Inquiring into the State of Large Towns and Populous Districts* (B.P.P., pp. 21, 30 and 138.)

15. J. A. Banks, *Prosperity and Parenthood*, Routledge & Kegan Paul 1954, pp.32-47.

16. *Statistics of Families in the Upper and Professional Classes*, C. Ansell, Jnr. (National Life Assurance Society, 1874), p.83.

17. F. Maurice (ed.), *Lectures to Ladies on Practical Subjects*, Macmillan & Colt 1857, p.304.

18. An income of £300 p.a. was considered necessary before the middle-class male could contemplate marriage. In 1865-6 there were 200,000 assessments for Income Tax under Schedule D which exceeded this amount. See Pelican Economic History of Britain, vol. 3, *Industry and Empire* by E. J. Hobsbawm, Penguin Books, p.156.

19. *Why Are Women Redundant?*, W. R. Greg, p.15.

20. *Report* for 1862 to 1872.

21. Greg, op. cit., p.18.

22. Ibid., p.39.

23. *Saturday Review*, 6 September 1862.

24. 'How to Provide for Superfluous Women', in Butler, op. cit., p.45.

25. *Edinburgh Review*, April 1859.

26. Greg, op. cit., p.26.

27. *Saturday Review*, 18 July 1857. At this time large numbers of watches were being imported from Switzerland, where they were made by women.

28. Anna Bronwell Jameson, *Sisters of Charity Catholic and Protestant at Home and Abroad*, Longmans, Brown, Green and Longmans 1855, pp.60-61.

29. J. S. Howson, *Deaconesses*, Longman, Green, Longman and Roberts 1862, p. xix.

30. The whole subject of nineteenth-century ultra-protestant fears on the subject of nunneries makes a fascinating – if sometimes disturbing – study. See Michael Hill, 'Religion and Pornography', *Penthouse*, vol. 6, no. 1, April 1971. The phamplet in question was a letter on *Convent Inquiry* by Charles N. Newdegate, MP, 1872.

31. *Convocation of Canterbury Report*, 1885, p.276.

32. See G. E. L. Cotton, *The Employment of Women in Religious and Charitable Works* (Lecture delivered before the Bethune Society, 5 April 1886).

33. H. P. Liddon, *Life of Pusey*, Longmans & Co. 1893-97, vol. 3, p.8.

34. G. W. E. Russell, *Arthur Stanton: A Memoir*. Longmans & Co. 1917, pp.57-8.

35. J. M. Neale, *Deaconesses, and Early Sisterhoods*, London 1869, p.4.

36. *Proceedings of the Church Congress Held at York, 1866,* York, John Sampson 1867, p.194.

37. Margaret Goodman, *Sisterhoods in the Church of England,* Smith, Elder & Co. 1863, p.268.

38. Its full title was the 'Ladies National Association for the Diffusion of Sanitary Knowledge'.

39. *Saturday Review,* 12 April 1862.

40. Quoted in the *Journal of the Workhouse Visiting Society,* February 1860. The Society's *Hints to Workhouse Visitors* recommended that as cod liver oil was beneficial but expensive it should be taken by the ladies and tactfully offered to the surgeon, whilst other worthwhile imports were back numbers of the *Family Friend* and Fry's Soluble Chocolate (see the *Journal of the Workhouse Visiting Society,* November 1861).

41. He was quoted, for example, in *My Life and What Shall I do with it?* by 'An Old Maid' (Longmans Revised Edition, 1862), p.119. This book was extremely influential in advocating suitable forms of philanthropy. Its first edition received an enthusiastic notice from the *Saturday Review,* 3 November 1860.

42. This is one of the interpretations put forward by Brian Abel-Smith in *A History of the Nursing Profession,* Heinemann 1960.

43. Florence Nightingale had originally toyed with the idea of forming a nursing sisterhood but her attitude eventually became more ambivalent, and sometimes openly hostile. One of her early matrons, Agnes Elizabeth Jones, was initially discouraged in her ambition to train as a nurse when she found that the only alternatives open were a high church sisterhood and a hospital in which she would have to join as a 'common nurse': as an evangelical, she chose the latter.

44. Rosalind Nash, *A Sketch of the Life of Florence Nightingale,* SPCK 1937, p.20.

45. This influence is, moreover, neglected in much of the existing literature. The surplus is not mentioned, for example, in A. Young and E. Ashton, *British Social Work in the Nineteenth Century,* Routledge & Kegan Paul 1956, or in David Owen, *English Philanthropy 1660–1914,* OUP 1965.

46. This was so despite the pioneering development of a body of knowledge by the Charity Organization Society. Cf. K. Woodroffe, *From Charity to Social Work in England and the United States,* Routledge & Kegan Paul 1962.

8 The Salvation Army and Social Questions of the Day

Christine Parkin

This study is concerned with the Salvation Army's approach to the problem of poverty during its formative years, from its foundation in 1865 to the launching of the Darkest England Scheme in 1890. Deeply involved in the squalor of the cities of nineteenth century England, General Booth's Army found itself forced to wage war against semi-starvation, filthy living quarters and the ignorance of the under-privileged as well as against sin and despair. The Army also had to find its place among those who preached other panaceas than the Gospel of Salvation from sin. Foremost among these were the advocates of national education, of the trade union movements, of co-operative enterprises of one kind or another and later on those who looked to socialism to provide a political solution. Even the Church of England, long divorced from the affairs of ordinary people and allied with conservative interests, was beginning to be involved in social matters. We are concerned, then, with the Salvation Army's attitude to these various enterprises and with the contribution the movement itself made to the thought of the period on this vital social issue.

As with many other aspects of his work, the social philosophy of William Booth, and of the movement he created, came initially from Wesleyan thinking and theology. This makes it necessary to consider in some detail the Wesleyan attitude to social questions, which in turn provides a useful parallel with Booth's approach and a valuable point of reference for his individual modifications. However, Wesleyan Methodism, as it had developed by the 1860s, existed in a social milieu which was rather different from the social environment of the Salvationists. For a point of contrast at that stage, a more interesting group are the Primitive Methodists, whose social composition was very similar to the Salvationists'. Before turning to Booth and the Army's response to social and economic affairs, a brief summary of the attitudes of these two Methodist groups will prove helpful.

To the church-goer of the late eighteenth century who was dissatisfied with the impersonal quality of the liturgy or dismayed by the attacks of the rationalists upon biblical authority, the message of Wesley and the evangelicals must have come as a new insight. For they preached the possibility, even the necessity, of a personal experience of conversion, which would give full assurance of salvation and provide an internal authority greater even than the authority of the written word. Wesley's religious assumptions began and ended with the individual. At first sight, then, the political implications of the Wesleyan movement were negligible. Some earlier religious revivals had achieved political significance by threatening the *status quo*. The political significance of Methodism was that it did not do so.

However, this did not mean that his preaching was to have no social repercussions at all, as Wesley himself perceived. For a converted man was a better member of society, hard-working and conscientious, thus lifting himself by his own efforts to a better standard of living. The economic position of whole communities might be transformed in this way. However, it was their individualism which made it difficult for Wesleyans to justify collective political activity to improve conditions, which they maintained would come about through self-improvement. Under the guiding hand of its nineteenth century leaders, particularly Jabez Bunting, Wesleyan government developed a rigid conservatism which discouraged political activity of all kinds likely to threaten the security of the state, including any united activity originating out of economic distress.

On the other hand, in spite of what amounted almost to repression of political activity, the impact of the Wesleyans on social development was not wholly negative. There is much truth in the assertion that the Methodists became the pioneers of much social reform. In the words of Raymond Cowherd: 'While they were piously renouncing political action, they were agitating for temperance, the abolition of the slave trade, the emancipation of the slaves and laws to protect the Lord's Day.'[1] This helps to explain the very large part played throughout the nineteenth century in achieving humanitarian and social reforms of all kinds.[2] But it was not until nearly the end of the century, through the Forward

Movement led by Hugh Price Hughes and Samuel Keeble, that Wesleyans became more politically conscious as well as more aware of the need for the church to take an active part in social reform.

The rigid and long-lasting conservatism of the Wesleyan Conference led to a series of secessions after the death of its founder as a result of which a number of other Methodist groups emerged. One of these was the Primitive Methodist Church, founded in 1811 and characterized by aggressive open-air evangelism which offended Wesleyan sensibilities. Most prominent in the Midlands and the north-east, it flourished mostly in small towns and among the rural poor and never penetrated in large numbers into the cities. Throughout its history, this group was markedly more democratic, both in its internal operations and in its political expression, than the parent body. Numbers of early trade union leaders came from its ranks and many of its ministers openly supported both the Chartist and the early trade union movements. Perhaps the long and consistent acquaintance of the movement with poverty, together with a historical dislike of autocracy, contributed towards the Primitives' battles against oppression in any form and their practical willingness to take political action if this were necessary. For example, the following appeared in *The Primitive Methodist Magazine* in the 1860s and showed the social concern of its members:

> Man is not all soul, but has a body as well, which demands a proper share of attention ... (The poor child) should certainly be taught contentment with his lot, but not such contentment as the heartless employer would have him practise, to live and die in the same position as he was when he began life, but to be contented to use his present lot as a stepping stone to something higher.[3]

In spite of official taboos, the Primitive Methodists remained politically conscious, reflecting the growing political awareness of the group to which they were primarily attached. Well might E. R. Wickham describe Primitive Methodism as 'the most chameleon-like' of the Methodist Churches:

> ... when the social group in which it was set became Liberal in politics, it became a great liberal Nonconformist Church, and when later the working class embraced Labour politics, the Primitives gave many men into their front ranks.[4]

From what has been said about the Primitives, it may be expec-

ted that their behaviour and development would be closely resembled by the Salvationists. Both movements had their roots in a
similar social environment, both had many members directly ex-
periencing the pressures of poverty, both were regarded in a
similar tolerant, half-amused manner by the poor themselves, and
in the early days of the Christian Mission[5] the two were often
confused. It was not at all unusual for the Christian Mission
evangelists to be nicknamed the 'ranters', like their Primitive Methodist brothers, nor was it surprising, for their mode of evangelism
took much of its character from the Primitives' techniques. And
yet, as it is hoped to show in the following pages, the attitude of
Booth and his Army to social questions, at least for its first quarter-
century, was far more akin to the Wesleyan outlook than to the
Primitive Methodist approach. Indeed, when the Army as a movement did turn its attention to the whole problem of the under-
privileged, the audacious scheme then envisaged still reflected far
more the conservative, patriarchal attitude of Wesley than the
politically-conscious attitude of the Primitives.

For almost the first twenty-five years of the existence of his movement, Booth remained convinced in practice that his message of
salvation was providing, albeit secondarily, one of the most effective weapons against the prevalence of poverty. He considered the
economic misery of those amongst whom he worked and diagnosed
its moral causes. He saw that drunkenness and vicious habits were
responsible for a great deal of poverty, and that the disruption of
family life among the poor was responsible for much more.[6] He
knew that the message he had for all men could change the habits
and circumstances of a life-time and replace a life of idleness and
promiscuity with one of industry and control. He was sure that
once he could change the character of the man, the nature of his
circumstances would, in more cases than not, change with him.
At the times when he was faced with the kind of misery whose
causes were purely economic, his main answer was the exercise of
Christian love through charity and every other evidence of care
and concern.

Booth's attitude was reflected very closely in that of his principal
followers. The writings of the Christian Mission evangelists as
they reported on their work reflect their thinking. In the main,
their attitude was fourfold. They saw society purely in religious

and moral terms and gave no importance to economic distinctions. They perpetuated Booth's and Wesley's individualistic concept, aware of the economic advantage that sometimes attended conversion for the individual, but they made no attempt to work this out into a systematic process. They saw the main relief of poverty in terms of the charity of one class towards another. But in spite of their lack of scientific principle they showed a real involvement in the plight of the poor, bewilderment over its cause, and frustration at being unable to relieve it.

In a report from Leicester in 1877, Evangelist William Corbridge described the scene at the end of one of his services:

> Three long rows of seekers, right across the Warehouse, nearly twenty in a row, some swearers, some drunkards, some thieves, some have been moral, some of the very poor, some in better circumstances.

It is clear that for him, moral distinctions were the most vital ones. For they reflected flagrant breaches of the law of God and a disregard for his authority which to the evangelists was a consideration in the future welfare of the soul. This also helps to explain the constant references in *The Christian Mission Magazine* to those whom it was thought were contributing towards moral degeneration, the publicans through their encouragement of drunkenness and all its consequences, and the secularists with all their persuasive arguments against the authority of the Father God. The fact that there is never a mention of such vices as swearing, nor of the incredibly low standard of wages for some people, shows equally that those who were exerting economic pressure on the poor were not nearly so liable for castigation as those who were exerting moral pressure upon them.

Much has already been said about the expected economic advantages which were attributed to true conversion. Further examples from the evangelists' reports could be given, of homes made bright and clean, of work obtained, of promotion and better circumstances achieved. In fact, Elijah Cadman, at the end of a long life in Salvation Army service which had included a period in charge of the Social Wing of The Salvation Army, went so far as to say that 'In all my days I've never found a truly converted, Christ-serving family actually destitute, and I've had some experience.' This is one of those bold statements that it would be very difficult to substantiate, and it is even contradicted by the experience of some of the other evangelists, but there is no doubt that they would have concurred with the general principle expressed. However, when material conditions did not improve, the evangelists' claim that they were of little importance anyway had some positive value. Once the blight of sin had been removed, even poverty was easier to bear: 'Hallelujah!', exclaimed one of the early converts. 'Our happiness don't depend on circumstances, the Christian Mission trains people above that sort of thing.'

The evangelists also expressed the evangelical belief in the duty of charity, a Christian duty for the rich which had its own particular merit, and which was the best means of alleviating the worst kinds of poverty. For in spite of their conviction that most poverty was the product of sin, the early Salvationists could not ignore the actual conditions of many among whom they worked. As in the case of other home mission evangelists, their very presence in the environment of the poor caused them to do what they could for those who were the unfortunate victims of their own or another's folly. In this venture they sought the assistance of the wealthy, endeavouring to place before them the true condition of the poor in the belief that when this was known liberality would increase. It was often the evangelists and others from middle-class backgrounds who were most stirred by the poverty and distress of the poor. For example, evangelist Mary Billups wrote to *The Christian Mission Magazine* in the following manner in the winter of 1871:

> The gentleman hastening home from the active scenes of the business life to the comfortable homestead, where bright fire, well spread meal, and cheeful faces await his return, gladly lays aside the momentary pang of pity he felt as on his way he gave the poor, half-starved crossing-sweeper a copper – and with a sigh of relief gives himself to the enjoyment of the cosy armchair and the newspaper ... What know these of the poor? Is it to them a fact that men and women are starving?... Nay, it is surely not, or purses would be more freely opened to those who willingly give themselves to the blessed work of relieving such.

This apparently naïve attitude should not be too lightly dismissed, for it represents the thinking of perhaps the majority of those involved in social relief programmes of the time. The application of scientific principles and the academic study of social problems was still in its infancy[7] and it was still felt most popularly that religious and humanitarian agencies concerned for the care of the soul as well as the body were the most capable of dealing with distress. Little was as yet being done to investigate the causes of poverty, but much was being done, if at random, to alleviate its worst miseries.

However, when all was done that could be done, there still remained for the evangelist the sight of many living in grinding poverty which the machinery at his disposal could not possibly alleviate. William Corbridge expressed the thoughts of many: 'I often wish the friends who send us relief could witness some of the cases I have to visit. Heaven only knows how my heart bleeds because we cannot do more than we do.' Nevertheless, the evangelists were comforted by their conviction that their most important, and vital, work lay elsewhere, that for them the only reality was in the power of the gospel, either to eliminate the effects of distress or to transform them. For one of Corbridge's converts the first was the case: 'I live in a queer den with a little chaff to sleep upon, and three bricks for a bolster ... and that ... is all the furniture I possess. But I am happy in Jesus.' Perhaps the last words in this connection, however, should be left to Mary Billups, who expresses the evangelists' constant faith:

> Frequently our hearts are rent with the extreme temporal distress of those who are anxious about their souls. Our inability to relieve the one renders it difficult to deal with the other. Nevertheless, our faith is unshaken in the all-sufficient power of the gospel to raise and renew and bless those most deeply sunk in misery and vice and crime! We shall go forward. Friends and brethren, pray for us.

Certainly at this stage, neither Booth nor his officers saw any room in their thinking for any other remedies for the problem of poverty. Although Booth himself had considerable sympathy for some of the panaceas which were advocated, particularly for trade unionism and co-operation, he did not, in his writings nor in his varied activity, ever refer to the possibility of bringing the weight of his authority in the religious sphere, at one time considerable, to bear upon the political or economic aims of other groups. He was never tempted to see the social responsibility of the church in this light, which is where, in practice, his attitude differs from that of the Primitives. By the same token, it is hardly surprising to discover that neither his officers nor his soldiers showed any significant interest in campaigning on behalf of trade unions, universal education, the labour movement or the like. There is no reference to any officer being a member, still less the local leader, of a trade union, nor of any other interest at a local level. There is not even any significant indication of what might be termed a reactive process, of officers or soldiers who, having had their social conscience stirred within the movement had left it to became active in social or political endeavour. Only in one instance is this known, that of an officer called Frank Smith, whose position will be more fully dealt with later. Most Salvationists quickly developed a social conscience, but this did not at any time lead them into other social or political fields.

On 30 August 1890, there appeared in *The War Cry* the first of a series of articles under the very modern-sounding title of 'Sociology'. It was announced that the series would be a study of the Lord's Prayer and its social implications and it was written by Frank Smith. Already a high-ranking and influential officer, Smith had returned from the command of the Army in the United States and was now responsible for the social welfare work in its infancy in the city of London. His series of articles, cut short at the end of the fifth, reveal a very different attitude from that which had been shown by the Christian Mission evangelists ten or twenty years before. Where the evangelists had paid little heed to the economic distinctions in society, for example, Smith saw them as of great importance, emphasizing as they did the degree to which the social order was contrary to the will of God. He ignored the individualist concept which saw economic advantage as one of the blessings which attended conversion and demanded that the rich as a group recognize their responsibilities towards the poor. He was not pleading for charity, but speaking of rights:

> The right we claim for suffering humanity is the right to live without pangs of hunger, the right of an opportunity to honest toil, and the right to maintain themselves and theirs in a position worthy of the creation of God and not, as so many are today, either in the vortex of destitution or on the verge of the over-hanging precipice of semi-starvation.

Thus Smith's concern for the poor must involve, not just the temporary, spasmodic relief that the evangelists felt incumbent upon them, but planned assistance, which would be engaged in by the rich on behalf of the poor. This must be undertaken as a religious duty in order to eliminate both extreme wealth and extreme poverty which were contrary to the will of God. Smith rejected the notion that resignation and submissiveness to poverty was in any way 'a *sine qua non* of indwelling grace'. Corbridge's

saint with 'three bricks for a bolster' but 'happy in Jesus' would
not have attracted his sympathy.

And yet Smith remained specifically religious in his approach
to poverty. Instead of stressing the religious duty of the poor, he set
himself to make the rich aware of their obligations. His appeal to
the wealthy in some way anticipates the position of twentieth-
century Christendom and the emphasis on the grace which comes
through service:

> If you want to find the Father ... you will find Him amongst the poor,
> the outcast, amongst the unwholesome crowds of vagrants and homeless,
> shoeless ones; and having found the Father, you will find Heaven.

Smith's approach to poverty has been discussed in some detail
because it helps to indicate better than anything else the change
which had taken place in the movement since its inception. However, it should not be imagined that Smith's voice was a represen-
tative one. His thinking was certainly to the left of the vast
majority of Salvationist opinion, to the extent that he eventually
felt himself compelled to resign. He is the only officer known, and
certainly the only prominent one, who eventually resigned and
devoted himself to secular politics. His resignation came at the
end of 1890, after the publication of the Darkest England scheme
which he had helped to inaugurate, and after it became clear that
it was not to be run on the lines that he envisaged. He disappeared
from the Army scene and became involved in local and national
government. A friend and confidant of Keir Hardie, he became a
member of the LCC and in 1929 MP for Nuneaton.

However, Smith's 'Sociology' articles do indicate a change of
attitude in the movement, which led directly to the Army embarking upon an extensive programme of voluntary welfare work.
From the very beginning of the movement in 1865, the Army's
weekly programme at every station had included some kind of
social relief project, dictated by the social and religious climate in
which it was operating. There were mothers' meetings and break-
fast or tea meetings, often with an overt philanthropic purpose,
even though the basic aim was evangelical. When the Christian
Mission became the Salvation Army, much of this activity disappeared, largely owing to Booth's distrust of the effects of charity
of this kind.

However, in spite of Booth's personal feelings, his officers soon found themselves involved in social relief work, which became more prominent as the movement increased in size. By the mid-eighties, ventures were started in various countries and on a small scale, which had in them the seeds of future institutional work. Most prominent of these ventures were the various efforts made to provide for prisoners after their release, which was especially important in Australia, and the crystallization of the numerous spontaneous attempts to give assistance to prostitutes to help them to leave their degrading way of life. Both of these efforts led eventually to the establishment of shelters for the destitute and of centres where food could be bought at nominal cost. There was also, attached to the men's shelter, an industrial factory where simple work was done in return for a standard wage. Opened in the spring of 1890, it was providing work for ninety men by the end of that year.

All of this represented what was for Booth a very significant change of mind from one of considerable doubt about the efficacy of any form of social relief for attaining his real purpose. He had felt that the various kinds of rescue work, usually undertaken as the result of a pressing sense of urgency, should not become central to the Army's life and programme. By the end of 1890, however, he was coming to a very different conclusion. This led to the publication, in October 1890, of a book written by Booth, in which he set out his plans for a scheme of social rescue work which aimed to take the whole destitute population of the country into its orbit. The title of the book was *In Darkest England and the Way Out*.[8]

The basic reason why Booth was persuaded to launch into a scheme of this scope was his observation of a phenomenon which recent studies in the sociology of religion have tended to confirm, that the very poor failed to join the Salvation Army, not because they were exceptionally sinful, but because they were exceptionally poor. He saw them flocking to the meetings led by his devoted officers, he saw the manifest desire of many to accept their offer of a new way of life opening through the gospel, he saw that in all too many cases circumstances forced them to drift away from its influence. His answer was logical, simple and devastating in its directness. He would set up machinery whereby the destitute and poor could be gradually and effectively trained to an industrious way of life, so that they would be better able to respond to the offer of salvation open to them. He had observed that in many cases religious commitment increased material prosperity; now he wanted to provide the means whereby a certain amount of material advancement would increase the possibility of religious commitment. This was made quite clear by Booth in a sentence in the Preface to *Darkest England.*

> In providing for the relief of temporal misery, I reckon that I am only making it easy where it is now difficult, and possible where it is now all but impossible, for men and women to find their way to the Cross of our Lord Jesus.

For Booth the basic factor was still the irreligion of the masses, not their poverty. In this, while he was open to considerable criticism from the more liberal sections of the British public, he was acting in a manner which would be understood by large numbers of them. For many of his readers his scheme would have the great advantage that it did not involve a betrayal of evangelical principles but still it provided an attempt to deal scientifically and yet with compassion with what was acknowledged to be an increasing evil.

Using Charles Booth's recent survey, *The Life and Labour of the People of London*, as his guide, Booth estimated that one in ten of the population of the country was living in destitution, or very close to it. These he labelled picturesquely 'the submerged tenth', demanding for them the same rights that were accorded to the London cab horse, a helping hand when he was down, food, shelter and work. Unlike the Charity Organization Society, he made no distinction between the deserving and the undeserving poor, stating that each individual must be given the same chance to set him on his feet.

The scheme, as outlined in Booth's book, is soon described. He envisaged the establishment of three separate units, taking the form of colonies, on the line of self-supporting communities which had occasionally been put into practice by others.[9] First would be the city colony, a network of agencies established in the hearts of the city, whose purpose was to draw in the destitute, find work for them, provide them with food and shelter and by encouragement and moral persuasion attempt to inculcate into them the desire to adopt a more regular way of life, together with the belief that this was possible. Those who gave adequate proof of response to the opportunity given would then be transferred to the second unit, the farm colony, which in many senses must be regarded as the focal point of the whole scheme. Here, away from the disintegrating influences of city life, Booth felt that it would be possible to build up a small, self-supporting community, where men and women could learn, first of all in the larger community and then if they wished in separate homes of their own, trades by which they could earn their own living, and also the forgotten art of mutual care by which alone the community could flourish. Booth could foresee the establishment of a flourishing farm, with all the home and cottage industries which could accompany it, resulting in a prosperous community which would provide a ready ground for evangelism. The third unit was the colony overseas, a tract of land in one of the developing colonies, to which the best farm colonists could be sent, ready equipped with the skills and tenacity to build for themselves a thriving community in a new land. At each stage, if they wished, the men and women could move out on their own to take up the threads of their old lives, but with new skills and attitudes.

It will be seen immediately that the heart of Booth's scheme was still the individualism in which he so firmly believed. He wished to restore to the individual his freedom of choice, so often stunted by temporal circumstances. He believed that in doing so he was furthering the interests of the individual and of the Kingdom of God. The focal point of his attention was 'John Jones, a stout stalwart labourer in rags, who had not had one square meal for a month, who has been hunting for work that will enable him to keep body and soul together and hunting in vain. There he is in his hungry raggedness, asking for work that he may live and not die of sheer starvation in the midst of the wealthiest city in the world. What,' asked Booth, 'is to be done with John Jones?'

In Booth's mind there were two great impediments which stood in the way of John Jones. One of them was the charity which was offered to him without thought for its effects. Booth had all the Charity Organization Society's horror of indiscriminate charity:

> I do not wish to have any hand in establishing a new centre of demoralization. I do not want my customers to be pauperized by being treated to anything which they do not earn. To develop self-respect in the man, to make him feel that at last he has got his foot planted on the first rung of the ladder which leads upwards, is vitally important, and this cannot be done unless the bargain between him and me is strictly carried

out. So much coffee, so much bread, so much shelter, so much warmth and light from me, but so much labour in return from him.

Secondly, and perhaps more importantly, Booth believed that John Jones' chances had been considerably reduced by the process of industrialization. For the introduction of the machine had resulted in the mushroom growth of large cities, destroying the sense of community which had been one of the most important features of town and country life. His *Darkest England* proposals aimed to redress the balance and to provide by artificial means the mutual care and concern which was evident in the town:

> ... it will be noticed that most of the suggestions which I have put forth in this book are based upon the central principle, which is that of restoring to the over-grown and, therefore, uninformed masses of the population in our town the same intelligence and co-operation as to the mutual wants of each and all, that prevails in your small town or village. The latter is the manageable unit, because its dimensions and its needs have not outgrown the range of the individual intelligence and ability of those who dwell therein.

Booth aimed to restore the dependence of the various classes upon each other, not in any sense of subservience, but to remind each group, as well as each individual, of their inter-dependence. A very important feature of his scheme was that much of the work of the city colony was to be provided by the collection of waste from the houses of the middle classes which could be turned into something which was productive for those living in the hostels and other institutions.

Finally, Booth believed that the town was but a larger expression of what was really the vital unit of social life, the family. He aimed to restore to those who came into his care a sense of belonging to a social grouping which would be in the truest sense the focal point of confession, of mutual care, of real friendship. Booth expressed his feelings in his own, typical manner:

> What we want to do is to exemplify to the world the family idea. 'Our Father' is the keynote. One is our Father, then all we are brethren.... We cannot know better than God Almighty what will do good to man. We are content to follow on his lines, and to mend the world we shall seek to restore something of the family idea to many hundreds of thousands – ay, millions, who have no one wiser or more experienced than themselves, to whom they can take their sorrows, or consult in their difficulties.

The elements of the scheme show Booth's indebtedness to the

Wesleyan concept. He did not depart for one moment from the individualism which marked Wesley's theology, and he retained within the framework of his scheme the conservative, patriarchal approach to human misery. Here was no blue-print for a social revolution, no encouragement for the breakdown of the social order. The prevailing class structure is made the focal point of fruitful co-operation, rather than an element of friction. The destitute and poverty-stricken, although their right to work is fully expressed, are still looked upon as erring children, whose one true salvation is to return to the Father God. And yet Booth departed from Wesley in the very conception that such a scheme was not only necessary, but that it was his responsibility to produce it. For Booth, unlike Wesley, had been forced to the conclusion that poverty bred sin and as such he had no alternative but to fight poverty with all the audacity and on the same kind of universal scale that he was daring to fight sin.

Booth's concern for the relief of poverty led him also to examine and comment upon various methods which had also been put forward as possible solutions to the 'social problem'. Each of them was rejected, not because of their lack of effectiveness, but because they were not specifically suited to the immediate and urgent purposes which Booth had in mind. One example must suffice, his comment upon the aims and activities of the socialists. Rather strangely, he allied their attitude with that of some religious societies:

> This religious cant, which rids itself of all the importunity of suffering humanity by drawing unnegotiable bills payable on the other side of the grave, is not more impracticable than the socialistic clap-trap which postpones all redress of human suffering until after the general overturn. Both take refuge in the future to escape a solution of the problems of the present, and it matters little to the sufferers whether the future is on this side of the grave or the other. Both are, for them, equally out of reach.

When the sky falls we shall catch larks. No doubt. But in the meantime?

The implementation of the *Darkest England* scheme falls outside the scope of this present study. However, it should be noted that Booth appealed for £100,000 to commence operations and that this was eventually subscribed. This did not take place without fierce debate in the press, which was particularly virulent in *The Times*, where it was kept alive by a series of hostile letters written by Thomas Huxley. However, on the strength of the contributions, many of the proposals made in the book were put into practice, including the farm colony, which was opened at Hadleigh in Essex in 1891. Tentative plans were also made for establishing a colony overseas, but these did not come to fruition. Booth's book became the blue-print for the Salvation Army's extensive welfare work and, even though his plan in its entirety was not put into operation, it can be said to have had its influence through this work on the development of twentieth-century state social welfare programmes.

Booth's vision, however, of men and women lifted by the scheme from poverty and sin to independence and righteousness had only limited success. For in the end it was not poverty so much as social habit that kept the poor out of the churches, and even Booth, with all his ingenuity and understanding of the poor, was unable to dispel this. He was on surer ground with his bright 'corybantic'[10] Christianity, his uniforms and street processions drawn from the culture of the poor than he was with his social rescue enterprises. In the long run, they provided a channel of service for his devoted officers and soldiers, the answer to a cry of need, rather than a new method of salvation.

The Salvationists' approach to poverty indicates that, in this field at least, they remained characteristically fundamentalist in their apolitical approach to social problems, in their fierce conviction that only the cure of the soul could achieve lasting results. Yet in spite of their aloofness from political controversy and their lack of interest in economic agitation, they became more involved with the practical problems created by poverty than many of their religious contemporaries and through this they learned to regard the care of the soul as more than a spiritual problem. Today still regarded as one of the foremost voluntary agencies, the Salvation Army is committed to twentieth-century methods for the care and rehabilitation of the poor. For its ability to adapt to changing circumstances the movement is much indebted to its founder who, unlike many visionaries, had no interest in the creation of a future utopia, but was concerned solely with the practicalities of the present.

NOTES

1. Raymond Cowherd, *The Politics of English Dissent*, Epworth Press 1959, p.17.
2. On this subject see Kathleen Heasman, *Evangelicals in Action*, Geoffrey Bles 1962.
3. E. S. Shields, 'The Training of Children', *The Primitive Methodist Magazine*, 1866.
4. E. R. Wickham, *Church and People in an Industrial City*, Lutterworth Press 1969, p.133.
5. The Salvation Army was the Christian Mission from 1865 to 1878, and its officers were known as evangelists.
6. Out of a sample of 40 case-histories taken from Booth's *How to reach the Masses with the Gospel* (1872), 20 (50%) attributed their poverty to drunkenness or disruption of family life. In comparison, Charles Booth in *The Life and Labour of the People of London* (1889), estimated that 36·5% of all those in poverty attributed this to vicious habits or to family circumstances. It would seem, then, that William Booth placed greater relative importance on these two factors.
7. The Charity Organization Society was founded in 1869, although its attempts to bring scientific principles to bear on the giving of relief was not followed up by adequate investigation into its results. See S. and B. Webb, *English Poor Law History*, part II, vol. I (reissued 1963 by Frank Cass & Co.). Charles Booth did not commence his work until the 1880s.
8. Published in London by the Salvation Army, the book reached five editions and sold over 200,000 copies. The title was inspired by the publication of Stanley's *Darkest Africa* of the same year. The book has recently (1970) been re-published in paperback by Charles Knight & Co.
9. In the appendix to *Darkest England*, Booth quotes from E. T. Craig, *History of a Co-operative Farm*, the description of a farm colony experiment in Ireland earlier in the century. He may also have used Herbert Mills' *Poverty and the State*. Mills was a Unitarian minister settling unemployed Londoners on the land in co-operative estates. German Rappists, American Amarites and English Shaker communities may also have influenced him. See Chapter 9 of Howard Steele, *I was a Stranger* (NY 1954).
10. Thomas Huxley's expression.

9 The Cult, the Cultic Milieu and Secularization

Colin Campbell

Introduction

Cult has long been the Cinderella in the family of terms that constitutes the taxonomy of religious collectivities. Consistently overlooked in favour of her 'big sisters' – sect, church and denomination – she has been relegated to a minor place within the sociology of religion's 'household' and entrusted with merely menial tasks.[1] Recently, however, there have been signs of a change of heart. Sociologists have begun to show more interest in cults and cultic phenomena either as examples of cultural deviancy or as empirical evidence with which to deny the hypothesis of secularization.[2] In addition, there has been at least one serious attempt to reformulate the concept of cult and to develop an adequate typology.[3] This re-awakening of interest in the cult can be seen as a somewhat belated response by sociologists to the changes that have occurred and are still occurring in the popular cultural scene in contemporary society. Stimulated by the increasing influence of non-Christian religious ideas and the weakened position of the churches as agencies of cultural control, cultic beliefs like astrology and witchcraft have 'hitched a ride' on the developing counter-culture and spread themselves more widely throughout society. The cultic has therefore become a far more visible component of the total cultural system and the lack of a genuine sociological theory of the cult has become a very obvious lacuna in the sociology of religion.

The concept of cult derives from Troeltsch's tripartite division of religious phenomena into church religion, sect religion and mys-

ticism.[4] The latter, in its pure form, is not represented by organizations at all, but to the extent that these arise they approximate
to the cult in their structure. Troeltsch's original formulation has
been employed and modified by Becker, Mann, Marty, Martin,
Yinger, Jackson and Jobling and Nelson.[5] At the same time, there
has been a discernible tendency to move away from Troeltsch's
emphasis upon the close association of mysticism and the cult
and to use that term to refer simply to any religious or quasi-reli-
gious collectivity which is loosely organized, ephemeral and
espouses a deviant system of belief and practice.[6] As a result two
contrasting conceptions of the nature of cults now exist. The first
view, which is closer to Troeltsch's original position, regards the
distinctive characteristics of cults as being found in association
with and deriving from, the nature of mystical religion. The
second view, as contained in the writings of Lofland, Stark and
Taylor Buckner, presents the special character of cultic groups as
stemming from their deviant or heterodox position in relation to
the dominant societal culture.[7] Although some writers appear to
include both views in their accounts of cults and there has been at
least one attempt to fuse them together into a single 'synthesized'
conception, they clearly remain analytically discrete perspectives
implying contrasting hypotheses.[8]

That they are so frequently associated is probably due to the
historical accident that has caused mysticism to approximate to a
deviant religious tradition in the majority of western societies. If
indeed this is the case then we would expect to be able to find
mystically-based cultic groups which do not occupy a deviant status
in relation to the orthodox culture of the larger society as well as
deviant cults which do not espouse mysticism. Examples of the
former phenomenon would appear to abound in India and in the
Buddhist societies of south-east Asia even if it is more difficult to
find examples closer to home, while those groups which espouse a
deviant scientific belief-system, such as the flying saucer groups,
appear to fit the latter category. Given that the Troeltschian interpretation of cults as the organizational response associated with
mystical religion may well suffer from the limitations which arise
from a consideration of specifically Christian movements of the
sixteenth and seventeenth centuries, it would appear as if the view
of cultic phenomena as primarily deviant is to be preferred. At
the same time, it should not be forgotten that mystical cults may

well constitute an important element of the deviant culture in such societies as Britain and America.

Sociological accounts of the cult tend to describe it as individualistic and loosely structured, in contrast to the communal and cohesive organization of the sect. Also unlike the sect, the cult makes few demands on its members, is tolerant of other organizations and faiths and is not exclusivist. Members do not act in common as a group so much as share 'a parallelism of spontaneous religious personalities'.[9] Membership of such groups changes rapidly and the groups themselves are often transient. Studies of individual cults have born out this general description and reinforced the picture of these groups as precariously balanced in relation to the containing society.[10] Cults, it is argued, tend to succeed very quickly and take over the characteristics of sects or else fade away in the face of societal opposition or the absence of a charismatic leader.[11] Faced with these conclusions it is perhaps understandable that the study of cults has tended in some cases to be absorbed into the analysis of sectarianism.[12]

However, it is by no means obvious that the correct strategy for the development of a genuine theory of cultic phenomena is to follow the example set by the development of theories of sectarianism. That is, to accumulate case studies prior to the establishment of suitable typologies and the generation of hypotheses concerning origin, maintenance and extinction of the various types. The contrast between cults and sects is sufficiently great to suggest that alternative strategies may be more appropriate. For while sects are usually clearly circumscribed entities with specifically formulated belief systems and organizational structures which have a tendency to persist over time, cults by contrast tend to have undefined boundaries, fluctuating belief systems, rudimentary organizational structures and are frequently highly ephemeral. They therefore present a sharp contrast with sects as convenient and suitable subjects for sociological research. There is, however, an alternative method of approaching the study of cultic phenomena.

Given that cultic groups have a tendency to be ephemeral and highly unstable, it is a fact that new ones are being born just as fast as the old ones die. There is a continual process of cult formation and collapse which parallels the high turnover of membership at the individual level. Clearly, therefore, cults must exist within a milieu which, if not conducive to the maintenance of individual cults, is clearly highly conducive to the spawning of cults in general. Such a generally supportive cultic milieu is continually giving birth to new cults, absorbing the debris of the dead ones and creating new generations of cult-prone individuals to maintain the high levels of membership turnover. Thus, whereas cults are by definition a largely transitory phenomenon, the cultic milieu is, by contrast, a constant feature of society. It could therefore prove more viable and illuminating to take the cultic milieu and not the individual cult as the focus of sociological concern.

The cultic milieu

The cultic milieu can be regarded as the cultural underground of society. Much broader, deeper and historically based than the contemporary movement known as *the* underground, it includes all deviant belief-systems and their associated practices. Unorthodox science, alien and heretical religion, deviant medicine, all comprise elements of such an underground. In addition, it includes the collectivities, institutions, individuals and media of communication associated with these beliefs. Substantively it includes the worlds of the occult and the magical, of spiritualism and psychic phenomena, of mysticism and new thought, of alien intelligences and lost civilizations, of faith healing and nature cure. This heterogeneous assortment of cultural items can be regarded despite its apparent diversity, as constituting a single entity – the entity of the cultic milieu. There are several sources of this unity.

At the basis of the unifying tendencies is the fact that all these worlds share a common position as heterodox or deviant items in relation to the dominant cultural orthodoxies. This fact gives rise to a common consciousness of deviance and the need to justify their own views in the light of the expressed ridicule or hostility of the larger society. The spokesmen for the various cultic movements thus have a common cause in attacking orthodoxy and in defending individual liberty of belief and practice. Arising from this there is a prevailing orientation of mutual sympathy and support, such that the various cultic movements rarely engage in criticism of each other. On the contrary they display a marked tolerance and receptivity towards each others' beliefs which, although partly stemming from this common concern with liberty of belief and resistance to any suggestion of dogmatism, also receives a great stimulus from the presence of the mystical tradition. Since this tradition emphasizes that the single ideal of unity with the divine can be attained by a diversity of paths it tends to be ecumenical, super-ecclesiastical, syncretistic and tolerant in outlook.[13] These tend, in fact, to be characteristics of the cultic milieu in general whether or not the belief content is mystical in the sense of pursuing the goal of ecstatic experience. As a result, the fragmentary tendencies present in the milieu because of the enormous diversity of cultural items are more than counteracted by the continuing pressure to syncretization.

Syncretization is then further facilitated and re-inforced by the over-lapping communication structures which prevail within the milieu. More than anything else the cultic world is kept alive by the magazines, periodicals, books, pamphlets, lectures, demonstrations and informal meetings through which its beliefs and practices are discussed and disseminated. However, unlike the sectarian situation these communication media are not bounded by the framework of the beliefs of a particular collectivity but are generally open. Thus not only does syncretization mean that cultic teachings are frequently mutually supportive (i.e. visitors from outer space prove to be psychic and mediums confirm that there is life on other planets), but the literature of particular groups and movements frequently devotes space to topics outside its own orbit, includes reviews of one another's literature and advertise one another's meetings. As a direct consequence of this individuals who 'enter' the cultic milieu at any one point frequently travel rapidly through a wide variety of movements and beliefs and by so doing constitute yet another unifying force within the milieu.

Lastly, the cultic milieu is manifestly united by a common ideology of seekership which both arises from and in turn reinforces the consciousness of deviant status, the receptive and syncretistic orientation and the interpenetrative communication structure. The concept of seekership has been employed by Dohrman, Taylor Buckner and Lofland and Stark, and the latter in particular have developed it to apply to persons who have adopted a problem-solving perspective while defining conventional religious institutions and beliefs as inadequate.[14] Such persons are defined as 'searching for some satisfactory system of religious meaning to interpret and resolve their discontents'.[15] If this conception is widened beyond the restriction to a religious frame of reference, then it can be seen that this notion of seekership prevails throughout the cultic milieu. Once again mysticism supports this ideology for the belief in the multiplicity and diversity of paths to spiritual enlightenment supplants the distinction between believer and unbeliever with the conception of degrees of 'seekership'. However, the basic seekership belief that truth (or enlightenment) is an esoteric commodity only to be attained after suitable preparation and a 'quest' exists outside the purely mystical religious tradition. It can apply equally well to the search for interpretations and explanations of non-religious phenomena and in situations where there is no expectation of 'revelatory experiences' and even in the context of the pursuit of worldy success, health or consolation.

The culture of the cultic world

Given that the ideology of seekership provides a common and unifying style and that the processes of syncretization are continually mutating whatever new cultural items enter, it is still necessary to describe the culture of the cultic world in a substantive fashion. This is clearly a difficult task and until such time as a detailed cultural map is drawn up it can only be attempted in a very general fashion. Basically cultic culture can be described as falling in the property space bounded by a religion-science axis and an instrumental-expressive orientation axis, taking for granted the prior criterion of societal deviancy. Thus there are items which are primarily deviant science, those which are deviant religion and there are both instrumental and expressive concerns in relation to each category. There are in addition cultic movements and belief-systems which represent blends of science and religion and display combinations of instrumental and expressive orientations. Attempts to classify cultic beliefs on the basis of these two axes will therefore only result in a very rough approximation to reality, especially as it is likely that it is just those systems of meaning which are able to blend both cultural traditions and both orientations which will be the most successful.

As has already been indicated, the most prominent part of the deviant religious component of the cultic world is mysticism. This is the religious response which Troeltsch identified as concentrating solely on the individual's relationship with the divine and through an emphasis on first-hand experience tending to neglect the historical, ecclesiastical and ritual concerns of religion. It has no need for dogmas, sacraments, ministry or indeed any formal organization, and as such it appears excessively individualistic. Although it is separated from the mainstream of religion by its rejection of the importance of the fellowship of believers, it does in fact include a belief in a spiritual fellowship but one mediated by the divine. These characteristics cause it to be totally ecumenical, super-ecclesiastical, syncretistic and tolerant in outlook. In all these characteristics mysticism represents almost the complete antithesis of the religion of the sects.

The basic beliefs comprising the mystical position are that the religious ideal is a state of unity with the divine; this ideal is potentially attainable by all: that there is an underlying unity of all consciousness and life and that no matter how diverse or how many versions of truth there are, all can lead to the same all-encompassing truth. Such a position leads not only to a depreciation of history, ritual and organization but also to a general indifference to all secular affairs except the most personal. Social, economic and political problems can only be resolved when a spiritual reformation has occurred at the individual level, and this requires that the spiritualization of personal life should be the principal aim. This in turn can cause the mystical to be closely associated with the erotic and the sexual while opposing materialism. Almost all these assumptions are contrary to the primary premises of Judae-Christian religion and have been rejected by that tradition as heresies. It is not surprising, therefore, that we should find that they flourish in the cultural underground of an officially Christian society. Other world religions like Buddhism and Hinduism have mysticism as their central ingredient and these religions and their teachings are widely disseminated throughout the cultic milieu comprising one of the principal components of that culture. In fact certain teachings of Buddhism and Hinduism, which are notably absent from the Christian tradition, like re-incarnation and the prohibition on the taking of animal life, are almost the hallmarks by which the cultic religious groups identify themselves. Although mysticism may be the dominant religious component in the cultic milieu it is not the only one. The other forms of 'deviant religion' which are well represented are the pre-Christian pagan traditions of magic, witchcraft, sun worship and the like. Rarely, however, do any of these teachings appear in their pure form but the rampant syncretism of the cultic milieu means that mysticism and magic, meditation and mediumship, astrology and ahimsa, all are likely to appear in association with one another.

They are also likely to appear in conjunction with 'non-religious' beliefs and practices, for the other important ingredient of cultic culture is 'deviant science and technology'. Orthodox science is now at least as important as orthodox religion in defining what is truth and what is error in contemporary culture, if not more so. Scientific 'heresies' abound in the cultic fringe. Of course mystic religion itself could be regarded as scientifically unsupportable, but the true heresies are not so much religious beliefs of this kind but beliefs held to be 'purely' scientific which are repudiated by the spokesmen of scientific orthodoxy; the flat-earthers, or the flying saucerians who hold that extra-terrestrial vehicles actually exist. Fully-fledged scientific theories also abound, notably concerning 'ethers', 'emanations', 'fifth senses', and astral planes together with the many and varied interpretations of the nature of time and space.

Lastly, there exists the underground technology which has been built on this deviant science, principally medical and psychiatric, but there are also technologies of communication, transportation and divination.

The institutions of the cultic milieu

The institutions of the cultic milieu can be viewed, like its culture, as encompassed by the religion-science and instrumental-expressive axes with the conception of seekership once again acting as a unifying factor. A variety of organizational forms can be seen within this framework and it is by no means obvious that the traditional conception of the cult is the dominant type. Fundamentally it is the case that the formal character of the cultic institutions derives from the nature of the cultural tradition of which they represent deviant forms. Thus, if it is heterodox science, then like para-psychology there will tend to be 'colleges' and 'institutes' like the College of Psychic Science and the Institute for Occult Sciences offering quasi-educational courses, lectures, demonstrations and facilities for research. If it is heterodox religion then one finds 'orders', 'lodges', 'fellowships', and 'brotherhoods' like the White Eagle Lodge, the Order of The Cross and the Rosicrucians.

Whatever the nomenclature, however, the majority of these organizations share the same characteristics; they are organizations for 'seekers', offering aid, support, facilities and a form of fellowship to those in search of truth. The exceptions to this are the revelatory cults which have adherents rather than seekers and promulgate *the* truth as it has already been revealed, together with the social institutions associated with the practice of deviant science and technology. The former, like the Aetherius Society, have many of the characteristics of a sect since belief in a revealed truth leads to a believer-nonbeliever distinction, rather than the notion of the degrees of seekership prevailing in the cultic milieu in general. The latter are merely institutions for the practice of a deviant technology like faith healing, chiropractic, naturopathy or mediumship and the appropriate individual categories are those of practitioner and client. Numbered here would be the numerous practices of the mediums, astrologers, graphologists, diviners and healers of all sorts, together with the many clinics, nature cure resorts and other establishments offering these services on a residential basis. It is probably at this point that the cultic milieu comes most directly into contact with the larger society as a consequence of a general demand for the unorthodox services which it offers. Apart from these personal service institutions it would appear as if the organizational form most typical of the cultic milieu is not the cult but the 'society of seekers'. Indeed the cult, in the form of a group offering a particularized and detailed revealed truth, represents something of an aberration from the basic principle of tolerance and eclecticism which is prevalent in the milieu in general and this could possibly be one reason why it tends to have such a short lifespan.

The nature and problems of cultic organizations derive primarily from the fact that they attract and recruit seekers. Seekership is probably the one characteristic that all members of cultic groups have in common, and while this facilitates the formation of groups it poses special problems for their maintenance. Seekers do not necessarily cease seeking when a revealed truth is offered to them, nor do they necessarily stop looking in other directions when one path is indicated as *the* path to the truth. They may in fact have lost sight of their original aim and through the 'displacement of goals' have come to accept seeking itself as the primary end. Because of this, groups face continuing pressure to widen their concerns and explore new cultic regions. Thus a group of seekers may join together out of a common concern with flying saucers, but then expand their interests to encompass all kinds of occult phenomena. Such a 'strain toward variety' may cause the group to eventually lose its focus of concern altogether and finally disappear back into the general milieu from which it arose.[16] Alternatively, if the group manages to resist these pressures and maintain its specific original focus of concern then it has the increasingly difficult task of finding something new to discuss. It is in this context that there exists the greatest possibility of an individual laying claim to some special truth and presenting himself as a revelatory 'channel'.

Another response to this dilemma is to institutionalize seekership within the organization. By creating several categories of membership corresponding to different degrees of initiation into new areas of knowledge it is possible to control the seekers' exploration of new 'mysteries' and so create within one organization the life-history that frequently occurs within the milieu in general. Skilful control of this process can convince the seeker that all he will ever need to know will eventually be made clear to him and he can be induced to develop an even greater commitment to the organization in terms of personal identity and (not least) money. Such a response clearly requires a secretive or semi-secretive aura and this in turn leads to the need to demonstrate that the organization's claims are genuine. There is, therefore, frequently a heavy emphasis upon the instrumental benefits of membership of such an organization.

In line with the distinction between the cult proper and the society of seekers there is an associated difference between the adherent to a particular brand of cultic culture and a seeker actively committed to a quest within the culture but uncommitted to a specific version of 'the truth'. It is the former whose particularized loyalty helps to bring the cult into being out of the general milieu but it is the latter who support the milieu itself by attending lectures and demonstrations and answering advertisements. There is, however, a third category of person whose support helps to maintain the cultic milieu in existence and this is the passive consumer of the 'products' of the culture. Unlike the seeker, such a person does not possess the intensity of commitment to the quest to actively invest a considerable amount of time, emotion and money in exploring the milieu. Instead his interest in the mysterious and the bizarre is merely a general one which he satisfies through subscription to magazines which are principally commercial rather than ideological in orientation (*Witchcraft* and *Man, Myth and Magic* are only the most recent and most publicized of a long line of such magazines). Or his involvement is that of the *ad hoc* concern typical of a client seeking the services of a professional practitioner. Magazines like *Fate, Prediction* and *Zodiac Monthly*, for example, which are totally commercial in their production style and bear little resemblance to the highly committed cultic house journals *Psychic News* or *Occult Gazette*, carry several pages of advertisements on behalf of many psychic consultants and healers including pyromancists, palmists, trance mediums, tarot experts, graphologists and absent healers as well as the more conventional clairvoyants and astrologers. It is this substantial commercial substructure which is one of the principal reasons why the cultic milieu continues to survive.

Secularization and the cultic milieu

Some of the sociologically most interesting questions one can ask about this milieu concern not its internal anatomy but its relationship with the containing society and its orthodox culture. How does it manage to survive in face of the continuing disapproval and even outright hostility of the organizations representing cultural orthodoxy? Through what channels are new cultural items introduced into the mileu? What are the circumstances which facilitate the transformation of deviant cultural items into variant or even dominant ones? What general functions, in fact, does the milieu fulfil? Although one can speculate on any one or more of these themes, it is clear that at present we lack the information to answer such questions. That we should seek to answer such questions would seem to follow from any commitment to explore the dynamics of socio-cultural systems. Among the hypotheses that suggest themselves concerning the cultic milieu one might pick out the following:

1. That it is a major agency of cultural 'diffusion' facilitating the accommodation of 'alien' cultural items into a host culture.
2. That it is a major agency of cultural 'innovation', new items

arising as a result of the processes of syncretization and 'revelation'.

3. That it functions as a cultural 'gene pool' for society, enhancing society's potential for cultural adaptation by transmitting and creating numerous cultural 'mutations'.

4. That it functions as a 'negative reference group' for the spokesmen of cultural orthodoxy, facilitating adherence to dominant scientific paradigms by practicing scientists and associated practitioners.

5. That the cultic milieu flourishes in relation to (a) the amount of 'alien' culture contact and (b) the disintegration of dominant indigenous culture.

6. That the cultic milieu acts as a source of renewal for ailing orthodox belief systems.

7. That cultic movements represent a general response to 'psychic deprivation'.

There is a general question underlying specific hypotheses such as these concerning the nature and extent of a societal cultural underground. If one starts with the premise that all societies will possess variant and deviant cultures in addition to a dominant one then the assumption of the universality of an underground cultic milieu appears, *a priori*, justifiable. But the nature and extent of such a milieu and the precise form of its relationship with the dominant orthodoxy are by contrast subject to much variation. The content of the counter-culture is clearly in part a product of the form of orthodoxy itself, just as the extent of such a culture is limited by the repressiveness of the agencies of orthodoxy. A consideration of the functions of the cultic milieu is therefore dependent in the first instance on analysis of the total cultural system of which the milieu is a part. Clearly this is a tall order indeed, but if one were to attempt this for British society then, at the very least, it would be necessary to relate both orthodox science and orthodox religion, firstly to each other and secondly to their unorthodox forms. The only concept that seems at all capable of fulfilling such a role is secularization and despite the notorious uncertainties and ambiguities surrounding the usage (and abusage) of this term it does seem worth speculating on how the postulated processes of secularization might relate to the position of the cultic milieu in contemporary society.

Primarily it would seem that the structural changes associated with secularization have been to the advantage of cultic culture. The decline in the power and influence of the Christian churches has inevitably weakened their role as custodians of 'truth' and reduced the extent to which they can draw upon societal support for forays against indigenous 'pagans' and 'heretics'. Thus although the churches still condemn such unChristian systems of thought as astrology and witchcraft these condemnations remain unsupported by secular sanctions and unnoticed by the public in general. Thus the principal bulwark against heresy and superstition has greatly diminished and the many pre-Christian and non-Christian varieties of religious belief and practice are free, for the first time in many centuries, to spread throughout society. In addition, the relativism and tolerance of cultural pluralism which, it is claimed, are concomitants of secularization, have greatly assisted the increased acceptability of these 'heretical' beliefs. Increased acquaintance with other world religions as a result both of the importation of ideas and the immigration of adherents has helped to raise the average threshold of tolerance of deviant religious views while robbing Christianity of its position as the automatic yardstick of what is normal in matters of religious belief and practice. The natural consequence has been that cultic beliefs of all kinds are now closer in cultural distance to the prevailing orthodoxies of society than they were at the turn of the century. What has been traditionally treated as categorically deviant and subject to secular sanctions as well as ecclesiastical wrath is gradually becoming merely variant. Although various occult phenomena fall into this category witchcraft is the best illustrative example and it is interesting to speculate on whether the British pattern of institutionalized dissent can actually stretch so far as to accommodate the total rehabilitation of witchcraft.[17]

There is, however, another strand of secularization theory, which would appear to argue against the increased accessibility of cultic culture. This is the identification of secularization as a cultural process (or processes) of rationalization stimulated and supported by the social institution of science and those that derive from it. From this standpoint it could be argued that it is misleading to view the accessibility of cultic beliefs from the perspective of their relationship to religious orthodoxy since the religious world-view, orthodox and unorthodox, is itself being steadily displaced

by a rational scientific *weltanschauung*. Scientific orthodoxy and
not religious orthodoxy is thus the proper yardstick for the identification of cultural deviance and judged by this standard such
systems of belief and practice as the occult must be regarded as
just as deviant as before, if not actually more so. Support for this
argument is found in the fact that sectarian and cultic movements
find themselves sanctioned by the secular authorities if they
attempt to implement deviant scientific theories even though their
'religious' deviance goes unpunished.[18] If, therefore, scientific
orthodoxy has replaced religious orthodoxy as the dominant cultural tradition in society one would expect the cultic to be no
more 'accessible' now than in former decades.

This aspect of secularization theory has the implicit assumption
that as the scientific world-view has significantly displaced the
orthodox religious perspective on man and the universe it will have
no difficulty in overcoming the heterodox versions prevailing in
the cultic milieu. The decline in the power and influence of the
churches is thus counter-balanced by the rise of the power and
influence of the scientific community. However, as soon as this
assumption is made explicit it is possible to observe the many
difficulties which it presents. The basic incompatibility of science
and religion is the central tenet underlying this assumption and
although such an incompatibility can be demonstrated at a philosophical level it is by no means clear that the scientific and religious outlooks are behaviourally incongruous.[19] It is even less obvious that religion in all its forms should necessarily be in conflict with
the scientific perspective. The potential for conflict would, in fact, appear to be greater for religions which emphasize a personal, and
transcendental conception of God than those which hold to an impersonal, non-intervening and immanent notion of the divine. Even
then some transcendental theologies are potentially more likely to
come into conflict with science than others. It would indeed be un-
warranted to assume that the conflict between evangelical Christianity and science which occurred in the nineteenth century was in any
way the type-case of relationships between religion and science.
If we accept that science's potential for conflict with religion varies
according to the nature of the religion concerned then it could well
be the case that science is less likely to come into conflict with
some of the religious systems prevailing in the cultic milieu than
with the prevailing religious orthodoxy. The non-historical char-

acter of mystical religion, for example, means that a conflict similar to that which existed between Christianity and science over evolution is unlikely to occur. However, even if one were to assume that rationalization was occurring and the religious world-view was steadily being replaced by a 'scientific world-view' it is still by no means obvious that this is the same view as that which prevails within the scientific community. The changeover from a religiously based to a scientifically based culture does not remove the problem of maintaining a dominant orthodoxy in the face of the continuing threat of heterodoxy. In this respect the central question becomes, how effective is science as an agency of cultural control? Clearly effectiveness in this sense refers both to the problem of maintaining adherence to the dominant paradigms within each scientific discipline as well as, more importantly, maintaining adherence to the canons of scientific procedure, the premises of scientific enquiry and the ethos of science in general. There is, however, the additional problem of enforcing these norms on those outside of the scientific community and it is here that the contrast with the church is most noticeable. For it is to be doubted whether scientists as a body can compare with the churches in either their desire or their ability to repress heterodox views in the society at large. In part one could argue that the fundamentally democratic ethos of science means that the authoritarian measures employed in the past by the churches are not available to them. In addition, unlike the church, they lack a thoroughgoing mandate for concerning themselves with the beliefs of non-scientists. Thus, although they may have measures for enforcing orthodoxy upon the scientific community, for example by effectively ostracizing the 'heretic', even this conformity may be achieved at the price of exacerbating the problem of heresy in society at large. It is only in fact in the realm of applied science and particularly with regard to the practice of medicine that one finds a situation which in any way resembles the traditional manner in which the churches attempted to control the spread of heresies such as witchcraft. But even here secular sanctions against those who practice a 'false' art or science of healing are not very severe or all-embracing and the trend is, if anything, towards greater tolerance of such heterodox systems as homeopathy, chiropractic and acupuncture. In sum, it does not appear as if science will necessarily be able to enforce any more cultural conformity upon society than the churches were able to do; indeed they could well be less effective.

There remains the question of whether it is reasonable to assume that the scientific viewpoint will spread through society even without any determined efforts being made to suppress heresies. Might not the enormous influence and prestige of science together with expanding institutions of education result in the gradual acceptance of the orthodox scientific outlook as 'demonstrably superior' to any other? Once again the argument is more complex than it might at first seem. The demonstrable superiority of science is in many cases just not demonstrable or in other cases only demonstrable to other scientists. Even more important, the inferiority of alternative systems may only be clearly demonstrable to other scientists. Even where a system is seen to be inferior to orthodox science in its explanatory power it may be preferred because it is more easily understood, more accessible or more comprehensive. The principal difficulty with this hypothesis, however, is that there is no guarantee that even those people who are impressed by the demonstrable superiority of science and as a consequence desire to hold a scientific outlook will in fact be in a position to distinguish between what are orthodox and what are heterodox scientific views. They may, as a consequence end up believing in flying saucers and ESP because of the convincing scientific 'evidence'. Thus there are good grounds for doubting whether an increase in the prestige of science will automatically lead to a consolidation of its position as a widely accepted belief-system.

Summary and conclusion

An adequate conceptualization of the cult and some formulation of hypotheses concerning cultic phenomena is becoming an increasingly necessary task as traditionally cultic beliefs become both more visible and more accessible within society. The established approach to the study of cults, which takes the highly successful study of sects as its model, appears to promise less than an approach which concentrates on the cultic milieu in general. Such a milieu is defined as the sum of unorthodox and deviant belief-systems together with their practices, institutions and personnel and constitutes a unity by virtue of a common consciousness of deviant status, a receptive and syncretistic orientation and an interpenetrative communication structure. In addition, the cultic milieu is united and identified by the existence of an ideology of seekership and by seekership institutions. Both the culture and the organizational structure of this milieu represent deviant forms of the prevailing religious and scientific orthodoxies in combination with both instrumental and expressive orientations. Two important elements within the milieu are the religious tradition of mysticism and the personal service practices of healing and divination.

A consideration of the relationship of this milieu to orthodox culture suggests that the imputed processes of secularization may be creating circumstances favourable to the growth of the milieu and the further expansion of cultic beliefs throughout society. The changeover from a dominant religious orthodoxy to a dominant scientific orthodoxy does not seem to correspond to any greater control of heterodox societal beliefs, for while the decline in power of organized ethical religion appears to have removed the most effective control over heretical religious beliefs, a growth in the prestige of science results in the absence of control of the beliefs of non-scientists, in an increase in quasi-scientific beliefs. Ironically enough, therefore, it could be that the very processes of secularization which have been responsible for the 'cutting back' of the established form of religion have actually allowed 'hardier varieties' to flourish, or possibly created the circumstances for the emergence, not of a secular scientific society, but of a society centred on a blend of mysticism, magic and pseudo-science.

NOTES

1. See H. Becker's remark that cult is a 'less useful' as well as less used concept in sociology (T. F. O'Dea in the *International Encyclopaedia of the Social Sciences*).
2. John Lofland, *Doomsday Cult*, Prentice-Hall, Englewood Cliffe, NJ 1966; David Martin, *A Sociology of English Religion*, Heinemann and SCM Press 1967.
3. G. K. Nelson, 'The Spiritualist Movement and the Need for a Redefinition of Cult', *Journal for the Scientific Study of Religion*, vol. 8, no. 1, spring 1969; 'The Concept of Cult', *Sociological Review*, New Series, vol. 16, no. 3, November 1968.
4. E. Troeltsch, *The Social Teachings of the Christian Church*, Macmillan 1931.
5. L. Von Wiese and Howard Becker, *Systematic Sociology*, NY 1932; W. E. Mann, *Sect, Cult and Church in Alberta*, University of Toronto Press

1955; Martin E. Marty, 'Sects and Cults', *The Annals of the American Academy of Political and Social Science*, CCCXXXII, November 1960, pp.125-34; David Martin, *Pacifism: An Historical and Sociological Study*, Routledge & Kegan Paul 1965; J. Milton Yinger, *Religion, Society and the Individual*, Macmillan, NY 1957; J. A. Jackson and R. Jobling, 'Toward an Analysis of Contemporary Cults' in *A Sociological Yearbook of Religion in Britain*, ed. David Martin, SCM Press 1968; G. K. Nelson, op. cit.

6. Lofland, op. cit.; J. Lofland and R. Stark, 'Becoming a World-Saver: A Theory of Conversion to a Deviant Perspective', *American Sociological Review*, vol. 30 (6), December 1965, pp.862-75.

7. Lofland, op. cit.; Lofland and Stark, art. cit.; H. Taylor Buckner, 'The Flying Saucerians: An Open Door Cult' in *Sociology and Everyday Life*, ed. S. M. Truzzi, Prentice-Hall 1968, pp.223-30.

8. G. K. Nelson, art. cit. (1969).

9. E. Troeltsch, op. cit., p.744.

10. Leon Festinger, Henry Riecken and Stanley Schacter, *When Prophecy Fails*, University of Minesota Press 1956; Lofland, op. cit.; Taylor Buckner. art. cit.

11. Charles Y. Glock and Rodney Stark, *Religion and Society in Tension*, Rand McNally & Co., Chicago 1965, p.257; Martin E. Marty, op. cit.

12. This appears to be the general trend of Bryan Wilson's work; see 'A Typology of Sects', *Acts de la X Conference Internationale (1969)*, Rome, CISR (1969), pp.29-56.

13. See Troeltsch, op. cit., p.745.

14. H. T. Dohrman, *California Cult,* Beacon Press, Boston 1958; Taylor Buckner, art. cit.; Lofland and Stark, art. cit.

15. Lofland and Stark, art. cit., p.868.

16. Taylor Buckner, art. cit., p.229.

17. Can we, for example, envisage a time when covens will be registered as religious bodies for tax purposes?

18. The treatment of scientology in Australia and Britain is an interesting example of this.

19. See, for example, the discussion in Glock and Stark, op. cit., pp.262-88.

10 The Catholic Apostolic Church: A Study in Diffused Commitment

R. K. Jones

Origins

THE origins and development of the Catholic Apostolic Church have been relatively well documented, although the most recent important study is now over a quarter of a century old.[1] The two men who feature prominently in the movement are Edward Irving and Henry Drummond; without these two it would have neither originated nor have been given any impetus towards its perpetuation.

Edward Irving was born in Annan, Scotland, in 1792. His father was a tanner, and his mother, Mary Lowther, was the daughter of a small landed proprietor. He was successful at school and came under the influence of Adam Hope, a Burgher Seceder. His biographies record him as often walking with Hope to the neighbouring village of Ecclefechan, to Sunday worship at the little kirk of the True Seceders. At the age of thirteen he went to Edinburgh University, from which he graduated in 1809. In the following year he obtained the mastership of the school at Haddington where he stayed for two years, studying in his spare time for the ministry and giving lessons to one Jane Baillie Welsh. It is a period rather obscurely documented but by all accounts he fell in love with Miss Welsh, who was later to marry Thomas Carlyle, another famous pupil of the Annan school and subsequently a friend of Irving. In 1812 Irving acquired the mastership of a new school at Kirkcaldy where he is reported to have been strict with his pupils. One particular pupil, Isabella Martin, the parish minister's daughter, Irving eventually married.

Except for a few Seceders religion in the Annan area was dormant[2] but in 1815, when Irving obtained his licence to preach, the

Evangelical Revival was sweeping the kirk. In 1819 he went as assistant to the famous Dr Chalmers, who was minister of St John's parish church in Glasgow. Chalmers' achievement was a new kind of parochial system, in appearance a microcosm of the welfare state. It was a complex system embracing the task of poor relief in a parish of 10,000, and was organized with a series of elders, deacons, teachers, and 'social workers'. Irving's contribution was practical rather than ideological, although when he was with Carlyle in Glasgow he apparently commented that if the plight of the poor was not remedied they would soon sink into that of the Irish. As a conservative and anti-liberal it is certain that he was moved profoundly by the plight of the Glasgow poor. Glasgow at this time was almost in a state of civil war, spurred on by the revolutionary weavers and cotton-spinners. Mrs Oliphant[3] records that 'Nothing less than the horrors of the French Revolution floated before the terror stricken eyes of all who had anything to lose.' Irving was touched by the people of the parish of St John's 'in the midst of nakedness and starvation'.

In 1822 Irving was called to be minister of the Caledonian Chapel or Asylum in London, and was inducted. There were 50 in the congregation, but Oliphant says that Irving was tired of 'the common stick of dry theology, the certified soundness of dull men'.[4] By the end of the year he was famous throughout London, and was variously described as handsome, eloquent and vitriolic. A contemporary account, cited by Drummond, has this description:

> Sunday after Sunday the mean-looking, dingy chapel was thronged with statesmen, philosophers, poets, painters, and literary men; peers, merchants, and fashionable ladies were mingled with shopkeepers and mechanics, while many hundreds were unable to obtain admission.[5]

Brougham, Canning, Mackintosh, Wilberforce, were only some of the famous who flocked to hear him. *An Argument for Judgment to Come* was published in 1823, together with his *Orations*, which was a protest against the visions of judgment of Southey and Byron. In October he married Isabella, having been unable to obtain release from what subsequently was regarded as a rash betrothal. Several biographers maintained that he was always in love with Jane, and she herself wrote: 'If I had married Irving the tongues would never have been heard.'

Irving's apocalyptic period dates from 1826, although it is true to say that to some extent the whole age was at this time apocalyptic. The French Revolution was seen as a sign or portent of the impending end of the world, and the arts produced not only the pictures of Danby and Martin, but Byron's *Heaven and Earth* and Moore's *Love of Angels*. James Hair, in his book *Regent Square*, writes

> If Irvingism is to be traced to its original germ, so far as any system can be traced to an individual, it may be found in Irving's religious experience, and in his consequent mode of apprehending divine truth not by open spiritual vision, but through a human vision.[6]

It was in 1826 that Irving became familiar with the work of the Spanish Jesuit Lacunza (pseudonym, Aben Ezra, sometimes Juan Josefat Ben-Ezra) which he translated under the title *The Coming of the Messiah in Glory and Majesty*. While attending a conference at Albury in the same year he met the second person who was later to become prominent in the Catholic Apostolic Movement, Henry Drummond, MP. The conference was to study unfulfilled prophecy.

In 1827 Irving moved to a new church in Regent Square; but his star was falling, and the congregation soon settled at some 1,000 'sittings'. In 1828 he published his *Lectures on Baptism*, which approximated to the theology of the sacramental party of the Church of England. In the same year the restless Irving journeyed to Scotland to proclaim the Second Advent. Oliphant records that Irving expected the Second Coming to occur in his lifetime, an event he eagerly anticipated.[7] He was welcomed in Edinburgh, Carnwath and Bathgate. However, the death of 35 villagers in a throng at Kirkcaldy, due to the collapse of the church gallery, cast a shadow over the tour.

At this time rumours of heterodoxy and controversy on the nature of Christ were directed at Irving. Though glorying in the divinity of Christ, Irving held that the nature of the body of the Son of God was 'one with us in all its infirmities and liabilities to temptation ... we argue for an identity of life ...' This view was attacked by a certain Mr Cole, and by J. B. Haldane in his *Refutation of Mr Irving's Heretical Doctrine* (1828). Irving replied in *The Orthodox and Catholic Doctrine of Our Lord's Human Nature* (1830) and *Christ's Holiness in the Flesh* (1831). The concept of the holiness of Christ through the operation of the Holy Ghost led eventually to 'perfectionism' in the Irvingite circle, and ultimately to the belief that 'gifted' persons were mouthpieces of the Holy Ghost when 'in the power'.[8]

> I believe that my Lord did come down and toil and sweat and travail, in exceeding great sorrow, in this man of temptation, with which I and all men are oppressed; did bring His Divine presence and death possessed humanity ... and in that very state which God had put it after Adam had sinned, did suffer its sorrows and pains, its anguish, its darkness, wasteness, disconsolateness and hiddeness from the countenance of God: and by His faith and patience did win for Himself the name of the Man of Sorrows and Brother and Finisher of our faith.[9]

Events were building up against Irving. John McLeod Campbell, minister at Rhu, with his doctrine of the Universal Love of God (that this love was not confined to the elect); Thomas Erskine of Linlathen; Hugh Maclean of Dreghorn; Scott of Woolwich; all were ministers of the Church of Scotland condemned for some form of heresy by the General Assembly of the Church. A. J. Scott was Irving's assistant, and he had urged the latter that apostolic gifts – healing, prophecy, and glossolalia (speaking in tongues) – were given for all time and were lost only by lack of faith.

The presbytery of London, comprising six men at least one of whom was personally hostile to Irving, challenged the heretical views. Whatever the verdict of the presbytery would be, any such challenge was unthinkable in terms of the consequences it would have for Irving. Finding no help from friends in the National Scottish Church, Irving nevertheless insisted, contrary to public opinion, that at that time the spiritual or apostolic gifts were being restored to the church.

Glossolalia and other manifestations

The 'unknown tongues'[10] were first heard on 28 March 1830 from one Mary Campbell, a pious consumptive. Mary's sister Isabella of Fernicarry had died some time previously and was revered as a saint. Her minister, Robert Story, documented her life in his book *Peace in Believing* and the burn near to where she lived became a shrine. About the same time, near Rosneath in Port Glasgow, two illiterate brothers named Macdonald came home from work and miraculously transformed their dying sister to health with the words 'Arise and stand upright'.

Shortly after the miraculous events the Macdonalds and Mary

Campbell began speaking with tongues which were attributed variously to the dialect of the Pelew Islanders, Turkish and Chinese. The account of the Macdonalds' tongues is recorded by a Robert Norton, MD, in his *Memoirs of James and George Macdonald*. Mary Campbell not only spoke with tongues but also exhibited automatic writing, and at Helensburgh people of all classes flocked to hear her. A similar crowd gathered at the house of the Macdonalds at Port Glasgow, and some members of the Albury group arrived from London. These members of the Prophetic Movement were all middle class, although they made use of these manifestations among the peasantry. It was concluded that the glossolalia were the voice of God, and that they were also the means of the evangelization which was to prepare for the Second Coming. F. M. Davenport in his book *Primitive Traits in Religious Revivals* (1906), mentions similar outbreaks of glossolalia in certain Mormon communities which occurred almost simultaneously in the United States of America. At the same time in London a Miss Elizabeth Farncourt, the daughter of an Anglican clergyman, was miraculously healed. Two more instances of glossolalia followed, those of a Miss Cardale and a Mr Taplin. These early manifestations were initially confined to small closed prayer groups, but in October 1831 the church in Regent Square was disrupted by an outbreak of glossolalia. Although Irving critically examined the increasing incidence of glossolalia, he concluded that they were indeed valid 'signs', and that the original pentecostal gifts were still manifest. The accounts of the manifestations in Drummond and Oliphant are psychological rather than sociological.

The Albury circle was composed of nobility, lawyers, Members of Parliament, doctors, ministers of religion and teachers; nevertheless they welcomed the 'signs'. Irving viewed the Regent Square utterances as the work of the Holy Ghost, but others strongly denied this, and as opposition to Irving grew, he was finally charged with allowing unlicenced persons to interrupt public services. He was found unfit and deposed from his charge and his trial before the presbytery of Annan resulted in a similar verdict of guilty. At the time the Annan verdict was declared Irving had left Regent Square church and had taken the majority of the congregation with him. He found temporary accommodation in a large bazaar in Gray's Inn Road, in premises which had been used by Robert Owen. In the autumn of 1832 he moved again, this time to a picture gallery in Newman Street. On his return from Annan his Newman Street congregation refused him permission to exercise any priestly duties, although they granted him the position of deacon – the lowest order in the newly emerging hierarchy. A month later, in March, Drummond[11] related that Irving was 'called and ordained angel or chief pastor' of the Newman Street congregation. He neither wrote nor appeared publicly again, and in 1834 he died. He himself had never exhibited any supernatural manifestations, and at the end he was forced to comply with those who had. He was buried in Glasgow cathedral, and Oliphant records that crowds waited for a miracle at his tomb.

Of particular interest in the glossolalia outbreaks is the case of Robert Baxter, a High Anglican and a solicitor. He became a member of the Regent Square church and himself manifested utterances which he later came to doubt as being from God, and which he subsequently repudiated. These early manifestations were accepted as genuine pentecostal manifestations by the early leaders of the church, and many were later to become accepted viewpoints.

The charismatic period

A new movement was beginning. Both the glossolalia and the Prophetic School were personal manifestations of quality without an institutionalized machinery. Between 1830 and 1833 there were neither leaders, hierarchy or movement. The 'routinization' was to become eventually manifest in a highly elaborate liturgy and office.

The Albury group, concerned with the study of prophecy, was organized and sophisticated, compared with the sporadic outbursts of the 'tongues'. It was at Albury that the liturgy and doctrines were formulated. It was from Albury, also, that the government of the Catholic Apostolic Church was initially exercised. The group first met in 1826 and annually after that for five years. Although concerned with prophetic writing they were also particularly anxious to receive guidance on the imminence of the Second Advent. Shaw, following C. W. Boase's *Supplement to the Elijah Ministry*, says they were agreed upon certain points:

(1) Premillennialism: that is, instead of the world becoming better gradually till the Millennium arrives, the present dispensation is to be destroyed. (2) That judgments are coming upon Christendom during which

period the Jews will be restored to Palestine. (3) That the judgment will fall chiefly upon Christendom, the people of God according to their privileges being held responsible. (4) That at the termination of the judgment the Messiah will come. (5) That the Millennium will then be ushered in – a season of blessedness to all mankind and every creature. (6) That the vials of the Apocalypse began to be poured out at the French Revolution (1793), since the great period of 1260 years commenced in 533, when Justinian gave special recognition to the Papacy.[12]

An account of the proceedings is given in the *Dialogue on Prophecy*.

Henry Drummond, MP, was the driving power of the Prophetic Movement. Two years after Irving's death he rushed to inform the Archbishop of Canterbury that the end of the world was near, and he was not disheartened by the fiasco of prophesying and glossolalia. The Napoleonic wars hastened the feeling of imminence of the end and apocalyptic fervour; indeed, L. W. Scholler records some remarkably parallel spiritual occurrences in Bavaria in 1827–1828. Hatley Frere, a member of the circle, had emphasized unfulfilled prophecy, especially in the *Book of Daniel*: It was to him that Irving had dedicated his *Babylon and Infidelity Foredoomed*. According to Oliphant, Irving substituted for the millennial reign of Christ 'the idea of a dispensation drawing towards its close, and .... of an altogether glorious and overwhelming revolution yet to come, in which all the dead society, churches, kingdoms, fashions of this world, galvanically kept in motion until the end, should be finally destroyed.'[13] The books of *Revelation* and *Daniel* were taken as symbolizing the ending of the reign of the saints which, it was asserted, lasted until 1793. To some extent the period following the Napoleonic wars was one of economic and industrial unrest, and even people such as Thomas Arnold wrote: 'I believe that "the day of the Lord" is coming'. Timothy Dwight, President of Yale, often gave sermons on the imminence of the "Day of the Lord" which were influential.'[14]

The official organ of the Albury meetings was *The Morning Watch*, edited by a Mr Tudor, who later rose to eminence in the Catholic Apostolic Church. According to Oliphant[15] the early numbers were monopolized by Irving: 'his name occurs, not so much as an authority, as an all influencing, unquestionable presence ...' Irving contributed articles on the humanity of Christ, inquiries about the 'spiritual gifts', and accounts of miraculous cures; there also appeared his series *Old Testament Prophecies*

Fulfilled in the New. In 1832 it was to condemn the General Assembly of the Church of Scotland which was about, like the 'veil of the Temple', to be 'rent in twain'. It was in every respect also the organ of the original expelled community, controlled by the wealthy originator of the Albury band, Drummond. In 1833 *The Morning Watch* came to an end, having fulfilled its original intention of sustaining and perpetuating the spiritual utterances of the Albury school of Prophets, and introducing these utterances to the general public. The main subscribers were needed in other offices in what was emerging substantially as a new religious sect. Tudor himself became an elder of the new movement and declined to transfer the office of editorship to any other person.

One Nicholas Armstrong, a minister of the Anglican church and later an apostle of the Catholic Apostolic Church, preached: 'Our inheritance shall be dominion over the creation; we shall rule angels: we shall rule the earth.'[16] There was increasing stress on 'signs' of the Second Coming. As Drummond says, there was a craving, by the Albury School, 'for the Gifts of the Spirit and an atmosphere conducive to charismata'. The Prophetic Movement did not last long. The title Catholic Apostolic Church originated as a clerical error, but from these fragmentary emotional beginnings an institutionalized, hierarchically differentiated organization rapidly developed. 'This Church is Catholic in its use of ancient creeds and liturgy, based on Roman, Greek and Anglican rites; lights, incense and vestments are used. It is Apostolic in its permission of "tongues" ... and in its deacons, elders, prophets and apostles.' The Second Coming was expected at the death of the last apostle but when this time passed the movement abandoned any conversionist policy it might have had, either towards the church authorities or laity.

The belief structure and organization

The Catholic Apostolic Church believed in a restored apostolate, ecumenicalism, and an imminent Second Coming. The wanderings of the homeless congregation, headed by Irving, had a precedent in the early Unitarians, many of whom after the Toleration Act of 1689 had left established churches and taken their congregations with them. It maintained some allegiance with the Scottish Presbyterians, but gradually evolved a form of worship and a pattern of church life that were highly articulate and organized. As Whitley points out, this early congregation stressed two basic facts: (1) the permanent authority of the Bible; (2) the continued experience of the church as the Body of Christ and the Temple of the Holy Ghost.

It was soon obvious that members from various streams were beginning to flow into it, among them Baptists, Anglicans, Congregationalists and Roman Catholics. It was from these early migratory congregations that the 'seven churches of London' were formed; it was from them that the twelve 'apostles' were drawn. There was a heterogeneity of origin unparalleled in any other sect. There were two foci: (1) London was the 'primitive' establishment; (2) Albury was the centralized headquarters for operations. As we have already mentioned, it was at Albury that the development of worship and belief were formulated and thence came the original Albury Prayer Book. By 1837 there existed a lithographed form of communion service and in 1843 the first edition of *Offices and Liturgy of the Church*, prefaced by an exposition, appeared, though there were subsequent amended editions.

Several writers have pointed out that the architecture of the movement is ordered and set out for liturgical worship. Molloy in 1892 brought out clearly the architectural hierarchy.[17] At the top of the chancel steps were seven seats, the centre seat being for the angel or bishop, the six others being for the elders. Below, in a parallel line, were seven other seats for prophets. Lower still, there were seven more seats for deacons, the centre one being occupied by the chief deacon. This arrangement represented 'a threefold cord of a sevenfold ministry'. The angel ordered the service while the prophets spoke when the spirit moved them. The elders took it in turn to expound. The bread and the wine were given by the angel to the elders, by the elders to the deacons, and by the deacons to the congregation.

After the death of Irving there was a rapid development of the movement. The full number of apostles was called and a council was formed at Drummond's residence at Albury, on the model of the Jewish tabernacle. Documents of intent were sent to the Archbishop of Canterbury, the Pope, and the Emperor of Austria. In 1840 the apostles suspended the council.

'Holy elements' were always present during the services. The act of worship emerged as a highly formalized order of service, with the eucharist eventually establishing itself as the central action, accompanied by an elaborated liturgical formula. The liturgical sources included those of the Roman Catholics, Anglicans, Eastern Orthodox, and Lesser Eastern. In 1850 the Catholic Apostolic Church adopted the reservation of the sacrament. Before this, in 1838, there emerged a doctrine something akin to that of baptismal regeneration, and the setting up of altars demarcating areas of sacred territory. 'Sealing' (the imparting of the Holy Ghost through the laying on of hands) was adopted in 1845, along with the introduction of chrism (consecrated oil). Elaborate vestments were introduced in 1842, altar lights and incense in 1852, and holy water in 1868. *The Liverpool Review* for 1888 has the following:

> From recent statistics, the community appears to be making steady progress. It claims to have among its clergy many of the Roman, Anglican, Scottish and other churches, the order of these churches being recognized by it with the simple confirmation of an 'apostolic act'.[18]

Tithing, prayers for the dead and infant baptism were also introduced. In 1892, according to Molloy, there were 47 congregations in this country numbering 6,000 communicants. There were congregations in Ireland, Scotland, America, Germany, France, Canada and Switzerland.

The distinctive belief of the movement is the stress placed on the act of sealing – an act, like most of the rituals mentioned, which no longer takes place because the original apostles have died and cannot be replaced. This, as we learn from Revelation 7.2,3,4, had a distinctly adventist connotation, together with the stress placed on four of the gifts of the Holy Ghost, i.e. tongues, miracles, healings and prophecy. The church is elected from the world and is a divine society which is also holy, catholic and apostolic. It is a universal church exercising its function through the fourfold agencies of apostles, prophets, evangelists and pastors, and the corresponding fourfold ministeries.

The ministry of the Catholic Apostolic Church, under the second calling of the apostles, comprised the angel bishop or chief officer of the local congregation, the priest or presbyter, and the deacon. The subordinate office of underdeacon, now all that remains, is not a sacred order of the ministry, nor is that of deaconess.

In terms of eschatological commitment the Catholic Apostolic Church is adventist, believing firmly in the hopes of the early Christians. The millennium is stressed, and heavy reliance is placed on Daniel, Revelation and the description of the Tabernacle (Heb. 8.5; Ex. 25.9; 26.30; 27.8). Indeed, the whole structure of the movement, as represented in some of the architecture of the buildings, is referred symbolically to the biblical descriptions of the tabernacle.

The Catholic Apostolic Church does not believe in the separate education of the young, and Sunday schools are not advocated. Each location on the strata is fixed, and 'the rich (will) be beloved by the poor, and the poor comforted by the rich'. The movement is curiously uninvolved with social matters, preferring a conservative policy in relation to the social order and to the distribution of property. It is anti-socialist,[19] anti-temperance, and anti-Salvation Army. It is ritualistic, authoritarian, and there is a spiritual obligation to tithe.

The emergence of the sect

The nineteenth century in England was, contrary to preceding centuries and to the situation in Europe, characterized by a substantial period of peace which was broken only by the Boer and Crimean wars. The influence of the changes which were occurring in Europe found expression in a reform of England's constitutional and political system, and simultaneously with an unprecedented rate of industrial expansion and invention. Notwithstanding, the abuses which were so much a part of the eighteenth century were perpetuated into the beginning of the nineteenth century. The French Revolution was, in fact, still making its impact at the time of the emergence of the Catholic Apostolic Church, and contributed to the period of nineteenth-century English history the two great ideals of nationalism and liberalism. This era saw the emergence of secular orientated political theories such as communism, socialism and anarchism. Side by side with the growth of intellectual discovery there existed a singlemindedness which manifested itself in the military, political and cultural colonization of much of the world. The attitude of the bishops to the events which culminated in the Reform Bill of 1832 made the church as an established institution increasingly unpopular. The rapid social change that followed the major industrial advance perplexed and alienated those caught up in the great migration into the urban areas, and shifted the balance of power from the landed aristocracy to the middle classes. The weak position and contribution of the Church of England after its emergence into the nineteenth century failed to counter the social conditions and the 'new awakening' which sowed the seed for the evangelical and anglo-catholic revivals and the emergence of politically active Labour and Chartist groups.

To some extent the Catholic Apostolic Church pre-empted the subsequent movements of Tractarians and Plymouth Brethren. All were initially upper-class movements, and two at least were to some extent motivated by the frustration inherent in the clerical profession at this time. Upward mobility was virtually impossible[20] and the poverty of the clergy stood in stark contrast to the affluence of the church hierarchy.

Although often called 'Irvingites' the movement denies this name, claiming instead that it originated through divine intervention rather than through the agency of any individual. Because it emphasized the importance of manifestations Irving had to bow to those who displayed these manifestations: thus Irving's contribution was in the fostering of spiritual persons who were either driven out of their existing congregations because of the exercise of spiritual gifts or who saw that the movement, in the form of Irving's original congregation, was rich 'in its numbers, ministries and gifts'. Drummond describes him as 'the forerunner and prophet of a new dispensation rather than a founder of a new sect'.[21] Nevertheless, the movement inherited and still displays much of the influence of Irving.

It denies, also, that it is a sect. Although professing they are not a sect, its members share many of the beliefs which characterize sectarian groups. For example, they believe in the imminent Second Coming[22]; their interpretation of the scriptures is fundamentalist; they interpret political events, e.g. revolutions, as 'signs of the times'; they are more willing to accept and emphasize prophecy than churches; they exhibit some intolerance of dissenters; they accept only the nicene, athanasian and apostles' creeds; they emphasize the doctrines of the permanence of the gifts of the apostles, prophets, evangelists and pastors in the church (the pentecostal endowments are seen as being still with the church); the supreme authority in the church is exercised by twelve apostles elected, not by men, but by God; the fourfold ministry, that of apostles, prophets, evangelists, and pastors, and the powers and gifts of the Holy Ghost are to prepare and perfect the church for the Second Advent.

Denying their separatism, despite their separatist characteristics, they see the present period with only a handful of worshipping congregation as a sign that the Lord's coming is imminent. It is to the Second Advent that they now look, and to the establishment of his universal kingdom of righteousness and peace. The hope of this imminence encourages them to penitence for sins which have marred his work, and to watch and pray for his appearance which is now nearer than they first believed. The movement is undeniably a separate gathering claiming a special core of knowledge. Most certainly it is not exclusive, and many of its members today are also members of the Church of England. Its membership is voluntary and yet presumably its members gather together because to do so offers some distinctive reward: the number of children at a service is striking. Authority within the movement is both charismatic and hierarchically sanctioned, and it possesses a formally instituted leadership role.

It is not, in Niebuhr's sense, a 'conflict society' in opposition to an institutional church. It is opposed to the idea of conversion in a salvationist sense and displays no fervour of adherence. Its membership, contrary to the assertion of Werner Stark and others that *all* sects are proletarian in origin, is middle class both in its original founders and in its present composition. Its original apostles comprised an aristocrat, a Member of Parliament, a solicitor, Anglican priests, advocate of the Scottish Bar, a father of the British Bar, an artist, a minister of the Scottish Church and a wealthy Northumberland landowner. The ministry of the Catholic Apostolic Church is purported to be prophecied by Malachi 4.5, and is based on the construction of the tabernacle. Each apostle was given a portion of the world as his 'tribe'.

Between 1839 and 1840 Cardale, the chief apostle, was forced to recall the other apostles from their work abroad in order to deal with the crisis of rebellion, which arose because some members regarded the council at home as the authority rather than the apostles who were dispersed throughout the world. It was essentially a dispute for authority between the prophets and the apostles.[23] Drastic changes were introduced and the council was discontinued until 1847; in fact it never regained its original position.

By 1860 half of the original apostles were dead, and at this stage schism arose on the continent. The German Catholic Apostolic Church felt that more apostles ought to be elected or called to bridge the gap, while Cardale in England stood firm in the conviction that twelve and twelve only had been called. The German faction based its policy on the claim that the number was exceeded many times in the New Testament (Acts 1.26; 13.2,3; 14.14 etc.). In 1865 the German splinter group became the General Christian Mission and in 1908 the New Apostolic Church. It is a conversionist schism, working chiefly among Germans and those of German extraction. It is interesting that in Britain, Canada and America members of the movement were often able to carry out their obligations at the same time as holding offices or ordination in the Anglican and Episcopal churches, although the American Protestant Episcopal Church was less tolerant. In the Apostles Council in 1881 there were 31 members, representing Russia, France, Denmark, Germany, Britain and America.

Because they are the 144,000 mentioned in Revelation, members believe they are to be the rulers of the church. They are diligent in stressing anonymity in their writings, and display complete uninvolvement with social problems. As Shaw says, '... the Catholic Apostolic Church is an emergency group, having come into being in view of the imminence of the Second Advent.... To all appearances the church is dying out, and the people are content that it shall be so.'[24]

The Catholic Apostolic Church was, in the beginning at least, the forerunner of later pentecostalist sects. The movement is unique because it combines a naïve pentecostalism with a highly sophisticated ritual and liturgy. Irving's own theology was influenced not only by sixteenth-century Scottish theology but also by his sympathy with the Prophetic Movement. The new sect, were it but known, was sowing the seeds of its later demise, by its emphasis on biblical literalism and the apostolic order of the early church.[25]

Sect compliance can generally be seen as resulting from what Etzioni calls by normative commitment. However, as Wilson has pointed out, normative commitment is not a phenomenon which possesses unitary characteristics. Commitment is positive involvement, and positive direction with a high intensity.[26] Commitment varies not only in degree but also in kind. Wilson suggests that 'Men may be primarily committed in different ways – emotionally, intellectually, ritualistically, morally or communally, to take some obvious respects'. Some sectarian commitments will emphasize one such way or ways, while others will emphasize other diverse commitments such as status, moral excellence, sobriety, etc. As Wilson points out, there may be various forms of commitment to religious movements which are neither religious nor normative. Often there is an open and relatively flexible framework of commitment, but 'in the last analysis sectarian commitment is always voluntary'.[27]

Compliance and commitment

The members of the Catholic Apostolic Church have a diffused commitment for several reasons: historically, there has always been a close doctrinal, liturgical and membership tie, e.g. many of the original members were Anglican and subsequently it has not been in the least incongruous to hold membership in both the movement and the Church of England. The movement has never stressed exclusion or separateness, but rather has seen itself in the role of innovator, as the vehicle of the apostolic age and of the Holy Ghost. The Catholic Apostolic Church was according to its self-image called into existence by God. It possessed a highly formalized, professional, hierarchically differentiated ministry – the incumbents of this office often being simultaneously holders of a priestly office in established churches. As a movement it does not fit happily into any of Wilson's types. It is actively opposed to a conversionist policy and to its concomitant doctrines. Although it is an adventist group it accepts the existence of the established churches, and it is not so much hostile as indifferent to the wider society. Although it has introversionist characteristics, it is not an introversionist sect; neither is it gnostic. In a sense it is occupying a uniquely marginal position in the church-sect typology.[28] On the other hand, its members do make special claim for their position in relation to the rest of Christendom.

Present position

Shaw quoted from *The Manchester Guardian* of 12 December 1934:

The Catholic Apostolic Church now awaits dissolution within ten years, not because it has no funds – the tithe every member gives made it comparatively affluent – nor from the lack of devotees, but simply because the belief on which the church was founded was that the Second Advent was at hand. Twelve apostles were appointed who alone had the power to ordain, and as the last apostle died in 1901 all the surviving ministers are either elderly or aged. The youngest in London is sixty-five. The one in charge of Paddington Catholic Apostolic Church is eighty-nine, and one who conducted services in Gordon Square last week – there are still services every day – was ninety. These men are carrying on because there is none to succeed them, and it is realized the time is approaching when there will be none to do the work.

Some ten years later there were still some thirty-five churches in use. Shaw wrote in 1935:

> It is not likely that there are more than a few thousand of them all over the world. By marriage some are indeed admitted into the group if so desired. Probably few people marry outside, those who do so being disposed to give up their Catholic Apostolic views.[29]

Today there is no church which offers a full service, and the number of extant congregations, although probably not more than six in number, is not known for certain. The belief in the Second Advent is stronger than ever, the decline in the congregation being read as a portent of the imminence of the events which herald that belief. The general pattern seems to be that worship is carried out by members of the Catholic Apostolic Church in the congregations of the established churches, principally the Church of England, and its adherents, unable as they are on the whole to meet for worship in their own churches, come together for meetings of prayer in each other's houses. (See Appendices A and B.) The cycle of the movement has ordained that its end bears remarkable similarity to its beginnings, since it was through precisely such private prayer meetings that the movement originally came into existence.

Conclusions

The circumstances which precipitated the emergence of a value-orientated movement such as the Catholic Apostolic Church and the period in which it emerged were characterized by a surfeit of new movements, with several value-oriented beliefs crystallizing into actual movements in the 1820s to 1840s.[30] Structural conduciveness was afforded by the preoccupation of the times with milleni-alism and prophecy, and religious ideology was not yet separated from the political sphere to the extent of value-oriented movements being excluded as conveying both secular and religious protest. Religion, being one of the dominant interests of society in the early nineteenth century, afforded a situation which was structur-ally conducive to the emergence of a religious value-oriented movement, but one which nevertheless afforded a camouflaged vehicle of protest for covert political anxieties. It was an attempt at a bourgeois revolution in Britain developed 'under the guise of a religious reformation'[31] specifically precipitated by the relative inflexibility of the governing aristocracy which was in effect block-ing the social mobility of the bourgeoisie.

The emergence of the Catholic Apostolic Church at this point in time was due, if we follow the model afforded by Smelser,[32] to the impotence of the middle classes in trying to restructure the social situation, to their inability overtly to express disapproval over matters of social concern, and to their inability to modify the normative structure, the facilities, or the mobilization compon-ents available in the action system.[33]

The sources of strain within the social system might be located in the inability of middle-class elements to cope with the rapid technological, constitutional and industrial changes which were occurring. This was a period of organizational strain, both economi-cally and in terms of actual physical deprivation. The social and revolutionary changes manifested themselves in a period of norma-tive disorganization. These strains are 'multiple and complex' and occur in clusters which 'accumulate in different sequences ... (and) ... vary in strength and significance'.[34] When some or all of these conditions of conduciveness and strain appear we get the crystalli-zation of value-oriented beliefs which can be precipitated by such factors as give some indication or 'reading' of a group's direction. For example, the glossolalia outbreaks, initially among the peasantry, were interpreted by the middle-class Prophetic Move-ment as being manifestations of the voice of God, but also the means for the evangelization which was to prepare for the Second Coming. The movement's mobilization for action was facilitated by its flexibility regarding its own role and it saw itself principally as innovator and heralder of the apostolic age and Holy Ghost; and in relation to the latter, it has never advocated a separatist policy. Once established, it swiftly put into operation formally instituted leadership roles and established procedures for financing itself. The gradual demise of the movement was due to its belief in the imminence of the Second Advent, and not to its inability to adapt to existing institutions. Nor was it due to the disruptive effects of successive leaders and leading bodies, to any change in strategy or tactics (this the movement has persistently refused to do), or to the early schism which resulted in the secession of the continental branch. Originally a reformist and innovating value-oriented movement, it increasingly adopted a negative and retreatist position. It was, in fact, a value-oriented movement which arose in a structural situation which was conducive to its initiation, and which also insulated, isolated and accommodated it.

APPENDIX A

Schedule of Churches in 1947 – England

Church in:

Albury (Apostle's Chapel, d. 1837)	in use
Barnsley	let
Barrow-in-Furness	let to Anglicans
Bath	in use
Batley	in use
Bedford (d. 1838)	in use
Birkenhead	in use
Birmingham	in use
Blackburn	in use
Blackpool	in use
Bolton	in use
Bradford	in use
Bridgnorth (d. 1836)	closed. Let to Anglicans
Brighton	in use
Bristol	in use
Burnham-on-Crouch	in use
Buxton	closed. Let to Plymouth Brethren
Cambridge	in use
Chatham	in use
Cheltenham	closed. Let to Anglicans
Chepstow (d. 1838)	demolished
Chester	closed. Let to Corporation
Coventry	let to Welsh Presbyterians
Eynsham (d. 1837)	in use
Huddersfield	let
Isle of Wight (Ryde)	in use
Ipswich	in use
Keighley	let to local organization

Leeds	in use
Liverpool	in use
Lymington (d. 1838)	closed
Manchester	in use
Morley	in use
Newcastle-on-Tyne	in use
Nottingham	in use
Oldham	closed
Plymouth	let to Baptists
Romford	in use
Sheffield	in use
Sunderland	let
Southampton (d. 1836)	destroyed by enemy action
Southsea	let to Anglicans
Southwark	destroyed by enemy action
Stoke-on-Trent	in use
Swallowcliffe	demolished
Swindon	let to Anglicans
Uxbridge (d. 1850)	demolished
Walsall	let to Anglicans
Ware	in use
Wem (d. 1839)	record of land purchase only
Weston	let to Anglicans
West Bromwich	let to Elim Church
Wigan	in use
Wolverhampton	in use

LONDON

Church in:

Bishopsgate	damaged by enemy action
Camberwell	let
Central London (Gordon Square)	in use
Hackney	in use
Islington	in use
Kentish Town	let to Anglicans
Paddington	in use
Westminster	let to Roman Catholics
Wood Green	in use

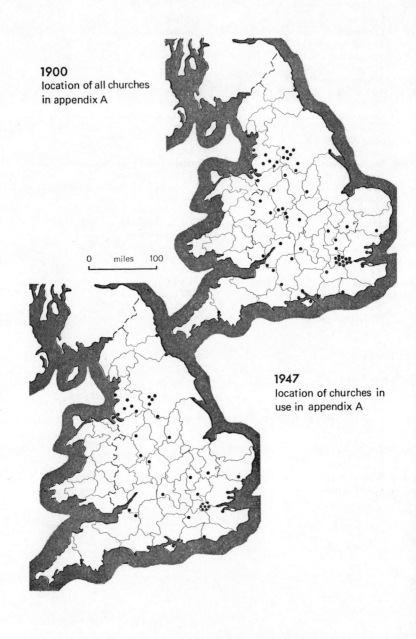

1900
location of all churches
in appendix A

0   miles   100

1947
location of churches in
use in appendix A

APPENDIX B

Schedule of Churches in Use in England by Catholic Apostolic Community in 1965

Apostle's Chapel, Albury, Surrey
Church in Hackney, London, E8
Church in Paddington, London, W2
Church in Liverpool
Church in Eynsham, Oxfordshire
Church in Clifton, Bristol (sold in 1967)
Caretaker's home, Summer Hill, Birmingham

Out of a total of some sixty-four churches in England, some dating from 1836, thirty-five were in use in 1947. In 1965 there were six churches and one caretaker's residence in use. There are now no churches in which full services are held and the number of extant worshipping congregations is not known, although it must be very small. Most of the members now worship in the established churches, notably the Church of England, but many also attend private prayer meetings, often in each other's houses, which is how the movement originated. The congregation in Liverpool, for example, meets in the church for worship every third Sunday in the month, and its members otherwise attend their own Anglican churches.

1965
location of churches
in use; appendix B

0   miles   100

In the United States of America there are now some 2,500 members in 2 churches. The New Apostolic Church of North America, a schismatic off-shoot from the parent body, spread to America via German immigrants, and currently has some 700,000 members internationally with members in 4,500 branches in 23 countries. In America there are 18,041 members in 165 churches and 35 missions.

APPENDIX C

Social Composition

The Catholic Apostolic Church is declining rapidly. Today there are probably only some five or six extant groups left in Britain. In America there are some two churches left in existence. The total number of sect members is probably round about 4,000–5,000 altogether. The original churches were predominantly concentrated in the south of England although the general spread was by no means meagre in other parts of the country.

The congregation observed in a non-participant manner by the author contained some 41 members. Eighteen of these were women and 15 were men. There were 8 children aged 14 and under. About 15 of the members were apparently over 65.

Nearly all the members were middle class with the exception of two adults with their four children. This particular congregation was situated in a down-town district. Most of those present appeared to have come considerable distances to worship there.

NOTES

I am grateful to Dr Bryan Wilson for his customary thoroughness in reading and commenting on an early draft of this article. The maps were drawn by John Hunt, Cartographer at the Open University.

1. The standard works on the Catholic Apostolic Church and Irving are as follows:

> M. O. W. Oliphant, *The Life of Edward Irving*, Hurst & Blacket, 5th edition 1864.

> Richard Garnett, article on *Irving* in *The Dictionary of National Biography*, Smith, Elder & Co. 1892.

> Thomas Carlyle, *Reminiscences*, ed. C. E. Norten, Macmillan 1887, sections on *Irving* and *Jane Welsh Carlyle*.

> Andrew Landale Drummond, *Edward Irving and his Circle*, James Clarke & Co. 1937.

More recently, there is Professor Shaw's historical account of the movement, and Whiteley's small but significant introduction to Irving:

> P. E. Shaw, *The Catholic Apostolic Church*, King's Crown Press, NY 1946.

> H. C. Whitley, *Blinded Eagle*: An Introduction to the Life and Teaching of Edward Irving. SCM Press 1955.

Relevant correspondence can be found in the Clement Boase Collection in the British Museum.

2. Drummond, passim.

3. Oliphant, op. cit., p.53.

4. Oliphant, op. cit., p.74.

5. Drummond, op. cit., p.49.

6. James Hair, *Regent Square*, London 1889, p.42.

7. Oliphant, op. cit., p.198.

8. Drummond, op. cit., p.113.

9. Edward Irving, *On the Orthodox and Catholic Doctrine of Our Lord's Human Nature*, London 1830, p.2.

10. Admirably documented by Drummond, pp.165-74. Also Oliphant, pp.327-9. The Camisards, Fox, Joan of Arc, Swedenbourg, Southcott, the Shakers, the Mormons, etc. all manifested glossolalia at some stage.

11. Drummond, op. cit., p.231.

12. This also appears in a similar form in Edward Miller, *The History and Doctrines of Irvingism*, 2 vols, London 1878.

13. Oliphant, op. cit., p.93.

14. Stanley, *Life*, p.174. Dr Bryan Wilson drew my attention to Dwight. See also: Kenneth Scott Latourette, *A History of Christianity*, Eyre & Spottiswoode 1964, p.1044.

15. Oliphant, op. cit., p.258.

16. Drummond, op. cit., p.134.

17. J. F. Molloy, 'The Catholic Apostolic Church', in *Faiths of the Peoples*, vol. 1, Ward & Downey, pp.74-101.

18. *The Liverpool Review*, 9 June 1888, p.11.

19. Shaw, op. cit., pp.219-23.

20. Donald Capps, 'John Henry Newman: A Study of Vocational Identity', *Journal for the Scientific Study of Religion*, vol. 9, no. 1, spring 1970, p.36.

21. Drummond, op. cit., p.231.

22. As a British millennial movement the hope of an imminent coming which never materialized at the time it was predicted but which is now felt to be very near bears similarity to the plight of the early Christians, the 'poor' and the 'saints' (Acts 1.4; 2.46f.) and also to such movements as Jehovah's Witnesses. (See Joseph F. Zygmunt, 'Prophetic Failure and Chialistic Identity: the Case of Jehovah's Witnesses', *American Sociological Review*, vol. 75, no. 6, May 1970, pp.926-48.

23. Shaw, op. cit., pp.98-102.

24. Shaw, op. cit., pp.234-5.

25. B. R. Wilson (ed.), *Patterns of Sectarianism*, Heinemann 1967, p.7.

26. A. Etzioni, *A Comparative Analysis of Complex Organizations*, Free Press of Glencoe, Illinois 1961, p.9.

27. Wilson, op. cit., p.7.

28. Warburton makes this point in relation to dual organizational commitment of members of the Faith Mission: 'To many of its followers it offers a communal type of religion to complement the more associational nature of the denomination. It is in this very special respect that the Mission clearly lies outside the sect-denomination typology, although like the Quaker movement it maintains co-existent sectarian and denominational traits'. T. Rennie Warburton, 'The Faith Mission: a Study in interdenominationalism', *A Sociological Yearbook of Religion in Britain 2*, ed. David Martin, SCM Press 1969, p.93.

29. P. E. Shaw, *The Catholic Apostolic Church*, Ph.D. Thesis, University of Edinburgh 1938, p.4.

30. C. E. Sears, *Days of Delusion*, Houghton Mifflin, Boston 1924, pp. xviii-xix.

31. L. Trotsky, *The History of the Russian Revolution*, tr. Max Eastman, University of Michigan Press, Ann Arbor 1957, Vol. 1, p.14.

32. Neil Smelser, *Theory of Collective Behaviour*, Routledge & Kegan Paul 1962, p.325.

33. Ibid.

34. Ibid., p.342.

11   The Bishops, 1860-1960: An Elite in Decline

James Bentley

'WE hear a good deal today of the poverty of the Church,' wrote A. G. Gardiner in 1907. 'The poverty is real; but it is not the poverty of money: it is the poverty of men.'[1] He was referring to the bishops, in particular to the Bishop of London. His was a widely shared opinion. In 1921 W. R. Inge observed that the nineteenth century had been 'an era of eminent bishops' – Wilberforce, Tait, Fraser, Moorhouse, Browne, Lightfoot, Westcott, Wordsworth, Selwyn and Goodwin. 'However,' Inge continued, 'the recent increase in the number of bishops has led to many inferior men being appointed, and the prestige of the office is nothing like what it was forty or fifty years ago.'[2] Six years later Dick Sheppard submitted his modest C. of E. reforms to the nation and to the forthcoming Lambeth Conference. 'Frankly,' he wrote, 'I doubt if any Bishop on the present Bench is capable of really leading the Church on the road of sacrifice. The Church needs a bigger man than any of its present Bishops.'[3]

By the mid-thirties this despondency had spread to some of the theological colleges. According to L. J. Collins:

> One evening, during my time as Vice-Principal of Westcott House, B.K. and I were in my room discussing the future of our ordinands. At B.K.'s suggestion we playfully selected twelve who would become bishops, the conditions for choice being (*a*) one who always said 'no' to anyone below him and 'yes' to anyone above; (*b*) one who was either of the family of a high-up ecclesiastic or of obviously respectable and privileged parentage and education; (*c*) one who could make no claims to intellectual attainments. We compared lists and found we had ten in common. All twelve on my list became bishops.[4]

Were these judgments accurate? Did the quality of the English episcopate decline rapidly at the beginning of this century? As a

Times leader observed in 1877, 'the world does not love Bishops over much'; they are always good for a cheap jibe.[5] Canon Collins' account certainly needs to be taken with a pinch of salt. At the Lambeth Conference of 1958 were 32 bishops who had been educated at Westcott House, but only 9 of these had been there when Collins was Vice-Principal. As for their intellectual attainments, two had 1st Class honours degrees and five had 2nds. Indeed, some writers have asserted that the twentieth-century archbishops and bishops of the Church of England have never been surpassed in quality.[6] In 1914 S. Baring-Gould, at the end of a detailed attack on the Victorian bishops, concluded that 'generally the type of our English bishops is now high; and under their direction no one need despair of the future of the Church in our land'.[7] In this paper I wish to ask whether and in what ways the quality of the bishops may be said to have declined and to examine what effect this may have had on their leadership of the Church.

At the beginning of this century men of short memories might be pardoned for erroneously supposing that there was an unprecedented decline in the leadership of the church. The church had lost three Archbishops of Canterbury who were, as Scott Holland observed, 'all men of singular mark, masterful, independent, and high-charactered'. This Scott Holland considered to have been 'a striking break into the Anglican tradition, which is apt to carry safe and unpronounced men to the chief places'.[8] Moreover, it should be remembered that the prestige of the twentieth-century bishops suffered in one major respect because of the inadequacy of their predecessors. The nineteenth-century bishops had lost the battle over science. When T. H. Huxley floored Wilberforce in 1860, Lady Brewster fainted with shock[9]; yet as a result of this conflict Wilberforce's immense qualities were eventually forgotten, replaced by an impression of his 'superficial cleverness'.[10]

The Victorians were aware of this stigma on the episcopate. On two separate occasions Lord Acton, the self-appointed patronage secretary to Mr Gladstone, suggested as bishops men he considered able to do something about the challenge of science. Liddon, he observed, 'is in no peril from the movement of modern Science. He has faced these problems and accounted for them.'[11] Of Frederick Temple Acton wrote, 'he has an arid mind, and a provincial note in speech and manner. But he also understands Science'.[12] Some bishops tried to grapple with science from the standpoint of the Society for Psychical Research. The Bishop of Ripon, who was Vice-President of the Society in 1885, maintained that 'Man's religious instincts are today recognized by science as part and parcel of his constitution'.[13] In 1887 he felt free to consult Huxley about a scientific reference in a sermon he was to preach before the House of Commons.[14]

But the stigma remained. In fairness to the bishops it should be said that the church in general would hardly have tolerated a man who had really faced up to the challenge of science. Thus, when F. W. Farrer wrote an article for Smith's *Dictionary of the Bible* questioning the universality of the Deluge, the publishers and editors were so alarmed that they postponed the article. In volume I they inserted instead of the article, '*Deluge:* see *Flood*'; when *Flood* was reached they inserted, '*Flood:* see *Noah*'; since *Noah* was already assigned to the Bishop of Worcester, Farrer's offensive article was then scrapped.[15]

In this way the early twentieth-century bishop started with a disadvantage not of his own making: his office had already been discredited. This, in turn, affected the quality of the men who wished to fill it. With the rise of science many felt, with Lord Kelvin in 1871, 'as if led out from narrow waters of scholastic dogma to a refreshing excursion on the broad and deep ocean of truth'.[16] At the same time the decline in the financial rewards of the clergy made a career in the church less attractive. In 1887 the Bishop of Lincoln wrote to his brother-in-law: 'Here we are in constant trouble from the agricultural distress, and I fear the social position of the clergy must suffer, and the social quality of them also. I only hope their spiritual power may be increased.' The situation did not improve. In 1900 the editor of Crockford's noted of the parochial clergy that, 'In too many cases they retain a mere pittance of starvation.'[17]

For these reasons, the number of boys entering the church's ministry from both the old and the new public schools declined steadily throughout the nineteenth century.[18] This decline was, however, concealed by the policy of many Oxford and Cambridge colleges of giving preference to ordinands.[19] Since the supply of these was drying up, many undergraduates selected because they were ordinands were inevitably of poorer quality than those coming up earlier in the century. From these men the future bishops were to be drawn. Corpus Christi College, Cambridge, which consistently favoured ordinands under E. H. Perowne, produced 11 bishops in the first 17 years of his mastership.[20] As a result Hensley Henson could write in 1925 that, 'The extent of the decline in social importance which has befallen the clergy during the last century is difficult to appreciate and almost impossible to overstate. It has marched with a continual lowering of their intellectual equipment until it would really seem impossible that we can fall lower.'[21]

Yet the decline in the quality of public school recruits to the ministry might easily have proved a blessing had the church set about recruiting its elite from outside that class. Faced with the same problem the Civil Service had begun to promote from 'the ranks', with the result that the proportion of its leadership drawn from the public schools declined sharply in the first half of the twentieth century.[22] The Church of England did nothing of the kind. According to a study of 43 diocesan bishops in 1958, '18 went to 12 well-known public schools – Eton, Winchester, Rugby, Marlborough, Malvern, Shrewsbury, Repton, St Paul's, Westminster, Merchant Taylors, Haileybury, and Bradfield. Of the rest, all but three went to (mostly well-known) minor public schools and grammar schools.'[23] In 1967 the percentage of bishops who had attended public schools was 75% – a percentage surpassed only by Judges, QCs, Conservative MPs and Directors of the Bank of England.[24]

There were, of course, few 'other ranks' from which the church could recruit its bishops, for by and large the bishops and the parochial clergy were drawn from the same social classes.[25] Some believed that this was changing. As early as 1863 the *Christian Remembrancer* was lamenting that 'It will very soon indeed cease to be taken as a matter of course that a clergyman is a gentleman.' Matthew Arnold imagined in 1887 that this was already happening. Forty years later the Bishop of London claimed to have a scheme to promote it. 'I do not want the ministers of the gospel in our church all drawn from one class,' he said. 'I believe that every man who has got a vocation for holy orders ought to have the way opened to him to become a minister of the gospel of Jesus Christ.' Whatever the bishop had schemed, it made little difference. In 1918 the Archbishop's report *Christianity and Industrial Problems* called for many more working-class ordinands. But as late as 1939 Hensley Henson was still putting the ordination of working men far into the future, on the grounds that 'Intellectual traditions take time to grow, and culture cannot be improvised.'[26]

Henson's assumption that the working classes had either no culture at all or none worth having indicates the kind of welcome such ordinands might have expected in the church. During the general strike of 1926 Dean Inge castigated those clergy who spoke in favour of the strikers as ' the new type of parson, sprung from the ranks and soured by poverty and thwarted social ambition'.[27] In any case no one suggested that working-class ordinands might be made bishops. By virtually limiting its episcopate to graduates of Oxford and Cambridge the church effectively prevented preferment of the new social classes. Even in the mid-1950s only about 9% of Cambridge undergraduates and 13% of Oxford undergraduates came from the families of manual workers.[28] Of the 43 diocesan bishops of 1958 21 had been to Oxford, 17 to Cambridge, and only 5 to other universities.[29] For the working class a career open to talents was thus hardly possible in the Church of England.

It is significant that those bishops who lamented the decline for the most part found other reasons than these to explain it. Hensley Henson followed Dean Inge in deploring that 'we still multiply bishopricks!', implying that the new suffragans were inferior to the old diocesan bishops. In fact, the increase in population during the nineteenth century clearly justified an increase in the number of bishoprics: at the beginning of the eighteenth century there were 27 bishops; at the end of the nineteenth century 35 diocesan bishops and 25 co-adjutors served a population that had increased fivefold.[30] An analysis of the bishops in 1958 showed little to choose between the social and academic backgrounds of both kinds of bishop.[31] Fifty years earlier the same was true. Men found no difficulty in moving from new to old bishopric, or vice-versa.[32] Diocesan and suffragan bishops were drawn from the same social group. Thus, Arthur Lyttleton, Bishop of Southampton from 1898 to 1903, was brother of the 5th Lord Lyttelton and nephew of Mr Gladstone. He had shared rooms with Harry Gladstone at Eton.[33] One of his brothers became headmaster of that college. One sister married Lord Frederick Cavendish; another married the Bishop of Winchester.

For those with the right background and connections preferment could be breathtakingly swift. Randall Davidson, who at the age of 53 became one of the youngest of modern Archbishops of Canterbury, had married the daughter of Archbishop Tait. Tait and Davidson's father were schoolfellows in Edinburgh, and their friendship had remained unbroken for 50 years. Davidson and Tait's son Crauford became friends at Trinity College, Oxford. These advantages served to overcome such disadvantages as Davidson's continual ill-health and his disappointing academic record. Small wonder that at the end of his life Bishop E. A. Knox of Manchester was still regretting that he turned down an invitation to tutor Crauford Tait in 1869.[34]

Archbishop Davidson exemplified above all what Sir Ivor Jennings described as 'the advantage of friendship or acquaintance with the Sovereign' as a prerequisite for preferment.[35] He 'began his life as a courtier'.[36] So did his successor. 'The Queen has taken a great fancy to Mr Lang,' wrote Marie Mallet in 1898. 'How soon will he be a Bishop?' Again, in 1900, she wrote, 'Mr Lang is here and preached very well this morning ... he is in high favour with all the Royalties and will soon be a Bishop.'[37]

A long tradition of aristocratic bishops had continued into the nineteenth century: Lord Alwyne F. Compton of Ely, Lord George Murray of Rochester, Robert John Lord Auckland and Lord Arthur Charles Hervey, successive bishops of Bath and Wells, for example (not to mention numerous lesser members of the nobility, such as the Hon. J. T. Pelham, Bishop of Norwich, and the Hon. H. M. Villiers, Bishop of Durham).[38] Along with the Cecil who was appointed Bishop of Exeter in 1916, Archbishops Davidson and Lang may be regarded as their twentieth-century heirs. The courtier-bishops of the twentieth century were not necessarily worse than the courtier-bishops of the nineteenth. But the persistence into the twentieth century of another tradition – the preferment of clerical schoolmasters – demonstrably led to the appointment of poorer men.

The mistake was a natural one. Many of the finest Victorian bishops and archbishops had been public school masters or headmasters – A. C. Tait, F. Temple, E. W. Benson, C. T. Longley and J. B. Sumner among the archbishops; Christopher Wordsworth, George Ridding and John Percival among the bishops.[39] But by the end of the century the supply was hardly equal to the demand. Fewer schoolmasters were taking holy orders: in 1890 the clerical masters of 22 leading public schools amounted to only 20% of the staff. According to T. W. Bamford: 'The insistence on having clerical heads with lay staff produced an absurd situation both for ambitious young men thinking of a teaching career as well as on the quality of the headmasterly ranks. By the 1880s and 1890s the governing bodies were appointing heads from 20% or less of the available pool and were therefore unnecessarily restricting their choice and appointing less competent people.'[40] Yet when governing bodies were scraping the barrel, the Church of England blithely continued to draw on this dwindling body of clerical schoolmasters for its elite. In 1900 the 34 archbishops and bishops of England and Wales included 8 former public school masters, 5 of them former heads; 25 years later the 45 archbishops and bishops included 9 former masters, 7 of whom had been heads.[41]

By this time such appointments were being criticized. 'There is a not unreasonable prejudice in the minds of many,' wrote Maurice Fitzgerald in 1928, 'against the appointment of a schoolmaster, or a College don.'[42] This feeling was by no means universal. In 1936 Norman Sykes, at that time Professor of History at London University, approved of the fact that in 1895 13 bishops had been 'headmasters, professors, or dons.'[43] In 1939 Henson wrote: 'The appointment to London is excellent. How the headmasters are romping in!' As late as 1946 he could write: 'I do not think experience favours the elevation of parish priests. Schoolmaster bishops, professorial bishops, and even decanal bishops have a better record than the waxing number of exhausted missionaries and popular parish priests.'[44]

In these ways, then, the Church of England ensured that the quality of her bishops declined in the twentieth century. Her leaders had failed to cope with the challenge of science, leaving the church intellectually discredited. The number of bishops had been increased to provide for the new urban population, but no serious attempt was made either to recruit or promote members of the new class. Instead the church preferred to draw on the public schools at a time when boys of increasingly inferior calibre were offering themselves for the ministry. The system of preferment, with its overtones of nepotism and connection, often made next to no assessment of the ability of these men. Finally, the tradition of preferring clerical schoolmasters was not abandoned, even though the supply of these was drying up.

One would not be so ready as Hensley Henson to judge the 'record' of these men; yet, as the reasons for their decline reveal, they belonged to a limited social group, so that in 1958 A. M.

Ramsey, the future Archbishop of Canterbury, found in them a 'tendency to be "of a type" – lacking the marked differences and clashes of individuality which, in a period a little earlier, assisted the church's vigour of mind and appeal to the community.'[45] It is pertinent to ask what was the effect of their social background on the way they led the church.

Few were able to free themselves from this background and upbringing. Straton of Newcastle, according to Bishop E. A. Knox, 'never quite forgot that he was a Plantagenet, or that he had received Edward, our Sovereign Lord, an unexpected guest dropping in on him in the Isle of Man'.[46] Some of the courtier-bishops displayed a touchingly optimistic view of the possibilities of the monarch as evangelist – Boyd-Carpenter thanking Edward VII in 1907 for his stand on behalf of morality, Archbishop Lang issuing a 'Recall to Religion' in connection with the coronation of George VI,[47] and Archbishop Fisher declaring of the coronation of Elizabeth II (seen by millions on television) that 'Her peoples by this solemn rite are drawn into a new relation to their Queen and to God.'[48]

Leaving aside such naïvety, the utterances of the bishops tended to do no more than support the prejudices of their peers. Lord Halifax said of Archbishop Garbett that his speeches in the House of Lords had 'the valuable quality of producing on his hearers the impression that it was all very much what they had been inclined to feel themselves'.[49] There could be an understandable remoteness from the concerns of ordinary life among bishops such as Lord William Gascoyne-Cecil of Exeter, of whom Henson said : 'He has been too much surrounded by adulatory sycophants and social inferiors : and the supremacy inherent in the episcopal office has fitted in but too easily to the general disposition to play the autocrat, and ignore counsel.'[50]

In 1960 the Bishop of Southwark wrote : 'If the bishop has had a privileged education and if he has been divorced from a working-class milieu, his values will be biased towards the Establishment. . . . He thinks he is a political neutral, but in fact he is a nexus of social relationships which produce a particular outlook. It is unlikely that he will be an active protagonist of the middle classes; it is more subtle – he will unconsciously voice their opinions and set the seal upon their values.'[51] In this respect the church had not changed for a hundred years. In 1877 Matthew

Arnold saw it as 'an institution devoted above all to the landed gentry, but also to the propertied and satisfied classes generally; favouring immobility, preaching submission, and reserving transformation in general for the other side of the grave.'[52] As a result, church-going remained inevitably a middle-class practice.[53]

Unfortunately, the great proportion of the population did not belong to this class. At best the conservative aristocratic attitude to the new social classes was one of paternalistic goodwill.[54] At worst it was a blend of fear and self-interest. William Thomson (Archbishop of York from 1862 to 1890) is described on his memorial in Sheffield Cathedral as 'The People's Archbishop'. He visited workshops and factories, and at his funeral sixteen working-men carried his coffin to its last resting-place. But he was totally opposed to strikes and found the Paris Commune execrable. In 1871 he addressed the working-men of Sheffield: 'I seem to hear already the mighty tread of the up-coming multitude, the future working-men of England. I listen to hear how they march. Are they coming in a noisy and confused rabble, with no rhythm in their tread, with loud and angry voices as they come? They are marching under the wrong commander; they are marching without officers, without drill.'[55] So, under his guidance, sixteen new churches and three missions were built in Sheffield. Thomson displayed an ignorance of working-class aspirations and attitudes perhaps unavoidable in a man of so different a background. Henry Hayman, headmaster of Rugby, had observed: 'I will venture to say that there is little of that honourable love of truth which distinguishes English public schoolboys to be found in the homes of the lower middling classes.'[56] If that was believed to be true of the lower middle classes, small hope for the workers. 'Have we any right to be surprised,' asked Bishop J. C. Ryle of Liverpool, 'if the working classes ... live without religion ... left to themselves?'[57]

Few seem to have supposed that God might be active among the urban proletariat without benefit of the church. In 1907 Henry Scott Holland preached a remarkable sermon on 'God in the Town', in which he said: 'We must look to these towns of his in order to see what man has best to tell us about God.' But these ideas were not taken up by an English bishop until E. R. Wickham wrote about the encounter of the Christian faith and modern technological society in 1959.[58] Instead middle-class church-goers naïvely equated the presence of God with church-going. 'A vast number of English working men,' said Ryle, 'never go either to church or chapel, and, to all appearances, live and die "without God".' 'When I say come back to your church,' preached Winnington-Ingram, 'it is not contrary to saying come back to Christ.' As late as 1958 Bishop F. R. Barry of Southwell wrote of the world outside the church: 'It is nothing at all – just non-religion. The existence of God has no place in its scheme of things. This is the world surrounding the parish church.'[59]

In consequence an inadequate theology prevailed consisting chiefly of making the lower orders conform to the supposedly admirable morality of the upper classes by taking them out of their own environment into church, as brands snatched from the burning. Bishop A. C. Headlam believed 'that for the great majority of the people of this country the Sunday service is the only contact they can have with anything that will lift them above the trivial round of their daily life.'[60] Headlam was a distinguished theologian; but in common with most of his generation he rarely considered the theology of mission. As Professor J. G. Davies has pointed out, in the Protestant churches the concept of mission only arose in the eighteenth and nineteenth centuries. Only in the twentieth century did it become a subject for theological investigation. Until then mission chiefly meant foreign mission; and foreign missionaries had the same attitude to the objects of their mission as did the English churchmen to the proletariat. There is a direct comparison between the way colonial economies were forcibly orientated to the British economy at the same time as colonial ways of life were (it was hoped) transformed by mission schools, Bibles and hymns, and the way the middle-class church-goer at home regarded the unconverted working-man.[61]

The comparison is not fanciful. It was made by numerous Victorian clergymen (and not only clergymen: T. H. Huxley wrote that the Polynesian savage, 'in his most primitive condition', was 'not half so savage, so unclean, so irreclaimable as the tenant of a tenement in an East London slum').[62] The early foreign missionaries could be forgiven for not seeing God at work among tribes practising infanticide, self-torture, Ghat murders, suttee, etc.;[63] but for the most part the English working classes did not practise these things!

The clearest example of a twentieth-century bishop displaying

most of the inadequacies that have been described is the Hon.
Edward Carr Glyn. In 1896 Marie Mallet observed: 'I am surprised at Mr Carr Glyn's rise in life, I somehow don't fancy him
as a bishop. How careful Lord Salisbury is to conciliate the Broad
Church party.'[64] In fact, from the point of view of his suitability
for preferment, Carr Glyn's background was impeccable. Eighth
son of the 1st Lord Wolverton, he had married a daughter of the
8th Duke of Argyll and was educated at Eton and Oxford. He
was consecrated Bishop of Peterborough a year after Marie Mallet
made her comment and resigned in 1918. (He died in 1928). In
1913 Carr Glyn preached in Westminster Abbey on 'Patriotism'.
Having commended some remarks made by Lord Rosebery at
the Jubilee of Wellington College, the bishop set himself to apply-
ing these remarks to the proletariat. 'It may be true,' he said,
'that many of our misnamed working class think more of the
amount of wages they can earn than of the source from which
those wages spring, and on whose safety and security those wages
depend. We have to rouse in such as these the dormant patriotism
that has been choked by selfishness.' To this end he asked for
generous contributions towards the cost of building twenty-five
churches for the employees of the Naval Dockyards and their
dependants.[65]

The purpose of such churches was to give the working classes
what was called 'character' – or what an unfavourable observer
called 'the dry husks of a negative Puritanism'.[66] Most churchmen
would have agreed with Matthew Arnold when he said to the
London clergy, 'I regard the Church of England as, in fact, a great
national society for the promotion of what is commonly called
goodness, and for promoting it through the most effectual means
possible, the only means that are really and truly effectual for the
object: through the means of the Christian religion and of the
Bible.'[67]

Despite Arnold's great influence, few accepted his next point:
that the kingdom of God also called for 'an immense renovation
and transformation of our actual state of things'.[68] Many actively
opposed the idea. 'I pity those well-meaning people,' said Bishop
Ryle, 'who imagine that any legislation can ever drive evil out
of the world. There is a deep-seated cause of human misery which
baffles all their schemes: *that cause is sin*.' Boyd-Carpenter said
the same thing in a different way: he believed in 'making people

see the power – yea, shall I venture to say the omnipotence of goodness. . . . Thus will the social problems and thus will the economic problems be met, not by legislation, but by the spontaneous power of those who believe they were only put into this world to make it better.' Headlam was less rhetorical: 'We hear a great deal about the difference in wealth of rich and poor, but I never feel that the economic problem is the real one.'[69]

For most bishops the real problem was the 'spiritual' one. This was true for some of those who professed most expertise at taking the gospel to working men. The bishops and future bishops who were connected with Oxford House, the university's mission in Bethnal Green, all agreed in one way or another with E. S. Talbot that the reason for the House's existence was 'the preparation of character for . . . the reception of the religion of Christ' and not for any pioneer attempt to change the social structure of society.[70] Missions of this kind enabled many bishops to avoid their public responsibilities by concentrating on pietistic evangelism. In 1890 Alfred Barry, who had been Principal of Cheltenham College, resigned as Primate of Australia in order to become assistant Bishop of Rochester. He persuaded his old college to set up a mission in South London. At the inaugural meeting the bishop 'argued that the primary need was to preach the gospel to the poor and make available to them the gifts of the spirit, but in that context to bridge the class gap as well. There was great value in educated men showing that they treated working-class men and women as fellow men and women and doing acts of kindness.'[71]

Naturally, the church became virtually irrelevant to these men and women. At the Working Men's Conference of the Church Congress in 1898 the Archbishop of Canterbury said: 'Forgive me if I have taken the opportunity of calling you to something higher than mere conflict with the employing class.'[72] Two years later the first decision in the Taff Vale Case was announced; until the outbreak of the first World War industrial unrest produced increasing estrangement between employers and men. In 1913 Winnington-Ingram was given the opportunity of addressing three large gatherings of city men in the Guildhall. He had been Head of Oxford House from 1889 to 1898; his published works included *Work in Great Cities* (1896) and *The Church of the People* (1889). He urged four things on the city businessmen: (1) to see that their office boys overheard no filthy language; (2) to help stop obscenity on the stage and to stamp out prostitutes; (3) to avoid drunkenness; and (4) to come to church.[73]

Few bishops saw any theological inadequacy in this. Those that did could suffer for their insights, since a better theology might readily lead to criticism of the social and economic *status quo*. Joost de Blank, who was Bishop of Stepney from 1952 to 1957, observed: 'There is something wrong with a so-called conversion that . . . is concerned only with people's souls and takes no interest in their bodily welfare.'[74] In 1957 he was appointed Archbishop of Capetown. Six years later the South African government forced his resignation.

Bishops of similar insight could also suffer at the hands of an English government. In the 1930s the situation of the German Evangelical Church brought George Bell of Chichester to ask 'such fundamental questions as those respecting the nature of the church, its witness, its freedom, and its relation to the secular power'.[75] Nine years later Bell pursued these questions in the House of Lords and ruined his career. 'There is no doubt,' wrote his biographer, 'that his speeches on the war had destroyed his chances of succeeding to the primacy.'[76] In the judgment of a moral philosopher, 'he tested the moral significance of the Establishment to destruction'.[77]

The example of such men did not persuade every other bishop to abandon equivocation in dealing with an establishment of which they formed so integral a part.[78] At best they created a tradition that other men could acknowledge and respond to. Bishop Trevor Huddleston, himself *persona non grata* with the South African government, wrote in 1965: 'Looking back over the recent past and thinking first of those Christian leaders who have spoken to England and for England in her darkest hours, I would rather stand associated with Archbishop William Temple and Bishop George Bell of Chichester than with any other Christians of this generation.'[79] There were few enough others to stand associated with, few who shared the theological and social insights of these men. The more usual belief was expressed by Bishop F. T. Chavasse during the miners' strike of 1912: 'What we need is not a new method, but a new temper and a new spirit.'[80] Behind such an attitude were sound economic reasons; the good behaviour of the labouring classes had hidden financial benefits for their masters. 'If pure and undefiled religion prevailed everywhere,' wrote J. C.

Ryle, 'such plagues and pests and nuisances as quarreling, robbing, murder, drunkenness, fornication, swindling, gambling, idleness, lying, and cheating would be comparatively unknown. Half the prisons and workhouses would soon be shut up. Half the poor-rates would be saved.'[81]

J. C. Ryle affords the clearest example of theology as the handmaid of late-nineteenth century capitalism. His appointment had been nakedly political. In 1880 at the end of the Conservative ministry Disraeli had informed the Queen: 'The people of Liverpool are very anxious about their new Bishop. The Tories subscribed the whole of the endowment, and built the palace. Lord Sandon says his seat for Liverpool depends upon the appointment being made by your Majesty's present advisers.'[82] But Ryle's spirit lived on after him. In 1931 Bishop C. M. Blagdon of Peterborough described the reduction in unemployment allowances as 'a wholesome discipline and medicine of the soul'. Four years later Bishop J. G. Gordon of Jarrow informed the church assembly that the clergy were 'not to be concerned with making society fit for men, but with making men fit for society'.[83] And the leader of these men, Archbishop Randall Davidson, never managed to speak other than 'in the muffled accents of compromise with the world'.[84] *Very unfair.*

Davidson in some respects passed as a Christian Socialist. In the late 1870s he had served with twelve others (including Stewart Headlam, Scott Holland, Walsham How, Dean Church and J. B. Lightfoot) on a committee to consider the relationship of the church to the trade unions.[85] Its achievement was ephemeral. It is hard to make any other judgment on all the later nineteenth-century Christian Socialists. The Christian Social Union, formed in Oxford in 1889, is said to have included in its members sixteen of the fifty-three men appointed bishops between then and 1913.[86] But as Professor K. S. Inglis has pointed out, most of its members stood for social reform only 'so long as it was of a piecemeal, gradual and not very controversial kind'.[87] This seems to have been especially true of B. F. Westcott, who as Bishop of Durham presided over the CSU until 1900. Westcott's address on 'Socialism' to the Hull Church Congress in 1890 offended many Conservatives;[88] but according to one of his biographers, 'the CSU, under Westcott's lead, from the first steadily set its face against any direct application of its principles to the social and economic needs of the time ... So with careful admonition the good Bishop prevented any outburst of practical effort that would radically change our economic conditions.'[89] In the end it is difficult to see any practical difference between the attitude of bishops like West-cott and that described by the biographer of Bishop H. E. Ryle (Bishop of Exeter, 1901 to 1903, Bishop of Winchester, 1903 to 1911, the son of J. C. Ryle): 'By nature, training, and conviction he was undoubtedly Conservative, with a desire to maintain all that is best in our heritage from the past, while gradually removing proved abuses, and educating public opinion to aim at higher standards of morality, public and private.'[90]

It would, of course, be wrong to regard bishops like H. E. Ryle as the twentieth-century heirs of the CSU. That title belongs to an abler group of bishops, led by Charles Gore. Gore was certainly no lackey of the Establishment, as is shown, for instance, by his work in the House of Lords on behalf of conscientious objectors during the first World War. Under his leadership the Church of England, once regarded as the Tory party at prayer, became, 'at least in the persons of the Anglo-Catholic clergy, the Socialist party at Mass'.[91] In 1908 Gore was preaching to railway workers the right 'which God puts on the sanctity of his own name of Father ... the right ... to work and the right to an adequate re-muneration for work'.[92]

Gore's influence on William Temple has often been noted. Temple was also very much in debt to Bishop John Percival of Hereford.[93] Percival had been the favourite among Temple's various headmasters, and in 1905 the future archbishop attended the first national conference of the WEA largely because Percival was to take the chair.[94] A member of the CSU, Percival sat with four other CSU bishops on the committee that produced the im-portant 1907 report *The Moral Witness of the Church on Econo-mic Subjects*.[95] The following year, preaching in Westminster Abbey on 'The Lot of the Poor', he said that the seeds of social uplifting planted by Christ 'can only become effective through fundamental socialistic changes'.[96] In the same year Temple preached a sermon on 'Social Sin and Social Redemption' to the Scottish branch of the CSU, calling for complete reorganization of social and economic life.[97] Temple 'with all his limitations... was as distinguished a church leader as his age produced any-where in the world.'[98] In view of his rise to the primacy is it fair still to maintain that the English episcopate declined in quality?

In answering this question it is important to realize how much Temple, a headmaster and don, born into the purple, shared the limitations of his colleagues and in particular their remoteness from most of the people they were trying to serve. Percival could describe the masses as living in an 'inferno of manifold temptations, of struggling poverty and moral debasement ... untouched by any transforming influence from above'. They live, he said, 'close to our churches, but in another world, which is largely in every moral and spiritual sense an under-world'.[99] As one perspicacious contemporary observed of Gore, he was 'a democrat in conviction and practice' but 'an aristocrat in manner and origin'.[100] Even under Temple's leadership there could be no 'sufficiently skilful and sympathetic understanding by the churches of the working-class pattern of life, in which faith has to be born and the Christian community to grow'.[101] This led to Temple's reliance on committees and conferences which usually reported benevolently and long after the circumstances had changed. After the last of these Temple pathetically concluded that in the realm of industry and society at least it 'put the church on the map again.'[102] Not surprisingly a distinguished economist observed that the men responsible for this conference possessed 'a brilliance of intellect and imaginative grasp of problems unhampered by any solid knowledge of the realities of the issues with which they tried to grapple'.[103]

In the end Temple seems to have realized the futility of trying to promote social change by these methods. Inveterate conference-going and paper resolutions are no substitute for real political activity. Shortly before his death the Archbishop spoke to Canon L. J. Collins about his work. 'He had, he said, spent a lot of his energies in helping to set up at top level machinery whereby the church could function more democratically and more efficiently, and could let its voice be heard more certainly on social and political matters; but, were his life still before him, he would now concentrate on the problem of creating from below a body of Christians ready and determined to make effective use of this machinery.'[104]

In any case most bishops did not possess Temple's wide outlook and sympathies. Of the vast majority it could be said that 'the Bishop was a born Conservative, one who counted the cost of a disturbance of the existing relations at least as carefully as the advantage of the change proposed.'[105] A bishop like A. C. Headlam could carry this alliance with the powers-that-be to the extent of chiding Pastor Niemöller for persistently upsetting Hitler.[106]

The class alignment of these men was closely connected with their decline in quality; and because of this decline few of them had sufficient insight to see beyond their class alignment. Because men from other ranks gained no entry into the episcopate, notions acceptable to the generation of William Thomson and J. C. Ryle were allowed to persist unchallenged until well into the twentieth century. It was the professed aim of the bishops (derived ultimately from Thomas Arnold) that the church should articulate the religious aspirations of the whole nation – in the words of Archbishop Tait, to 'set forth that view of a comprehensive, loving, yet zealous Christian teaching which approved itself to the conscience and seeks to be embodied in the lives of the vast majority of intelligent persons throughout the kingdom'.[107] God was for them the ultimate sanction of national interests and institutions.[108] But in the end this amounted to sanctioning the institutions and interests only of one particular class.

NOTES

1. A. G. Gardiner, *Prophets, Priests, and Kings,* 1914, p.163. For another low estimate of Winnington-Ingram see *Letters of H. H. Henson,* ed. E. F. Braley, SPCK 1950, p.8; Henson had a low opinion of several other bishops – see pp.66,137.

2. In a lecture given in Manchester Cathedral, 3 June 1921, printed in *A Quincentenary Celebration, The Ancient Collegiate Church of Manchester,* Manchester 1921, p.228.

3. H. R. L. Sheppard, *The Impatience of a Parson,* 1927, p.226.

4. L. J. Collins, *Faith Under Fire,* Leslie Frewin 1966, p.48. He was Vice-Principal of Westcott House from 1934 to 1937. 'B.K.' is the Principal, B. K. Cunningham.

5. *The Times* leader, 31 May 1877. For an example of a cheap jibe see Earl Russell's letter to Bertrand Russell, 15 June 1925: 'I like your conclusive proof that bishops are more brutal than Aztecs who go in for human sacrifices.' *The Autobiography of Bertrand Russell,* Vol. II, Allen & Unwin 1968, p.175.

6. J. R. H. Moorman, *A History of the Church in England,* A. & C. Black, 2nd edition 1967, pp.416, 433. The Earl of Longford, *Five Lives,* Hutchinson 1964, p.70.

7. S. Baring-Gould, *The Church Revival,* 2nd edition 1914, p.210.

8. H. Scott Holland, *Personal Studies,* n. d., pp.202, 206. Scott Holland

underestimated the nineteenth-century bishops; cf. O. Chadwick, *The Victorian Church*, Vol. I, A. & C. Black 1966, p.476: 'The Palmerstonian bishops were good bishops.'

9. Ronald W. Clark, *The Huxleys*, Heinemann 1968, p.60.

10. The phrase is from S. C. Carpenter, *Church and People, 1789-1889*, 1933, p.471. For juster impressions of Bishop Wilberforce see Robert Blake, *Disraeli*, OUP 1966, p.510; S. Baring-Gould, op. cit., p.175; *Letters on Church and Religion of W. E. Gladstone*, ed. D. C. Lathbury, Vol. II, 1910, p.308.

11. *Letters of Lord Acton to Mary Gladstone*, ed. H. Paul 1904, p.184. This was far from true, as is shown by Liddon's distress over the publication of *Lux Mundi*: J. O. Johnston, *The Life and Letters of H. P. Liddon*, 1904, pp.360-81.

12. Op. cit., p.204.

13. *The Christian World Pulpit*, 29 July 1908, p.71. His presidential address to the Society is in the *Proceedings of the Society for Psychical Research*, Vol. 26, September 1912, pp.2-23.

14. Cyril Bibby, *T. H. Huxley, Scientist, Humanist and Educator*, C. A. Watts 1959, p.67.

15. F. W. Farrer, 'Men I have known' in *The Temple Magazine*, Vol. I, 1897, p.861. For Archbishop Tait's attempt to deal with the intellectual challenge of scientific thought see P. T. Marsh, *The Victorian Church in Decline*, Routledge & Kegan Paul 1969, pp.59-65. In 1882 Tait admitted that 'the age has become sceptical', ibid., p.283.

16. W. Thomson, *Popular Lectures and Addresses*, Vol. II, 1894, p.177. Cf. Henry Sidgwick's remark that 'In the present age an educated man must either be prophet or persistent sceptic – there seems no *media via*.': A. and M. Sidgwick, *Henry Sidgwick, a Memoir*, 1906, p.158.

17. G. W. E. Russell, *Edward King, Sixtieth Bishop of Lincoln*, 1913, p.128. *Crockford's Clerical Directory*, 1900, p. xv.

18. T. J. H. Bishop and R. Wilkinson, *Winchester and the Public School Elite*, Faber & Faber 1967, pp.63-70. T. W. Bamford, *The Rise of the Public Schools*, Nelson 1967, pp.215-6, 219-22. David Ward, 'The public schools and industry in Britain after 1870', *Journal of Contemporary History*, vol. 2, no. 3, July 1967, pp.37-52.

19. Sheldon Rothblatt, *The Revolution of the Dons,* Faber & Faber 1968, pp.63-5.

20. Ibid., p.65.

21. *More Letters of H. H. Henson*, ed. E. F. Braley, SPCK 1954, p.43.

22. T. J. H. Bishop and R. Wilkinson, op. cit., pp.40-41; cf. Sir Felix Pole, who joined the Great Western Railway as a telegraph clerk when a lad in 1891 and rose to the position of general manager: *Felix Pole, His Book*, Town & Country Press 1968.

23. D. L. Munby, *God and the Rich Society*, OUP 1961, p.162. For the years 1894 and 1922 see the evidence in T. W. Bamford, op. cit., p.222. F. R. Salter, *St Paul's School, 1909-1959*, A. Barker 1959, Appendix II, p.193, lists among its old boys six English bishops (including the then Dean of Bristol), one colonial archbishop and seven colonial bishops.

24. Public Schools Commission, *First Report*, Vol. II, 1968, p.236. The percentage of Heads of Colleges and Oxbridge professors drawn from the public schools was 49·3%.

25. In the sense of drawing on the parochial clergy many bishops were recruited from the other ranks. In 1900 26 of the 35 diocesan bishops pos-

sessed parochial experience (an average of 12 years each); 25 years later 29 bishops possessed parochial experience (an average of 10 years each): *Crockford's Clerical Directories* for 1900 and 1925.

26. *Christian Remembrancer*, October 1863, Vol. XLVI, p.395. Matthew Arnold, 'Last Essays on Church and Religion' (1877) in *Works*, Vol. IX, 1904, p.362. Winnington-Ingram in *The Christian World Pulpit*, 4 December 1907, p.354. *Christianity and Industrial Problems*, 1918, p.159. H. H. Henson, *The Church of England*, 1939, p.142.

27. Quoted from *The Sunday Express*, 1 August 1926, by John Oliver in *The Church and Social Order*, Mowbrays 1968, p.91. *Crockford's Clerical Directory*, 1967, p. vi, singled out W. Temple, Henson, A. C. Headlam and Dean Inge as the leading church spokesmen in the 1920s and 1930s.

28. S. Rothblatt, op. cit., p.22, based on *The Franks Report*, Oxford 1966, Vol. I, pp.63-96. The corresponding figure for the universities of Manchester, Leeds and Birmingham was one third. Cf. Ernest Raymond's novel, *The Witness of Canon Welcome*, 1950, about the careers of a middle-class vicar and his working-class curate. Raymond was himself ordained in 1914 and served as an army chaplain during the Great War: *The Story of My Days*, Cassell 1968, pp.114ff.

29. D. L. Munby, op. cit., p.162. D. H. J. Morgan, 'The social and educational background of Anglican bishops, continuities and changes', *British Journal of Sociology*, September 1969, pp.295-310, found that between 1860 and 1960 the number of bishops with a public school background increased, and that except for the year 1960 the percentage with an 'Oxbridge' background never fell below 90%. He failed to discover a bishop whose father had been a manual worker.

30. C. A. Lane, *Illustrated Notes on English Church History*, revised edition 1898, pp.550f. For various attitudes to the notion of increasing the nineteenth-century episcopate see K. S. Inglis, *Churches and the Working Class in Victorian England*, Routledge & Kegan Paul 1963, pp.31-3, and P. T. Marsh, op. cit., pp.204-7.

31. D. L. Munby, op. cit., p.163.

32. E. S. Talbot had been first diocesan bishop of Southwark, translated from Rochester in 1891. E. W. Benson, first Bishop of Truro, became Archbishop of Canterbury. E. A. Knox, Bishop of Manchester, had been the first suffragan Bishop of Coventry. W. W. How, suffragan Bishop of Bedford and first Bishop of Wakefield, declined the see of Durham. E. R. Wilberforce, first Bishop of Newcastle, was translated to Chichester in 1895. In 1911 F. E. Ridgeway was translated from Kensington to Salisbury and E. S. Talbot from Southwark to Winchester.

33. D. C. Lathbury, op. cit., Vol. II, p.184.

34. E. A. Knox, *Reminiscences of an Octogenarian*, 1934, pp.88-9.

35. W. I. Jennings, *Cabinet Government*, 1936, pp.346-8, which gives examples.

36. Sidney Dark, *Archbishop Davidson and the English Church*, 1929, p.166; cf. A. G. Gardiner, op. cit., p.126: 'He thinks in crowns and sceptres.' Davidson's rise would have been even more spectacular if Queen Victoria had had her every wish in this respect: Marie Mallet, *Life with Queen Victoria*, ed. V. Mallet, John Murray 1968, pp.92-3.

37. Ibid., pp.138, 179.

38. S. Baring-Gould, op. cit., p.171, gives a list of ten such Victorian bishops. For one humble aristocrat who refused elevation to the bench see Lord Frederic Hamilton, *The Days before Yesterday*, 1920, pp. 17-18. In

the twentieth century the number of bishops with fathers of landed or peerage connections declined sharply: D. H. J. Morgan, art. cit., p.297.

39. Other Victorian headmaster-bishops include Edward Maltby of Durham, Samuel Butler of Lichfield, Francis Jeune of Peterborough and George Moberly of Salisbury. Bishops who had taught at public schools include B. F. Westcott and Charles Wordsworth. For Prince Lee of Manchester see D. Newsome, *Godliness and Good Learning*, John Murray 1961.

40. Op. cit., p.55.

41. *Crockford's Clerical Directories* for 1900 and 1925. Twentieth-century headmaster-bishops include William Temple and Geoffrey Fisher of Canterbury, St John Basil Lynne Wilson of Marlborough, Bertram Pollock of Norwich, H. M. Burge of Oxford and Albert Augustus David of Liverpool.

42. M. H. Fitzgerald, *A Memoir of Herbert Edward Ryle*, 1928, p.146.

43. In *The Church and the Twentieth Century*, ed. G. L. H. Harvey, 1936, p.38.

44. *Letters*, pp.234, 180-81.

45. A. M. Ramsey in *The York Quarterly*, February 1958.

46. E. A. Knox, op. cit., p.305. Norman Dumenil John Straton, Bishop of Sodor and Man, 1892-1907, Bishop of Newcastle, 1907-1915, was in fact the son of a clergyman.

47. P. Magnus, *King Edward the Seventh*, John Murray 1964, p.395. Lang's action is approvingly cited in D. Webster, *What is Evangelism?*, Highway Press 1961, p.16; for an unfavourable contemporary view see *Chips: The Diaries of Sir Henry Channon*, ed. R. R. James, Weidenfeld & Nicolson 1967, p.104.

48. *The Archbishop Speaks*, selected by E. Carpenter, Evans 1958, p.231. For a later comparison of the church and the monarchy by Archbishop Fisher see *The Listener*, 25 September 1969, p.408.

49. C. Smyth, *Cyril Forster Garbett, Archbishop of York*, Hodder & Stoughton 1959, p.437.

50. *Letters*, p.28.

51. In *Bishops*, ed. Glyn Simon, Faith Press 1961, p.36. Cf. F. R. Barry writing as a chaplain in the Great War in *The Church in the Furnace*, ed. F. B. Macnutt, 1917, p.63; W. H. Hook's letter to Bishop Wilberforce in A. R. Ashwell, *Life of Bishop Wilberforce*, 1880, I. 225; and a former costermonger's remark to Henry Mayhew that 'the costers somehow mix up being religious with being respectable', quoted K. S. Inglis, op. cit., p.20.

52. Op. cit., p.356. Cf. G. W. E. Russell, *Some Threepeny Bits*, 1908, p.295: 'The Church continued, as a general rule, to be the close ally of the governing classes.'

53. See the excellent summary of statistics and evidence in H. Pelling, *Popular Politics and Society in Late Victorian Britain*, Macmillan 1968, ch. 2, esp. p.29.

54. Exemplified in the belief of Valdimaro Marquis di Furvanti that 'If you are born an aristocrat, it is not your fault, but it is God's will. Therefore you must have responsibilities. You must learn to lead people in reading the gospels and teaching the less fortunate the right way to live by example': quoted A. Sinclair, *The Last of the Best*, Weidenfeld & Nicolson 1969, p.179.

55. H. Kirk-Smith, *William Thomson, Archbishop of York, 1819-90*, SPCK 1958, p.102.

56. Quoted from *Can we adapt the Public School System to the Middle Classes?* 1958, by T. W. Bamford, op. cit., p.49.

57. *Principles for Churchmen*, 4th edition 1900, p.400. Cf. the revelation that the working class possessed ethical ideas by A. S. Headlam, 'The National Mission', *Church Quarterly Review*, vol. 83, 1916, pp.1-19.

58. Scott Holland, *The Christian World Pulpit*, 11 September 1907, p.162; for his contribution to the Christian social tradition see S. G. Evans, *The Social Hope of the Christian Church*, Hodder & Stoughton 1965, pp.165-7. E. R. Wickham, 'The Encounter of the Christian Faith and Modern Technological Society', a paper read at the first meeting of the European Council of Churches in 1959, reprinted in *Encounter with Modern Society*, ed. E. R. Wickham, Lutterworth Press 1964, pp.31-42.

59. Ryle, op. cit., p.396. Winnington-Ingram in *The Christian World Pulpit*, 17 December 1913, p.387. F. R. Barry, *Vocation and Ministry*, James Nisbet 1958, p.142.

60. Art. cit., p.10.

61. J. G. Davies, *Dialogue with the World*, SCM Press 1967, p.10. For the way English missionary schools evolved curricula modelled on English public schools and bearing little relation to local economic and social conditions see *Educational Policy and the Mission Schools*, ed. B. Holmes, Routledge & Kegan Paul 1968.

62. See the quotations in Asa Briggs, *Victorian Cities*, Penguin Books 1968, pp.315f. The quotation from Huxley is on p.315. Cf. E. B. Pusey, writing from Oxford: 'If I had no duties here, I would long ago have asked leave to preach in the alleys of London, where the gospel is as unknown as in Thibet.': H. P. Liddon, *Life of E. B. Pusey*, Vol. III, 1895, p.32.

63. See E. Daniel Potts, *British Baptist Missionaries in India, 1793-1837*, OUP 1967, ch. 7: 'Certain Dreadful Practices'.

64. Marie Mallett, op. cit., p.94; cf. the practice sixty years later, when 'the expected presence at Canterbury of one generally regarded as an Anglo-Catholic was to be offset by the appointment to York of one equally conspicuously associated with the Evangelical tradition': D. M. MacKinnon, *The Stripping of the Altars*, Fontana Books 1969, p.30.

65. *The Christian World Pulpit*, 30 April 1913, p.285.

66. G. W. E. Russell, op. cit., p.300; cf. the opinion of the bishops at the Lambeth Conference of 1897: 'It is character they need.': quoted in K. S. Inglis, op. cit., p.185; Mandell Creighton on the 'training of English character' in *The Church and the Nation*, 1901, p. 322; and J. Moorhouse, *Church Work*, 1894, pp.116-7, 225.

67. Op. cit., p.345; cf. J. R. Seeley, 'The Church as a Teacher of Morality' in *Lectures and Essays*, 1870.

68. Op. cit., p.368. Dean Church took Arnold's works with him among a few favourite books when he left London for the last time: B. A. Smith, *Dean Church*, OUP 1958, pp.189, 192. Mandell Creighton found his writings to be far more 'fruitful' than Ruskin's: L. Creighton, *Life and Letters of Mandell Creighton*, 1904, I. 325. Cf. F. A. Iremonger, *William Temple*, 1948, p.106. Characteristically, Liddon was not beguiled: J. O. Johnston, op. cit., p.358.

69. Ryle, op. cit., p.287. Boyd-Carpenter in *The Christian World Pulpit*, 23 July 1913, p.51. A. C. Headlam in *Church Quarterly Review*, vol. 83, 1916, p.12; cf. 'Economics and Christianity', *Church Quarterley Review*, vol. 103, 1926, pp.64-95.

70. K. S. Inglis, op. cit., p.157. For similar opinions from W. Walsham How, Lang and Winnington-Ingram, pp.157-8.

71. M. C. Morgan, *Cheltenham College, the First Hundred Years*, 1958, pp.128-9.

72. K. S. Inglis, op. cit., p.320. This was at a time when the rise of the Labour churches had been brought about by 'a directly felt need for a religious expression of the moral aims and moral unity of the working class'.: A. MacIntyre, *Secularization and Moral Change*, OUP 1967, p.25; cf. the Preacher's Plan for the Primitive Methodist Connexion of Brierley Hill, Staffs., 1900: 'Appleby's Hats are all made by Trades' Union Labour.'

73. *The Christian World Pulpit*, 10, 17 and 24 December 1913, pp.376-7, 385-7, 409-10. In the 1930s Winnington-Ingram and Archbishop Lang readily gave their support to the Buchmanites: J. P. Thornton-Duesbery, *The Open Secret of MRA*, Blandford Press 1964, pp.92-3. Lang's birthday message to Frank Buchman is in Peter Howard, *Innocent Men*, 1941, p.124.

74. J. de Blank, *This is Conversion*, 1957, p.72.

75. 10 May 1934, quoted in Mary Bosanquet, *The Life and Death of Dietrich Bonhoeffer*, Hodder & Stoughton 1968, p.141.

76. R. C. D. Jasper, *George Bell, Bishop of Chichester*, OUP 1967, p.285.

77. D. M. MacKinnon, op. cit., p.85.

78. See the various attitudes collected by Christopher Driver in *The Disarmers*, Hodder & Stoughton 1964, pp.193-200.

79. Letter to *New Statesman*, 23 July 1965. For the reaction of the Conservative establishment to Temple, see the diaries of Sir Henry Channon, op. cit., pp.337, 352, 396. Bell went as clerical student of Christ Church, Oxford, in the year Scott Holland became Regius Professor of Divinity. He worked on Temple's small committee that investigated the unemployment question in the 1930s: Jasper, op. cit., pp.14-15, 79.

80. J. B. Lancelot, *F. J. Chavasse*, 1929, p.210. Chavasse was Bishop of Liverpool from 1900 to 1923. Cf. Bishop H. L. Paget's comment that 'Kindness is a feeble thing when justice is asked for.': E. K. Paget, *Henry Luke Paget*, 1939, p.98.

81. Op. cit., p.288.

82. Quoted by R. B. Walker, 'Religious Changes in Liverpool in the 19th Century', *Journal of Ecclesiastical History*, October 1968, Vol. XIX, No. 2, p.198.

83. John Oliver, op. cit., pp.152 n.30, 157.

84. A. G. Gardiner, op. cit., p.128. For Davidson's claim to be a Christian Socialist see S. Mayor, *The Churches and the Labour Movement*, Independent Press 1967, p.220; but his cautious nature made him hesitate to pronounce openly on any social issue: Oliver, op. cit., pp.25 n.8, 27, 34, 93. In 1923 he contemplated resigning, on the grounds that he was out of touch with an increasingly social interpretation of Christianity; but he continued in office for another five years: ibid. p.66, with references to G. K. A. Bell, *Randall Davidson, Archbishop of Canterbury*, 1935.

85. P. T. Marsh, op. cit., p.91.

86. M. B. Reckitt, *Maurice to Temple*, 1947, p.138.

87. Op. cit., p.279; cf. H. Pelling, *The Origins of the Labour Party, 1880-1900*, Macmillan 1954, p.136: 'as time went on the distinctive vigour of the CSU seemed to weaken as its ranks opened to more and more members.'

88. *The Times*, 2 October 1890, p.7.

89. J. Clayton, *Bishop Westcott*, 1906, pp.160, 162-3. Even so, Lord Salisbury in 1890, having read some of Westcott's writings, put up considerable resistance to the Queen's suggestion that he should go to Durham: E. F. Benson, *As We Were*, 1934 edition, p.191.

90. M. H. Fitzgerald, op. cit., p.260.

91. H. D. A. Major in *The Modern Churchman*, Vol. XXI, February 1932, p.583. Gore became president of the CSU on Westcott's death. For his social thinking see 'Some Aspects of Christian Duty' in the 1889 Appendix to *Lux Mundi*; *Property: its Duties and Rights*, ed. C. Gore, 1913; and the Halley Stewart Lectures for 1927, *Christ and Society*.

92. *The Christian World Pulpit*, 14 October 1908, p.243.

93. Percival was assistant master at Rugby and headmaster of Clifton College. Educated at Appleby Grammar School, he took a double first at Oxford, becoming Fellow of Queen's and then President of Trinity. He was Bishop of Hereford from 1895 to 1918. A. G. Gardiner wrote that 'Dr Percival, Canon Barnett, and Dr Gore alone have the ear of the nation.': op. cit., p.164. In 1908 there was general surprise when he was not preferred to York: E. A. Knox, op. cit., p.306.

94. Iremonger, op. cit., p.74. In 1921 Temple wrote an important *Life of Bishop Percival*.

95. E. S. Talbot, Gore's friend and fellow-contributor to *Lux Mundi*, was amongst the CSU bishops on this committee. In 1895 he had written *The Religious Aspirations of Labour*. Successively Bishop of Rochester, Southwark and Winchester, he chaired the Archbishop's Committee that in 1918 produced the famous fifth report, *Christianity and Industrial Problems*.

96. *The Christian World Pulpit*, 28 December 1908, p.403.

97. Ibid., 30 September 1908, pp.214-6.

98. S. Mayor, op. cit., p.372.

99. *The Christian World Pulpit*, 28 December 1908, p.402.

100. Thomas Jones, *Whitehall Diary* ed. R. K. Middlemas, Vol. I, OUP 1969, p.16. At times Gore assumed that there were sins (such as fornication, drunkenness and violence) to which the working class leaned more than the rest of society: *The Reconstruction of Belief*, new edition 1926, p.969.

101. E. R. Wickham, *Church and People in an Industrial City*, Lutterworth Press 1957, p.217.

102. *Malvern 1941*, 1941, p.224.

103. D. L. Munby, op. cit., p.158. Examples of such trivial engagement with society could be multiplied. Archbishop Garbett, having addressed 400 Manchester businessmen at a luncheon club, a group of printers in Leeds and 800 members of the Institute of Personnel Management at Harrogate, noted in his diary, October 1950: 'I am sure the indirect value of these contacts is great, they show the church is interested.': C. Smyth, op. cit., p.432. After an NUR service at Chester Cathedral a railwayman wrote to Bishop Paget, 'You cannot think what this has meant to me, for it is the first time my church has ever shown any interest in my daily work.': E. L. Paget, op. cit., p.217.

104. L. J. Collins, op. cit., p.77.

105. S. Paget and J. M. C. Crum, *Francis Paget, Bishop of Oxford*, 1913, p.332.

106. Jasper, op. cit., p.100.

107. 'Thoughts suggested by Mr Mozley's Oxford Reminiscences', *Macmillan's Magazine*, Vol. XLVI, no. 276, October 1882, pp.422-3.

108. Mandell Creighton, op. cit., pp.213-5, 262-6.

12 Church Denomination and Society

David Martin

THIS essay falls into two clear sections: past and future. The first section is concerned with the differing ways in which Catholicism and Methodism have related to the total society. Catholicism and Methodism are taken as the typical 'church' and 'denomination' in the sociological usage of these terms. The second section is concerned with the manner in which they may confront the 'secular' as it exhibits itself in modern societies.

The Catholic Church has related itself to society in two major ways. First, it has attempted to dominate society at a high price in terms of the compromise of Christian ideals. These ideals have been maintained at the level of the family, albeit in a legalistic and restrictive manner, and very seriously diluted at the level of social stratification, economic forces and power drives. So far as stratification and the forces of power and wealth are concerned the Church has either thrown a cloak of Christian ideology over them or largely accepted their autonomy. To take examples only from the context of power relationships the Catholic Church can either relate political manoeuvres to the rhetoric of crusade, or it can accept the prudential calculations of nationalistic foreign policy as an independent arena of forces. Thus Cardinal Richelieu pursued a foreign policy based on the interests of France, not the interests of Catholicism. The autonomy of power and interest is present in both cases, but in the one case secularization is implicit, in the other case explicit.

This first type of relationship includes a sub-variety which arises under the impact of forces which seek to render explicit the autonomy of power, notably as focussed in the state. This can be achieved either by making the Church a sub-department of the state (Peter the Great, Henry the Eighth) or dissociating the Church from the state, as happened during the French revolution. If the former method is employed the state feels little need to dissolve a relationship in which it is the dominant power, and thus the stability of the relationship depends on other factors which in England, for example, made it enduring and in Russia eventually consigned the Church to positive persecution because implicated in the accumulating tyrannies of later Tsardom. If the latter method is employed the Church tends to retain a fairly close relation to conservative forces and to stand on the conservative side in a society racked by polarized politics. Eventually the politics of Christian democracy represent an attempt both to transcend this polarization, at least in its most acute form, and to give some expression to the massive presence which the Church retains in society.

The second major Catholic mode of relating to the wider society is the minority enclave, either a territorial enclave (Ireland, Quebec) or a social ghetto. The territorial enclave tends to be socially backward and to spawn nationalist movements; the social ghetto tends to be socially depressed and also – partly on account of that depression – to achieve some partial alliance with radical politics (England, Australia and to some extent the United States).

Like the Catholic Church, Methodism has two main stances *vis-à-vis* society. One is the small, socially depressed and often pietistic group huddled together in a society dominated by a national church or by the Communist party. Such a group is normally apolitical. The other stance is that of a largish minority dispersed at medium status levels in a pluralistic Protestant culture. The political expression of this minority varies with the stratum which is its carrier, but is hardly ever extremist and never explicitly involves the Methodist Church as a religious organization. For example where Methodism is lodged in the upper working class of (say) Yorkshire or Wales it is associated with liberal minded sections of the Labour Party. The overall drift – and the word drift is used advisedly – is towards liberalism, especially perhaps in those comparatively secure levels where it is combined with theological liberalism. Certainly in America Methodism (10% of the population) belongs to main-line Protestantism and fits easily into the atmosphere of liberal rhetoric in which political discussion must be cast.

All of which is obvious enough. But it is worth noting a pervasive contrast between a unitary, coherent Catholic pattern and a partly incoherent, flexible Methodist pattern of dispersal. The Methodist mode includes partial congruences, partial disjunctions, with the surrounding society adopted by individuals and groups without direct political support from the religious organization – apart from the social comment of its specialized agencies. Of course these varied modes are not immutable on either side, especially perhaps in Latin America. In that continent the Catholic Church struggles to extricate itself from often rurally based conservative forces (e.g. in Brazil) while the Methodist Church (e.g. in Chile) makes massive inroads amongst freshly-arrived urban migrants. Here the possibility of a common Christian-radical front is more likely than it was in Europe.

Having suggested these differing relationships to the total society it is now appropriate to consider how Catholicism and Methodism compare in their responses to social change both in terms of their own *internal* renewal and response to the dynamism of the wider society. Of course, so far as Methodism is concerned it is itself a movement of renewal. How then can it be renewed? Or does it perform its task and then relapse? Clearly periodic revivals are one method of Methodist renewal but not one which asserts new principles or contemporary relevance. Rather it harks back to what it believes to be the original impulse. In any case running parallel to these revivals has been a tendency to bureaucracy, centralization, and even, in some degree, intellectualization which was present very early in Methodism, and which forced both revival and reform into new groupings, often more localized, more democratic and more lay than the parent body; indeed some of them were not explicitly Methodist at all, though clearly within the charismatic wing of the same tradition, e.g. the Salvation Army and Pentecostalism. Moreover as each movement of revival hardened a new one stepped into the vacant role, affirming the primacy of heart-work and struggling against the tramelling of the Spirit by particular structures and forms.

The Roman form of renewal may take the form of a massive restatement by the whole Church, focussed in the Pope or a General Council, as it faces a whole range of contemporary problems which have come to a head: Trent, Vatican I and II, as well as the great reforming Popes. Or internal change may be channelled through new orders with a specific contemporary task. These orders may between them assert a whole variety of principles and objectives, including the ultimate irrelevance of the merely contemporary. Some may be concerned with reform, others organize charitable works, yet others deny the world or, on the contrary, attempt to penetrate the upper echelons of power. The orders resemble

Methodism in some degree, and more particularly, those orders founded in the same period, the Passionists and the Redemptorists.

To sum up: Catholicism organizes an array of varied principles derived from a richly various past, and emphasizes one or other as contemporary exigencies require, while Methodism exhibits a group of related attitudes consisting of a core and a periphery, from which a given range of inferences can be drawn according to time and place.

Both the characteristic Methodist and Catholic modes meet the 'world' armed with different advantages and disadvantages. So far as Methodism is concerned the tendency to disperse into a not markedly contrasting pluralistic society leads to absorption and erosion, especially when that society is socially and geographically mobile. Local cohesion is difficult to maintain in such circumstances. On the other hand, the notion of a doctrinal or psychological core with peripheral outworks means that no crisis of faith occurs when one of the outworks disappears. Temperance may have been a symbol of Methodist identity but a loosening grasp on the temperance ideal does not proliferate damagingly through the whole body of Methodist faith and morals. Similarly Methodists are not troubled by inflexible doctrines concerning divorce or the regulation of births. Since such matters are automatically given over to individual conscience there is no crisis either of faith or authority when changes occur in the wider society.

The Catholic position is largely the reverse. The ghetto, particularly separate education, maintains cohesion, although at enormous financial cost and maybe also at some cost in the acceptability of the community and the social mobility of its members. The 'total environment' held together by ecclesiastical authority as well as by ethnic identity protects its members, and even attracts outsiders who feel the pull of this protective security; but it can also build up tensions to the point of explosion, as well as encouraging extremism among radicals. Such an explosion will occur whenever a *single* point of doctrine is undermined simply because a hole in the dyke undermines the complete defensive system. And of course if some limited social mobility creates a Catholic middle class in closer contact with Protestants and humanists of similar status, then this is where the explosion is audible. What becomes audible dissent at this level is often unspoken divergence from Catholic norms at lower levels. Intellectuals begin by inventing verbal subterfuges and, when they can bear these no longer, erupt against authority; the working class either obeys or silently pursues its way in the usual manner of erring humanity. The Catholic system can cope with large-scale divergence, but it cannot brook overt disruption and challenge, and it is precisely this that occurs as more and more climb out of the overlapping ghettos of class and religious separatism.

No doubt Methodism also suffers somewhat from upward social mobility, but these are inaudible and unpublicized drifts towards Anglicanism or towards humanism or apathy. The educated laity easily feels at home with (and at least equal to) an educated ministry, and perhaps both are a little uncertain about their more unsophisticated brethren. No Methodist superintendent identifies a *consensus fidelium* amongst the less educated mass in order to rebuke arrogant middle-class dissenters. And the nearest approach to verbal subterfuge among middle-class Methodists is an agreement to use traditional language as a bond even when the content of the words differs both in meaning and in tone.

What now of the specific challenge of modern society in its liberal industralized, semi-affluent guise? I have already suggested that Methodism does not find too many points of incongruence, while for Catholicism the problem is the extent to which it follows in the same path. Of course, there is also the problem of revolution in developing countries, notably Latin America, and of countries in southern Europe where Catholicism was in a conservative phase at the point where radical social change erupted, but however important this turns out to be it is not the main focus of the present comparison.

Methodism in modern society is in the awkward position of a group whose point has been partly taken and which is left with a diminished specific *raison d'être*. In the Anglo-Saxon cultures where Methodism has its main provenance, liberal rhetoric, if not liberal achievement, is universal, and the noisy impotence of rebels – their attempts to be doctrinaire and violent – only witness to that universality. The Methodist emphasis often turns up like floating driftwood very far from home and with no identification marks to show their origin. For example, the elevation of conscience and sincerity over rigour and of informality over formality are two doubtful Methodist gifts to the world – including current student ideology. Likewise participatory democracy. As for those ecclesiastical virtues which look so enticing from outside – localism, the small cell, lay initiative – they can be strongholds of stagnation and introversion. Methodists know that an active laity is not necessarily the stuff of the Tolpuddle Martyrs, either politically or ecclesiastically. It is true that the Methodist Church has often been the poorer man's university, and the place where he spent his leisure, but both the education and the leisure facilities are overtaken by agencies technically superior if not always superior in content. Just as the Methodist emphasis has been partly taken over so has its social function. The question is as posed above: does Catholicism now travel the same road? And the further question is: are both doomed to absorption in what is called secular society.

To suggest possible answers to this latter question requires a detour to the opening section of this essay. There it was argued that the Church in the period of its greatest apparent power only maintained its ideals, in a somewhat repressive legalistic fashion, at the level of the family. Mostly it legitimated the secular system, and indeed received near-indelible stigmata from that system in the hierarchical organization of its own body. The dynamism of the gospel had to be carried first by dissident social groups, sometimes in partial alliance with heresy, and then later by incoherent diffusion and countless promiscuous unions with disparate ideological materials. Official Christianity was maintained largely by being spiritualized. This is true of every period in the history of the Church: social forces above the level of the family remained obstinately autonomous and secular in their resistance to Christianization. The Lutheran recognition of the dominance of the secular power was in one sense a retreat but also an admission of what was already and inherently the case. The near-theocracy of the papacy at its strongest represented an internal collapse before the secular imperatives of power and wealth whereby the Church itself became just such a structure; but the more usual pattern was one in which secular powers largely absorbed the Church in their own purposes and patterns of organization.

Nowadays when the autonomy of power and of economic forces is recognized and explicit, the privatization of religion becomes clear whereas before its reality was obscured. The medieval *de facto* is the modern *de jure*. Once the autonomy of the secular (meaning its resistance to Christianization) became clear, Protestantism, for which Methodism provides a characteristic example, handed matters over to the individual conscience, which meant religious adaptation to this and that stratum, its life-style, interests and political imperatives, with the moral disparities only noted and attacked by individuals. Such individual protest, often directed at the phenomenon of war but also to some extent at social injustice, failed to come to grips with the structural character of the problem. Catholicism, on the other hand, partly preserved formal elements from the medieval situation but also met the naked secularity of the world by reinforcing the organizational autonomy of the Church and its institutional fabric as well as by trying to enlist the state to shore up its obsessive concern with the integrity of the family.

Thus the basic situation has always been the same: religion has been largely unable to subdue the secular world above the level of the small community (the territorial village and the self-selected sect) and of the family. In an undifferentiated medieval society the ideological modalities of power, wealth and hierarchy were theological and the essence of secularization has been replacement of theological modalities by secular ideology. These have in turn tended to attack *either* the autonomous power of the state (liberal capitalism) *or* the autonomous power of economic forces (Marxism), whereas theology tried to attack both. They have not been much more successful than theology and to the extent that they have come near the achievement of their goal in one direction they have been more totally given over to the arbitrary market or to the totalitarian state on the other. By claiming to conquer where they have largely failed they are agents of mystification now just as theology was in the past, and a new secularization is required which is all too slow in coming.

Now that the Church and theology are partly freed from the stunting, distorting, mystifying task of legitimating the social and economic order, and now that the privatization of religion is clear, certain advantages accrue. The partial failure of the secular ideologies to humanize the state or economic forces gives us some measure of the problem, some index of the recalcitrance which Christianity faced, some compassion for its failure. The Church is also freed from the grip of its previous tasks, and even perhaps able to mount some critique of the new mystifications and legitimations propounded by 'secular' ideologies. And if the Church is not totally freed then at least a free religious style of radical thinking is available.

In so doing the Church is assisted by the growth of its specialist agencies, and retarded by a suburban familism where its constituency, the female, the old, the very young, and the lower-middle class is not easily shifted from the theology of comfort to that of challenge, and where privatized religion is almost celebrated. The specialist agencies also gain from the new loneliness of the clerical profession, which is partly hived off from its old social entanglements, and (where not recruited from ex-police inspectors) motivated by an activism which cannot be satisfied by the suburban parish or circuit. The new-style clergyman wants to be where the action is, partly to show he is a man, which is important for a profession operating in a female-dominated milieu, and partly because suburbia is defined as 'unreal'. Hence a movement of the socially engaged into the specialist agencies and a superstructure of ecclesiastical social commentary very much more radical than its social constituency. The Church now shares some of the moral advantages of the 'socially unattached' intelligentsia over the pragmatic limitations experienced by the practical politician.

These tendencies can have an effect on the 'spiritualized' condition of Christianity by translating its language and images into political and communitarian perspectives without remainder. To some extent this tendency is continuous with the liberal theology of the Kingdom of God on earth, but the desire to merge Christianity into secular categories is greater and the radicalism perhaps more marked. Put shortly, concepts like baptism become indistinguishable from birth, and the Church ceases to maintain a separate identifiable existence over against society. Communion would not differ from Community; in some cases it might not differ from Communism. Conversion would become merged in notions like maturity; holiness would approximate to psychological health, and Christian assurance to confidence. Sin is translatable into the terminology of alienation or neurosis. The peace of God may be either peace between nations or an unruffled temper. Grace can even be transmitted into moral and social graces. In sum, 'God' becomes a combination of the ideal society and the extrapolation of human potentiality and dominion: Durkheim and Feuerbach vindicated.

A sociologist as such can hardly comment on this possibility. He can, of course, point out that such a translation of Christianity, while initially dynamic in its release of the energy stored in theological concepts, also finally empties those concepts of their power. The reservoir is finally used up and the dialectic lapses.

13 Bibliography of Work in the Sociology of British Religion, 1971 Supplement

Robert W. Coles with the assistance of Hilary Graham

THIS bibliography is the third supplement to a bibliography produced by David Martin in *A Sociology of English Religion*, SCM Press 1967. The focus of the bibliography is, as before, on the contemporary religious situation in Great Britain, to which historical information is added selectively. We would welcome the co-operation of readers in the future in sending details of their publications in the field of the sociology of religion and of research endeavours in this general area.

1. General Surveys and Comments on Religion and Society

Banton, M., *The Coloured Quarter*, Jonathan Cape 1955

Brothers, J., *Religious Institutions*, Longmans 1971

Campbell, Colin, *Towards a Sociology of Irreligion*, Macmillan 1971

Campbell, Colin, 'Does Belief in God Make A Difference?', *Question*, ed. Hector Hawton, Pemberton Press 1972

Coleman, J. A., 'Civil Religion', *Sociological Analysis* 31 (2), 1970

Curtis, James, 'Voluntary Association Joining; A Cross National Comparative Note', *American Sociological Review* 36 (5), 1971.

De St Moulin, Leon, 'Social Class and Religious Behaviour in England', *The Clergy Review*, January 1968

Firth, R., Hobert, J., and Forge, A., *Families and Their Religions*, Routledge & Kegan Paul 1969

Gay, John, *The Geography of Religion in England*, Duckworth 1971

Hill, Michael, and Turner, Bryan, 'John Wesley and the Origin and Decline of Ascetic Devotion', *A Sociological Yearbook of Religion in Britain 4*, ed. Michael Hill, SCM Press 1971

Kokosalakis, N., 'Aspects of Conflict between the Structure of Authority and the Beliefs of the Laity in the Roman Catholic Church', *A Sociological Yearbook of Religion in Britain 4*, ed. Michael Hill, SCM Press 1971

Krausz, E., 'Religion and Secularization; a Matter of Definitions', *Social Compass* 18 (2), 1971

Little, K., *Negroes in Britain,* Routledge & Kegan Paul 1947

MacIntre, A., and Ricoeur, P., *The Religious Significance of Atheism,* Columbia University Press 1969

MacKenzie, C., *Catholicism and Scotland,* Kennikat 1971

Martin, David, 'The Secularization Issue', review article in *Encounter,* April 1971

Moore, R. S., 'Methodism, Class and Conflict', *Sociological Analysis* I (2), 1971

Pinder, R., 'Religious Change and the Process of Secularization', *Sociological Review* 19 (3), 1971

Pratt, V., *Religion and Secularization,* St Martins Press 1970

Robertson, Roland, 'The Influence of Religion', *New Society,* 6 January 1972

Sissons, Peter, 'Concepts of Church Membership', *A Sociological Yearbook of Religion in Britain 4,* ed. Michael Hill, SCM Press 1971

Stewart, C. W., *Adolescent Religion; A Developmental Study of the Religion of Youth,* Abingdon Press 1967

Turner, Bryan, 'Belief, Ritual and Experience; The Case of Methodism', *Social Compass* 18 (1), 1971

Vidler, A., *A Variety of Catholic Modernists,* CUP 1970

2. Historical Background

Akenson, D. H., *Church of Ireland; Ecclesiastical Reform and Revolution 1800–1855,* Yale University Press 1971

Crowther, M. A., *Church Embattled: Religious Controversy in Mid-Victorian England,* Anchor Press 1970.

Goulston, Michael, 'The Status of the Anglo-Jewish Rabbinate 1840–1914', *The Jewish Journal of Sociology* 10 (1), 1968

Lyons, F. S. L., *Ireland Since the Famine,* Weidenfeld & Nicholson 1971

Norwood, F. A., 'Wesleyan and Methodist Historical Studies, 1960–1970', *Church History* 40 (June) 1970

3. Statistical Material

Catholic Educational Council, *Catholic Education; A Handbook 1971*

Spencer, A. E. C. W., 'Report on the Parish Register. Religious Practice and Population Statistics of the Catholic Church in Scotland 1967', paper from the Pastoral Research Centre, Harrow 1969

4. Community and Parish Studies

Broady, M., 'The Social Adjustment of the Chinese Immigrants in Liverpool', *Sociological Review* 3 (1), 1955

Craven, Anne, *West Africans in London,* Institute of Race Relations 1968

Desai, Rashmi, *Indian Immigrants in London,* Institute of Race Relations 1963

Firth, Raymond, 'Two Studies of Kinship in London', *Monographs of Social Anthropology* No. 15, LSE 1956

Mogey, J. M., *Rural Life in Northern Ireland*, Routledge & Kegan Paul 1947
Nelson, Geoffrey, 'Communal and Associated Churches', *Review of Religious Research* 12 (2), 1971
Ng Kwee Choo, *The Chinese in London*, OUP 1968
O'Farrell, P., *Ireland's English*, Batsford 1971

5. Priesthood and the Ministry

Absalom, Francis, 'The Anglo-Catholic Priest; Aspects of Role Conflict', *A Sociological Yearbook of Religion in Britain 4*, ed. Michael Hill, SCM Press 1971
Bocock, R. J., 'The Role of the Anglican Clergy', *Social Compass* 18 (4), 1970
Hill, M., 'Typologie Sociologique de l'Ordre Religeux', *Social Compass* 18 (1), 1971
Hill, M., *The Religious Order in a Sociological Context: a Study of Virtuoso Religion and its Legitimation in the Nineteenth Century Church of England*, PhD, London 1971

6. Religion and Education

Murphy, J., *Church and State in Schools in Britain 1800–1970*, Routledge & Kegan Paul 1971
Musgrave, P. W., *Society and Education in England Since 1800*, Methuen 1968
Musgrave, P. W., 'The Relation Between the Family and Education in England; A Sociological Account', *British Journal of Educational Studies* 19 (1), 1971
Smith, R. V., *Religion and the Schools; From Prayer to Public Aid*, National School Press 1970
West, Vera, 'The Influence of Parental Background on Jewish University Students', *The Jewish Journal of Sociology* 10 (2), 1968

7. Religion and Politics

Campbell, F., and Campbell, C., 'Ireland's Durex Politics', *New Society*, 27 May 1971
O'Leary, C., 'The Northern Ireland Crisis and its Observers', *Political Quarterly* 42 (3), 1971
Rose, Richard, *Governing Without Consent; an Irish Perspective*, Faber 1971
Rose, R., and Unwin, D., 'What are the Parties Based On?', *New Society*, 7 May 1970
Whyte, J. H., *Church and State in Modern Ireland 1923–70*, Barnes & Noble Inc. 1971

8. Sects and Specialized Groups

Baron, R. V., 'Jewish Students; A Survey', *The Jewish Chronicle*, 16 February 1951

Buckle, Robert, 'Mormons in Britain; A Survey', *A Sociological Yearbook of Religion in Britain 4*, ed. Michael Hill, SCM Press 1971
Hill, Clifford, 'From Sect to Church', *Journal for the Scientific Study of Religion* 10 (2), 1970
Hill, Clifford, 'Immigrant Sect Development in Britain; A Case of Status Deprivation', *Social Compass* 18 (1), 1971
Oakley, R., 'The Cypriot Background', *New Backgrounds: The Immigrant Child at Home and at School*, ed. Robin Oakley, OUP 1968
Prais, S. J. and Schmool, M., 'Statistics of Jewish Marriages in Great Britain', *The Jewish Journal of Sociology* 9 (2), 1967
Prais, S. J. and Schmool, M., 'The Size and Structure of the Anglo-Jewish Population 1960–65', *The Jewish Journal of Sociology* 10 (1), 1968
Prais, S. J. and Schmool, M., 'Synagogue Marriages in Great Britain 1966–1968', *The Jewish Journal of Sociology* 12 (1), 1970
Prais, S. J. and Schmool, M., 'Statistics of Milah and the Jewish Birth Rate in Britain', *The Jewish Journal of Sociology* 12 (2), 1970
Scharf, B. R., 'Durkheimian and Freudian Theories of Religion; The Case of Judaism', *British Journal of Sociology* 21 (2), 1970
Sharot, S., 'Secularization, Judaism and Anglo-Jewry', *A Sociological Yearbook of Religion in Britain 4*, ed. Michael Hill, SCM Press 1971
Skultans, V., 'The Healing Process', *New Society*, 10 June 1971
Walker, A., and Atherton, J., 'An Easter Pentecostal Convention; The Successful Management of a "Time of Blessing"', *Sociological Review* 19 (3), 1971
Whitworth, John, 'The Bruderhof in England; a Chapter in the History of a Utopian Sect', *A Sociological Yearbook of Religion in Britain 4*, ed. Michael Hill, SCM Press 1971
Whitworth, John, *Religious Utopianism*, D.Phil., Oxford 1971.
Wilson, Bryan, *Religious Sects*, Weidenfeld & Nicholson 1970

9. Research in Progress

Absalom, J., *Anglo-Catholicism: Ideology and Influence*, Research in Progress, M.Phil., London
Carter, D., *Social and Political Influences of Bristol Church 1828–1914*, Department of History, University of Bristol
Coles, R. W., *Patterns of Culture and Commitment in the Church of England*, University of York
Cox, Caroline, et al, *Inter-Denominational Study of Theological Colleges* (Studying problems posed and experienced by an increasing number of named ordinands, their wives and families.) University of Newcastle
Dowling, W. C., *The Methodist Ministry Since Union*, Thesis research in progress at LSE
Foster, B., *A Study of Patterns of Christian Commitment*, University of Birmingham
Goodridge, R. M., *Comparative Religious Practice of Nineteenth-Century Bristol and Marseilles*, M.Phil. in progress at LSE
Hams, C. C., *Sociology of Religious Organizations. The Dioceses of Bangor*, UCW, Swansea
Hillyer, Ruth, *The Parson's Wife*, M.Phil. in progress at LSE
Hinings, C. R., *The Clun Valley Survey*, Research in progress at University of Birmingham

Hull, J. M., *Aspects of Religious Education with Special Reference to the Problems of Worship*, University of Birmingham

Hunter, John, *The Society of Friends in Birmingham 1815–1918*, PhD in progress at Department of General Studies, Wolverhampton College of Technology

Jarvis, P., *Religious Socialization in the Junior School*, M.Soc.Sc., University of Birmingham

Langstom, Paul, *The Determinants of the Pattern of Methodist Voting in the Unity Scheme at Circuit Level*, University of Keele

McCleod, D. H., *Membership and Influences of the Churches in Metropolitan London 1885–1914*, PhD in progress at Cambridge

Patterson, Sheila, *A Study of Migration to England*, Research in progress, Institute of Race Relations

Paul, L., *The St George's House Survey; The Role and Attitudes of the Clergy*, Queens College, Birmingham

Peel, John, *Hull Family Survey; Re-Study After Five years*, Department of Sociology, University of York

Pickering, W. S. F., *A Sociological Study of the Place of Married Students (and their wives) in Theological Colleges in Britain*, Department of Social Studies, University of Newcastle

Robinson, T., *The Formation of the Church of England Board of Social Responsibility*, University of Sheffield

Varney, P., *The Social Geography of South Norfolk with Special Reference to Religion*, MA in progress at Durham

Wollaston, B., *Church Arrangements in New Towns*, MA, London (projected)

Wright, D., *Different Personality Types of Religious Believer and Non-Believer*, Department of Psychology, University of Leicester